God's Book
of Prayers

Each and Every Prayer in the Bible

God's Book
of Prayers

Using The Very Words of God to Pray

written by God
via the hand of His servants
as prayed by people of the Bible
and extracted, compiled, and categorized by M. A. R.

WESTBOW
P R E S S
A DIVISION OF THOMAS NELSON

WestBow Press books may be ordered through booksellers or by contacting:

WestBow Press
A Division of Thomas Nelson
1663 Liberty Drive
Bloomington, IN 47403
www.westbowpress.com
1-(866) 928-1240

ISBN: 978-1-4497-5310-8 (e)
ISBN: 978-1-4497-5311-5 (sc)
ISBN: 978-1-4497-5312-2 (hc)

Library of Congress Control Number: 2012909335

Printed in the United States of America

WestBow Press rev. date: 7/11/2012

In honor of my grandparents,
James and Leona Baze,
the patriarchal pilgrims of
our family's Christian heritage;
along with my Daddy and Mama,
Guadalupe and Ruth Rodriguez,
who, for over half a century, have lived
an incredible life of faith and continue
the legacy as ministers of God's Word.

Contents

Acknowledgments

First credit goes to God the Father, the Lord Jesus Christ, and the Holy Spirit for the Very Words of God, inspiration, life, gifts, talents, health, etc., and all that I am. Second, to my wife, Margaret, who stood by me and allowed me to complete this project. Third, to my father, my children and brother Jimmy, who provided me with valuable encouragement and support and with proofreading and editing input; the rest of my family and others who gave encouragement and support and any other input; also San Antonio graphic designer Ed Garza, who rescued my initial Prayer Words Cloud and made it a sight to behold! Additional credits go to Saint Augustine, E. M. Bounds, Dave Drueding, C. S. Lewis, Herbert Lockyer, George MacDonald, Josh McDowell, Watchman Nee, Derek Prince, Leonard Ravenhill, Francis Schaeffer, and many others whose writings and teachings contributed much to my spiritual life and life in general. Much of my thoughts, speaking, writing, and indeed my life are a compilation of what I have learned; therefore, if I err in giving proper credit, my sincerest apologies. And special credit to my parents and grandparents for instilling religious virtue in my siblings, the rest of our family, and me.

Introduction

More than just a book, this is God's Very Book, mined from The Book that He Himself authorized and wrote. All that I have done (although that was quite a chore!) was extract the prayers out of His Holy Writ and place them, all of them, together into one volume.

About fifteen years ago, I wanted a book like this; however, I wanted to have it the easy way. I wanted to just go to the bookstore or online and buy it. After much searching and researching, I realized that the book just didn't exist. I still can hardly believe that four hundred years after the King James Version was published that such a volume, listing just the prayers of the Bible, was not available. If I wanted it, I realized I would have to put it together myself. So began this project at the end of the last century. Much time and effort has passed, and at long last, each and every one of God's Prayers are available, just the prayers, in this one handy volume before you.

Actually, there are two volumes, both of which have all the prayers of the Holy Bible. The larger one, *The Lord's Prayers*, lists all the prayers in biblical sequence with an exhaustive concordance of major and many minor words/phrases for easy reference and God-approved praying. The alphabetized listing also specifies which category of prayer each verse is in. The smaller edition, *God's Book of Prayers*, categorizes all the prayers of the Scripture and lists them in categorical sequence for easy reference and to be able to see each particular type of biblical prayer separated from the others. (See the section "How to Read the Lists in This Book" for further details.)

The electronic book version of *God's Book of Prayers* may also be used to search and find anything that one desires to pray about.

All editions exhibit some surface analysis of the prayers in the Bible through a pie chart showing the breakdown of all Bible prayers at a glance, a bar graph showing how many prayer verses each category contains, and two diagrams that show the most common words found in the prayers of Scripture.

Again, this book is a compilation of all the prayers in the Holy Bible, God's Very Own Words, pure and plain. Just the prayers in His Holy Word extracted for our enjoyment and benefit. Compiled mostly in an effort to aid in my own prayer life, I understand it will be used in many other capacities. And although I desired to use it in my own prayer life as appropriate, I understand the potential risk of appearing to limit the infinitely limitless God of the Bible; nevertheless, I present this volume.

Everything prayed in the Bible is documented here to indicate that these Very Words of God have already been approved by God, which helps ensure that He will honor His Own Words in your life, situation, or request. The implicit limitation comes when we do not find something in the Bible or our exact need is not referred to or prayed about in Scripture. For these matters, the idea in the apostle John's gospel John 21:25 comes into play, "And there are also many other things which Jesus did, the which, if they should be written every one, I suppose that even the world itself could not contain the books that should be written."

Also John 20:30 says, "And many other signs truly did Jesus in the presence of his disciples, which are not written in this book." Many other things have been and will be prayed about that are not written of in the Bible and thus are not in this present volume; however, that lack of documentation should not reduce by one iota our faith in and belief that The God of the Bible is concerned about you and your specific prayer and that He will answer. Of course, many things mentioned in the Bible that are not in the specific context of prayer may and should be prayed about (e.g., Colossians 2:2, 6–7 with myriad etceteras). Of particular note, those that are not included herein are most of the "prayers" of the apostle Paul.

The apostle Paul and others list many things they prayed for or about; however, they were not specifically quoted in the first or second person and thus do not meet the parameters for this book, although a couple are included. For all these various things, one need only consult any complete biblical concordance. Each one of us is unique and The Lord wants to hear from each of us on all matters in our life, even more so than any earthly father. As is recorded in Psalm 40:5, "Many, O LORD my God, are Thy Wonderful Works which Thou hast done, and Thy Thoughts which are to us-ward: They cannot be reckoned up in order unto Thee: if I would declare and speak of Them, They are more than can be numbered."

There are some sections of actual prayer that I have not placed into any category. A couple of these instances are Psalm 109:6–20 and Isaiah 7:12. I believe all will understand my reasoning, as the aforementioned appears to be a terrible display of man's vindictiveness and thus should not be repeated, even though the apostle Peter does refer to this exact portion of Psalm 109 (although not in prayer) when selecting someone to replace Judas Iscariot as one of the twelve, so I could be wrong. The reference from the book of Isaiah seems to be trying the patience of God as evidenced by the next verse, 13.

This book will only add to a host of books regarding prayer. This will differ, however, in that it will attempt to list every single prayer in the Bible, God's Book. (If you find a reference that is not listed, please do not hesitate to contact me so I can add your newfound reference to later editions of this work. Contact me at the website *www.GodsBookofPrayers.com*) It is written primarily in an attempt to give you *what* are the exact words that God has approved and chosen to use and to show *how* to pray using those very words.

Although it was not written primarily as a reference book, there is no doubt that it will be used in that capacity; however, my hope is that its main function will be in using The Very Words of God when praying. References to prayer were gleaned by reading and perusing the entirety of the Scriptures and by using common, and maybe some uncommon, words to indicate speaking to God and any of their respective past, present, future, etc. variations, such as:

answer, ask, beg, beseech, bless, confess, cry, entreat, hearken, implore, inquire, intercede, petition, plead, praise, pray, request, say, seek, speak, supplication, talk, thank, vow, worship, etc.

I also made heavy use of *All the Prayers of the Bible* by Dr. Herbert Lockyer as a source, so you will notice he is often quoted. While a marvelous devotional and expositional classic, Dr. Lockyer readily admits in his book, "it is impossible within the compass of this book [*All the Prayers of the Bible*] to enumerate all the prayers."[1] These new volumes, *God's Book of Prayers* and *The Lord's Prayers*, will once and for all time put the exhaustive list and only the prayers of the Holy Bible in one convenient volume for anyone to use and enjoy.

The pray-er (the one praying, you) should refer to the Scripture of their translational choosing for the exact wording as I have used the King James Authorized Version, with usage of the New International Version for isolated modern words. In some instances, whenever the same prayers are recorded elsewhere in the Scriptures but with slight word variations, I have placed them together with the differing word(s) in [brackets]. Even though the prayers are fully spelled out within, please see each prayer's referenced verse(s) and open up your own translated Bible and pray God's words for yourself.

As mentioned before, the list of prayers consists only of actual prayers that were spoken directly to God, whereas anything that was prayed about, but was not prayed in the first or second person, will not typically be listed (e. g., in Philippians 1:9, the apostle Paul writes, "And this I pray, that your love may abound yet more and more ..." and thus, Paul does not appear to be speaking directly to God about love abounding in others, so this prayer mention is not listed).

At times, it was difficult to ascertain what fell into what category of prayer, so there may be some disagreement as to what should and should not be considered as prayer or into what category(ies) I have placed them in. Please contact me via the website for any discussions regarding these instances, and Happy praying! May He give you the "Spirit of Prayer" as mentioned in Zechariah 12:10, and God will hear His Own Words in your prayers if you use the Bible (of course, it is very important to live the "ABCs of the Pray-er" as indicated within the opening guide of this volume), and from Psalm 20:5, may "The Lord fulfil all thy petitions" and answer your prayers, so "we will rejoice in thy salvation."

I conclude this introduction with some quotes (I love quotes!) from some well-known figures in Christendom regarding prayer:

"The praying voice is music in God's ears."[2]
Matthew Henry

"Prayer can transfigure a person's countenance and character."[3]　　　　　　　　　Herbert Lockyer

"The devil often laughs when we work, but he trembles when we pray."[4]

"Is prayer your steering wheel or your spare tire?"[5]
Corrie ten Boom

"Because we never know the ultimate effect of decisions we make, much prayer should be ours before the die is cast."[6]　　　　　　　Herbert Lockyer

"If we keep the channel to heaven open, God will care for all concerning us."[7]　　　　　Herbert Lockyer

"Prayer is more than a repair kit for our broken-down situation."[8]   Leonard Ravenhill

"Christ prayed not only to maintain His communion with God, and to obtain guidance and power from God, but also to perfect His Manhood."[9]
                                        Herbert Lockyer

"Have you ever learned the beautiful art of letting God take care of you and giving all your thought and strength to pray for others and for the kingdom of God? It will relieve you of a thousand cares."[10]
                                        A. B. Simpson

"There is something impressive about the solemn prayer preceding the removal of the Ark, and also sanctifying its resting place at night. The example of Moses in invoking the blessing of God morning and evening while on the march is worthy of emulation. As we begin each day we should entreat to our closet and commend ourselves and all we represent to God. At the close of the day, as darkness gathers, the grateful acknowledgement of the good providence and watchful care of God should also be ours."[11]
                                        Herbert Lockyer

"The prayer of the upright is his delight; it is music in his ears."[12]   Matthew Henry

Endnotes for Introduction:

1. Herbert Lockyer, *All the Prayers of the Bible* (Grand Rapids: Zondervan Publishing House, 1959), 103.
2. Matthew Henry, *Commentary on the Whole Bible* (1706).
3. Lockyer, *All the Prayers of the Bible*, 215.
4. Corrie ten Boom, *Amazing Love* (Grand Rapids: Fleming H. Revell, 1953), 41.
5. Corrie ten Boom, quote only.
6. Lockyer, *All the Prayers of the Bible*, 214.
7. Lockyer, *All the Prayers of the Bible*, 153.
8. Leonard Ravenhill, *Revival God's Way* (Minneapolis: Bethany House Publishers, 1983), 22.
9. Lockyer, *All the Prayers of the Bible*, 214–215.
10. A. B. Simpson, *Days of Heaven Upon Earth—A Year Book of Scripture Texts and Living Truths* (Brooklyn: Christian Alliance Publishing Co., 1897), February 6 page.
11. Lockyer, *All the Prayers of the Bible*, 40.
12. Matthew Henry, *A Method for Prayer* (Glasgow: D. MacKenzie, 1834), 286.

Rationale and Instructional Guide

Now, What Is Prayer?

The world abounds with a plethora of books, articles, sermons, programs, and on and on that answer this very question, and rightly so. Anything as important as prayer should be much written about and discussed. After all, what can be more crucial than interacting with God? As mentioned in Luke 2:37, the act of praying is to serve God. Therefore, prayer is indeed service to God. However, not wanting to overanalyze prayer, I have defined prayer for this project simply as communicating with God. I attempted to capture every instance of anyone communicating with God within the Bible.

Prayers found in the Bible may be categorized under many varying topics. I have chosen to categorize them into the following nine groupings: blessings, confessions, requests for insight, petitions, praises to God for what He has done or does, responses to God, thanks to God, worship of God for Who He is or His Characteristics, and general statements that any person speaking to another might mention. During the times when God was on Earth in bodily form (i.e., Jesus on Earth), some communications with Him were not considered by me to be classified as prayer, while others appeared to be traditionally accepted as prayers.

I did, however, attempt to find and list in the following tables every instance of anyone communicating with Jesus, whether I considered it as prayer or not. All communications with Jesus may be found either under the heading "Words Spoken to Jesus, Considered Prayer" or "Words Spoken to Jesus, Not Usually Considered Prayer."

Those that I considered as prayers are appropriately placed within the heart of this book, while those not considered prayers typically might not be found within. Several of Jesus' prayers could only ever be prayed by Himself or are solely regarding Himself and could never refer to anyone other than Our Lord; these are not included in the main lists of these volumes. However, some, if not all, are: John 17:2, 5, 21–22, 24, 25, 26; and Psalm 2.

Words Spoken to Jesus, Considered Prayer

Matthew 8:2b, 6, 8–9, 25b, 31; 9:18b, 27b; 11:3; 13:10, 36b, 51b; 14:28, 30b; 15:15, 22b, 23b, 25b; 16:16; 17:15–16, 19; 18:1, 21; 19:16, 18a, 20, 25b, 27; 20:21, 30b, 31b, 33; 21:9; 23:39b; 24:3; 26:22b, 25b
Mark 1:40; 4:38; 5:9b, 10, 12; 7:28; 8:29b; 9:11, 17b–18, 21b–22, 24b, 28b; 10:17, 20, 35, 37, 47, 48, 51b; 11:9–10; 12:28b; 13:4; 14:19b
Luke 5:8; 5:12b; 7:4b–5, 6b–8; 8:9, 24a, 28b, 30b, 31, 32b; 9:20b, 38–40, 54; 10:40b; 11:1, 27; 12:41; 13:23a, 35b; 15:12a, 18b–19, 21; 17:5, 13, 16, 37a; 18:18, 21, 38, 39b, 41b; 19:38; 21:7; 23:42
John 1:49; 3:4, 9; 4:11b, 12, 15, 49; 6:25b, 28, 34, 68–69; 8:33; 9:2, 36; 10:24; 11:3, 21–22, 27, 41b–42; 12:13; 13:9, 25b, 36a, 37; 18:38a; 20:16b, 28; 21:15b, 16b, 17b, 20b, 21
Acts 7:59b, 60a; 9:5a, 6a; 22:8a, 10a, 19–20; 26:15a

Words Spoken to Jesus, Not Usually Considered Prayer

Matthew 8:19b, 21b, 29; 9:28b; 12:2, 10b, 38, 47; 14:15, 17; 15:2, 12, 27, 33, 34b; 16:14, 22; 17:4, 10, 26a; 19:3, 7, 10; 20:22b; 21:16a, 20b, 23b, 27a, 31b, 41; 22:16b–17, 21a, 24–28, 36, 42b; 26:17b, 33, 35, 49b, 62, 63b, 68; 27:11b, 13, 40
Mark 1:24; 2:18, 24; 3:11; 6:35b, 36, 37b, 38b; 5:7, 31; 7:5; 8:4, 5b, 19b, 24, 28, 32; 9:5, 38; 10:2, 4, 28, 39a; 11:21, 28, 33a; 12:14–16, 19–23; 12:32–33; 13:1a; 14:12b, 29, 31, 45b, 60b, 61b, 65b; 15:2a, 4, 18, 29b–30
Luke 2:48b; 4:3, 6–7, 9b–11, 34, 41; 5:5, 30, 33; 6:2, 7; 7:40b, 43a; 8:20, 28b, 45b; 9:10, 13b, 19, 33b, 49, 57b, 59b, 61b; 10:17, 25, 27, 29b, 37a; 11:16, 45; 12:13; 13:1, 31b; 14:15b; 15:29–30; 17:20; 18:28; 19:39b; 20:2, 7, 21–22, 24b, 28–33, 39; 22:9, 33, 35b, 38a, 49b, 64–65, 67a, 70a; 23:3a, 9, 37, 39; 24:18, 19b–24, 29a
John 1:38b, 48a; 2:3b, 18, 20; 3:2b; 4:9, 11a, 17a, 19, 25, 31b; 5:7; 6:7, 9, 30–31; 7:3–4, 20; 8:4–7a, 11a, 13, 19a, 25a, 39a, 41b, 48, 52–53, 57; 9:2, 40b; 10:33; 11:8, 12, 24, 32b, 34b, 39b; 13:6b, 8a; 16:29–30; 18:5a, 7b, 19, 22b, 33b, 35, 37a; 19:3a, 9b, 10; 20:15b; 21:5b

Dr. Herbert Lockyer authored a beautiful poem regarding Jesus' Own Prayer Life wherein he rhymed all the places, times, ways, reasons, when, why, and people for whom Jesus prayed.

Who We Pray to Helps Make Us Who We Are

In praying to God, we should solely pray to The Only True God — The God of the Bible. Likewise, the proper way to pray to Him is through Jesus Christ. Jesus told us that no one comes to The Father but through The Son. Ephesians 2:18 lets us know that through Jesus we "have access by One Spirit unto The Father." Here we see the fullness of The Trinity and how They interact in prayers. The Spirit of God prays in us, while Jesus is in heaven, receiving our prayers, and Jesus, in turn perfects the prayers to The Father, while The Father hears and is The Giver of all good gifts. Or as Dr. Lockyer succinctly puts it, "The prescribed way to pray is in the Spirit, through the Son, to the Father."[1]

A beautiful example of humanity being laborers together with God is described in 1 Corinthians 3:9. In fact, part of the inheritance to which we were predestined is this working partnership with and for God. God "predestinated according to the Purpose of Him Who worketh all things after the counsel of His Own Will" (Ephesians 1:11). We already "know that all things work together for good to them that love God, to them who are the called according to His Purpose" and "how shall He [God] not with Him [Jesus] also freely give us all things?" (Romans 8:28, 32b).

Earlier (vs. 27b) and later (vs. 34b), Romans 8 also lets us know that The Spirit makes "intercession for the saints according to The Will of God" and that Jesus is He "Who is even at The Right Hand of God, Who also maketh intercession for us." If we pray in this way, then we are praying according to The Will of God. Remember that Jesus told us in Mark 11:24, "What things soever ye desire, when ye pray, believe that ye receive *them*, and ye shall have *them*." God, through John the Apostle (15:7), records Jesus as saying, "If ye abide in Me, and My Words abide in you, ye shall ask what ye will, and it shall be done unto you."

Never pray to other persons, creatures, objects, things, ideas, beings, etc. since God is the only One worthy, as mandated in Exodus 20:5 with a big reason why found in Romans 8:34. Martha, the sister of Lazarus, stated to our Lord Jesus in John 11:22, "But I know, that even now, whatsoever Thou wilt ask of God, God will give it to Thee." Jesus, in verse 42 of that same chapter, stated, "And [Father] I knew that Thou hearest Me always ..." When we pray to Jesus, we know that He is at the right hand of God the Father, and that "He ever liveth to make intercession for them...that come unto God by Him" (Hebrews 7:25).

Why Some of Our Prayers Aren't Answered

The psalmist could rightly advise in 37:4, "Delight thyself also in the Lord; and He shall give thee the desires of thine heart," and the king truly declared in Psalm 21:2 that God had "given him his heart's desire, and hast not withholden the request of his lips." How does this come about when we often ask and ask, pray and pray, and see no results? Several explanations could answer this dilemma.

What was the psalmist in 37:4 referring to when he penned the word "*also*" after "Delight thyself"? In a look at the preceding verse, we can conclude that he was referring to his admonition to "trust in The Lord". What is it to trust in The Lord but to have faith in Him? Trusting — or having faith in God — is one of, if not the main requirement, to successful praying. According to Hebrews 11:6, we must initially believe in the existence of God, and *then* believe the fact that He does hear and that He does answer our prayer. D. Elton Trueblood stated, "Faith is not belief without proof, but trust without reservation."[2] We also must learn and live

4

"The ABCs of the Pray-er" (later in this section) to line ourselves up with God's Will.

The great prayer motivator E. M. Bounds contributes to this theme in *The Necessity of Prayer* with, "[Faith] is the one great condition of prayer; the lack of it lies at the root of all poor praying, feeble praying, little praying, unanswered praying."[3] Hebrews 11:6 reads, "Without faith it is impossible to please Him: for he that cometh to God must believe that He is, and that He is a rewarder of them that diligently seek Him." Notice how we are to seek Him in order to receive an answer to our prayers or to receive a reward. The way is to "diligently" seek after God. Jesus requires us to "seek first," not necessarily first in time or order, but definitely as priority one, and then "all these things shall be added unto you" (Matthew 6:33).

The apostle James explains one shortfall of our praying in that we "ask amiss, that ye may consume it upon your lusts" (4:3). This term *lusts*, though seemingly similar to *desires*, paints an appropriate distinction between the two. As we delight ourselves in the Lord, we learn what pleases and is acceptable to Him. This then, causes us to want to long for and ask *only* for things that are in line with God's Will. These desires, or delights, but clearly *not* lusts, become our true requests, so that The Lord gives and does not withhold them from us. Lockyer again: "If we would have His will we must continue in living union with Him (John 15:7)."[4]

In a beautiful display, the writer of Psalm 21 shows some of these desires and delights which God has already fulfilled (rich blessings, life, victories, eternal blessings, gladness, joy, etc.) in the first half of the psalm and what God will do in the second half of the chapter. These desires and delights might be added to the "benefits" mentioned throughout Psalm 103 — forgiveness, healing, redemption, love, compassion, good food, renewal, and more — that we are told not to forget. We could consider this psalm a statement of the benefits package God offers the believer.

Other benefits of God's Word are listed in Proverbs 4:20-23. The Lord says,

> Attend to My Words; incline thine ear unto my sayings. Let them not depart from thine eyes; keep them in the midst of thine heart. For they are life unto those that find them, and health to all their flesh. Keep thy heart with all diligence; for out of it are the issues of life.

Indicating how we should speak in the next verse, God tells us to "Put away from thee a froward mouth, and perverse [corrupt] lips put far from thee." We should not speak evil of anyone but instead speak blessings to and for others as our Lord taught us by what He did and does, including on the last day He was on Earth. We can do this through our prayers to God, speaking His Very Own Words. Also, our Lord shows us that we can approach Him with peace, confidence, joy, boldness, and so many more positive ways in Hebrews 12:18–24, needing not be afraid at all.

David in Psalm 37:7 gives us another secret of successful praying: "Rest in the Lord, and wait patiently for Him," and "Wait on the Lord, and keep His Way" (v. 34a) since he had "not seen the righteous forsaken" (v. 25). Though we wait and rest in Him, we also "keep His Way." As James tells us that faith without works is dead, so prayer without action when required is negligent laziness. Jacob and Nehemiah offer two excellent biblical examples of this principle. Both prayed long and continuously, but they also put feet to their prayers. Jacob, after all night in prayer, planned and did what he could to calm his brother, Esau, while Nehemiah, pray-er of one of the longest prayers in the Bible, trusted in the Lord's protection, but he was also wise to arm himself and the builders. The whole of Psalm 37 is also froth with "Fret not," an important element in our attitude in prayer.

There remain instances when we truly do not know *what* (as in, what we pray for is bad for us) we are praying for. Dr. Lockyer points out that the mother of the disciples James and John came to Jesus "worshipping Him," yet Jesus proclaimed, "Ye know not what ye ask" (Matthew 20:20, 22). Commenting on Psalm 106:15 and Mark 5:18, 19, Dr. Lockyer states, "Every answered prayer is not necessarily for our benefit.

> That Power above, who makes mankind His care,
> May bless us most when He rejects our prayer."[5]

Jesus' Last Earthly Act Was to Bless Us

The Arbitrator that Job longed for is, in reality, Jesus, Who "lay[s] His Hand upon us both" [God and the one praying] (Job 9:32–35). Luke 22:32 describes Jesus praying for one of His disciples, while John 17:9 lets us know that Jesus prayed for all of His disciples. He doesn't stop His prayers with this group only; Jesus even prays for all of us who, throughout history, will believe on Himself through the word of the disciples, including the writings of Matthew, Mark, Luke, John, Paul, Peter, James, yea even all the agents God employed to pen Holy Scripture (see also John 17:20; Hebrews 7:25; and Romans 8:34).

Jesus started His risen life by comforting one of us, opening up the Scripture to a pair of us, helping the business enterprise of some, physically feeding others breakfast, restoring yet another, and, as if foretelling His eternal ministry, He concluded His stay on Earth and began His future life the same way, by praying, in fact *blessing*, those fortunate enough to be in attendance near Bethany when He ascended in the air from Earth to heaven on that historical day (see Luke 24:50–51).

Jesus continues His post-earthly risen life concerned about your comfort, your business, your cares, your restoration, your understanding of Scripture, your family, and your overall blessing. Remember that Bethany was the community where Martha was

7

from and who had issued the proclamation that God would give to Jesus anything that He asked. So what did Jesus ask for when He concluded His first earthly visit at this very locale? Nothing less than blessings for His people! And Jesus continues requesting this of the Father to this very day (Luke 24:50–51)! Blessed Savior and Lord *and* Blesser!!

John 12:50 tells us that Jesus speaks whatever the Father says to Him so that even the Father is directing Jesus to petition blessing for His children! What tremendous insight into the mind of God! Words cannot express this joy unspeakable and full of glory! I am confident that God perpetually honors His Word, wants to give the blessings to us that Jesus requested and requests, and that by expressing His Words in our prayers, we will garner blessings we have not imagined as well! May we not be like the disciples who did not believe the report of the one and of the pair who reported Jesus' resurrection. May we not choose to not believe that Jesus is now returned and is at the right hand of the God of the universe and eternity and is constantly praying blessings for us. Truly Jesus is the One Who initiated and perpetuates the expression, "God bless you!"

The First Mention of Prayer in the Bible

Outside of the conversations that Adam and Eve had with God, the very first mention of prayer in the Bible can be found in Genesis 4:26, "And to Seth, to him also there was born a son; and he called his name Enos: then began men to call upon The Name of The LORD." Interestingly enough, the named individual of birth in this verse is Enos, a name that literally means "to be frail." This perpetual, inherent frailty of humanity remains the cause of the necessity to "call upon The Name of The LORD." (An interesting study can be made of the meaning of names of the initial humans to include, but not limited to, Adam—man of earthly elements; Eve—life-giver; Cain—created; Abel—vanity; Seth—substituted; Enos—frail; Kenan—fixed, nest; and many more.)

God does not appreciate it when He calls out and speaks to us and we do not hear or answer or we hide from Him, so God would not do that to us when we pray to Him. (See Isaiah 66:4 and Genesis 3:8, 9 and Zechariah 7:11–13). Imagine when we take the time to honestly call out to Him and He hears His Own Words coming from our heart and lips. How pleased God must be that we not only know His Words, but that we love Them and Him enough to repeat them in blessing, confession, request for guidance, direction, insight, petition, praise, response, statement, thanks, honor, or worship of Him. As in the garden of Eden, God is calling to us to come to Him no matter where we find ourselves (see also Hosea 11:1).

Some Examples of Praying God's Very Words

God's Words are a great aid when in comes to praying. D. L. Moody is quoted as saying, "We must have a warrant for our prayers. If we have some great desire, we must search the Scriptures to find if it be right to ask it."[6] This book will also give ideas for what to pray for, and when at a loss for words, God's Word makes it easy. Just pray God's Words! Many of us already pray The Lord's Prayer, so let us take advantage of the entirety of the Scripture and pray all of The Lord's Prayers!

While putting together this work, I remember that it had not rained for quite a while in South Texas, in fact all over Texas, so I decided I would employ this technique of praying God's Very Words. Using the alphabetized list in the *The Lord's Prayers* volume of this project, I located all the verses that had the word *rain* in them and in my morning prayer simply parroted one of these exact verses to God. I did feel though that I was utilizing a seemingly superstitious behavior.

Jack Hayford, in his magnificent little book on prayer, *Prayer Is Invading the Impossible*, stated that when the disciples asked Jesus to teach them to pray, He "taught them nothing of mysticism, nothing of religious pretense, nothing of meditation, nothing of bizarre physical contortions, nor anything of memorized incantations attended by clouds of incense."[7] Thus, I am not advocating any of this and did not feel comfortable mainly with my attitude toward my "rain prayer." When it did not rain that day, I sensed and knew that my attitude and thoughts in approaching God was one of quasi-mysticism.

The next day after further reflection, I again prayed the very same verse from Jeremiah, although now feeling more comfortable with using the Very- Words-of-God-to-pray approach. I felt right with the Lord, especially when it proceeded to rain for the next two straight days in my hometown!

Another incredible example of the magnificent use of these books of God's Prayers was when I thought about my own mortality and knew that I could not physically continue in my current line of work. Being concerned about surviving economically, I looked to the Lord to give me peace and answers. Being raised in the church as a preacher's kid, I knew all the passages regarding God supplying all my needs, but I was thoroughly pleased and overwhelmed when He revealed Psalm 71:9 to me. David prayed, and I now pray regularly, "Cast me not off in the time of old age; forsake me not when my strength faileth." I cannot begin to recount the full benefit of my previous scriptural knowledge, along with this newfound prayer of mine, namely the peace, security, and joy I am granted at God's Very Words. The place to begin and end and continue in any endeavor, and in particular, prayer, is The Words of God.

E. M. Bounds wrote:

> Prayer draws its very life from the Bible and has no standing ground outside of the warrant of the Scriptures. Its very existence and character is dependent on revelation made by God to man in his holy Word. Prayer, in turn,

exalts this same revelation and turns men toward that Word. The nature, necessity, and all-comprehending character of prayer is based on the Word of God.[8]

Jesus told us that "heaven and earth shall pass away: but My Words shall not pass away" (Mark 13:31). Therefore, the prayers that are within the Scriptures will remain as well—another good reason to learn and use them in our lives. The sole thought in Ephesians 5:10 is to prove, or find out, what is acceptable, or pleasing, to God, and we know that Christ, The Living Word, and The Scripture, The Written Word, are indeed pleasing to The Lord.

Job did esteem the words of God's Mouth more than his necessary food (Job 23:12), while Jeremiah reciprocates Job's pleasure with God's Very Words in 15:16, pronouncing, "Thy Words were found, and I did eat them; and Thy Word was unto me the joy and rejoicing of mine heart ..."

A clear example of this biblical giant using God's Very Words in prayer can be found in Jeremiah 20:12 and 32:19 where Jeremiah echoes God's Very Words recorded in 17:10. John the Apostle also quotes The Lord Jesus in Revelation 2:23 from this same passage. Consider the prophet Daniel who prayed even though what he was praying for had been foretold in Scripture (Daniel 9:1–3). Jonah, apparently well versed in the Psalms, gleaned much of his prayer in the belly of the great fish from 42:7, 18:4–6, 22:23–24, and throughout Psalm 88 and 69. These serve as good examples for us to emulate.

As mentioned in the introduction, many things mentioned in the Bible that are not in the specific context of prayer may and should also be prayed about (e.g., Philippians 1:9, with thousands of others). Joyce Meyer, in her book, *The Power of Simple Prayer*, relates the powerfully beautiful story of someone who prayed Jeremiah 24:6 (God Himself was being quoted here, so it is not a prayer) for herself. God was so good to her and answered her multi-detailed prayer to the last jot and tittle.[9]

The ABCs of the Pray-er

As indicated earlier, praying God's Very Words is obviously not the only way to pray, but in my estimation, it is the best way, or at the very least, a highly effective method, given that one's heart is in the right condition. Next are some necessary attitudes, behaviors, and conditions that every "pray-er" (the one praying) should employ for successful praying.

The ABCs of the Pray-er (the Attitudes, Behaviors, and Conditions):

1. Faith in God
2. Spirit, directed by the Holy Spirit
3. Privacy of prayer
4. Obedience in life
5. Right motive
6. Repent
7. Forgive
8. Boldly
9. Sincerity of prayer and life
10. Persist in prayer
11. Pray according to The Will of God
12. Fasting with prayer
13. Humility of life and prayer (contrite
    and reverent submission)
14. Pray in Jesus' Name

To easily remember these ABCs, you may use the following acronymical sentence with each underlined letter being one of the fourteen ABCs for successful prayer: "For successful prayer, one must repent, forgive, boldly, and sincerely persist with faith in His Name." Of course, to remember the attitudes, behaviors, or conditions is not the goal for us, but by knowing them, it may help us to remember to live them out in our very life and so attain "the prize of the high calling of God in Christ Jesus" (Philippians 3:14b).

Jesus tells us that "out of the abundance of the heart the mouth speaketh." Praying God's Very Words is an example of the overflowing "good treasure of the heart" and "bringeth forth good things" (Matthew 12:35). Our Lord declares His Peace for us in Philippians 4:7 when we make known our requests unto Him, being "careful for nothing" (v. 6), and ultimately, He "shall supply all your need according to His Riches in glory by Christ Jesus" (v. 19).

Some input from others regarding the ABCs:

"I pray, listen, and obey."[10]

Paul (David) Yonggi Cho

"Lack of sincerity weakens the effect of prayer."[11]

Herbert Lockyer

Some differences between God and the judge in Luke 18:1–8— The judge avenged her because the widow troubled him and to prevent her from wearying him, while The Right Judge of all the earth (Genesis 18:25) is truly concerned about the oppressed and poor.

Some differences in the widow's relationship with the judge and ours with God—1) She had no given promises from the judge to plead, while we have God's Promises, which ignite our expectations and importunity. 2) The widow had no familial relationship with the judge, while we have been admitted into God's Family by adoption (Psalm 103:13). And 3) The widow had no one to help plead her case, "[b]ut we have an "Advocate *with* the Father"—resident at Court—to attend to our cause. He is at the Judge's right hand, "Great Advocate! Almighty Friend!" ...

> Then earnest let us cry,
> And never faint in prayer;
> God loves our importunity,
> And makes our cause His care."[12]
>
> Herbert Lockyer

"Unless the common course of our lives be according to the common spirit of our prayers, our prayers are so far from being real or sufficient degree of devotion that they become an empty lip-labour, or, what is worse, a notorious hypocrisy."[13]   William Law

"Some people think God does not like to be troubled with our constant coming and asking. The only way to trouble God is not to come at all."[14]   D. L. Moody

"If we knock, God has promised to open the door and grant our request. It may be years before the answer comes; He may keep us knocking; but He has promised that the answer will come."[15]   D. L. Moody

"Endurance in prayer is hard but fruitful."[16]

Herbert Lockyer

"Hypocrites never pray in secret."[17]

Herbert Lockyer

"If Christ had need of constant withdrawals from the gaze and glamour of the world, how deep must our need be of the 'desecularizing, decarnalizing process of which the desert seclusions of Jesus are the perpetual parable!'"[18]

Herbert Lockyer

"Pray more from conviction than from crisis."[19]

Peter Lord

'Tis not to those who stand erect,
Or those who bend the knee,
It is to those who bow the heart
The Lord will gracious be;
It is the posture of the soul
That pleases or offends;
If it be not in God's sight right
Naught else can make amends."[20]

Herbert Lockyer

"Every true prayer involves the submission of what it asks to the divine judgment."[21]   Herbert Lockyer

"What mistakes are prevented in any aspect of life, if only we acknowledge the counsel of the Lord, ere setting out on an undertaking! (Proverbs 3:6)"[22]

Herbert Lockyer

"If He [Jesus] had need of such a retreat, how deep must be our need of one."[23]   Herbert Lockyer

Help for Daily Living

Psalm 77 is a prayer for help. In verses 1–9, the writer implores the Lord for help and wonders if He has forgotten him. At verse 10, the writer decides to appeal to the things the Lord has done in days gone by as a way of reminding himself that God is still with him and can do it again. Verses 16–19 tell us that The Way of The Lord is often trod with difficulties, but that He is always with us, even if God's "Footsteps are not known" or seen, much like the famous poem.

15

Likewise, verse 20 concludes, telling us, "Thou leddest Thy People like a flock by the hand …"

See also Psalm 81:7 for answered prayer and how God deals with us sometimes. He "proves" us to see if we trust Him, and at the end of 81:10, He promises us "open thy mouth wide, and I will fill it." The Lord will fill it "with the finest of the wheat: and with honey out of the rock should I have satisfied thee"! (Psalm 81:16, emphasis mine). If we would but listen to Him, as in 81:8, 11, and 13.

Daily we encounter situations in which we need assistance. In referring to the "armour of God" (Ephesians 6:10–20 and 1 Thessalonians 5:8, where the apostle Paul gets the idea from Isaiah 59:17), an argument can be made for the union of the two offensive weapons we possess in proclaiming our declarations and petitions using The Word of God in our prayers. After all, Paul writes, "And take … The Sword of the Spirit, which is The Word of God: Praying always with all prayer and supplication in The Spirit," while Isaiah, after mentioning some components of the armor of God earlier, relays God's Message in 59:21, "My Spirit that is upon thee, and My Words which I have put in thy mouth, shall not depart out of thy mouth …"

The famous Hebrews 4:12 passage refers to The Word of God again as a sword and further down in verse 16 gives us the confidence to "come boldly unto the throne of grace, that we may obtain mercy, and find grace to help in time of need." After stating in Ephesians 6:18, "Praying always with all prayer and supplication … for all saints," Paul indicates specifically what it was he wanted prayed for for himself in verses 19 and 20. And no matter what happens or how we are treated, we should always pray and be consistent (see Daniel 6:10 and Acts 4:18–31; 5:27–42).

Our Lord is very much concerned with our daily living. Dr. Lockyer teaches, "We have not to wait, however, for our King to hold out His golden sceptre. At all times and in all places, the way is open to the mercy seat where Jesus answers prayer."[24] Whatever we are involved in in our lives and at any given moment, we can express our prayers to the Everywhere and Anytime God. He wants to hear from you whether you are at home, at school, at work, at church, traveling, resting, with family, with friends, etc., and even when you are playing, you can be praying!

Other Ponderings on Prayer

Prayer has long been likened to railroad tracks. Though the locomotive is mighty, powerful, and great, it can go nowhere without rail lines. If we lay no tracks in prayer, God will not work. The work of God is a joint effort (1 Corinthians 3:9). It is recorded that the disciples asked Jesus to teach them one specific thing. What was that one thing?

Prayer. Jesus taught us some principles of prayer in Luke 11 and 18. Lesson One is *to pray*. Lesson Two is *to pray always*. While we are experiencing the first and second lesson of prayer, God will teach us how to sharpen our ax of prayer so that we are more effective in tumbling the works of the Enemy. God said in the Old and New Testament of the Bible, "My House shall be called … the [My] house of prayer" (Mark 11:17; Isaiah 56:7).

Watchman Nee taught that once we know the will of God, we should pray according to His will. Prayer has been said to change things; however, prayer only changes things inasmuch as it rights what we on Earth or the Enemy of our soul has damaged. Prayer does not change what God has willed. Prayer merely releases The Will of God on Earth as it is in heaven. Prayer turns the world right side up. In case you do not know The Will of God in a particular matter, you can always pray, saying, "Your Will be done, Lord." However, we do not need to focus on areas where we do not know The Will of God, as there are enough areas for prayer where The Will of God is clearly known or easily discerned.[25a]

Nee explained our joint effort with God in prayer in this four-step process:

17

1) God establishes His Will in heaven;
2) God reveals His Will to His children;
3) We pray for God's Will to be done;
4) God accomplishes His Will on Earth.[25b]

Will God accomplish His Will without our prayer? More and more I am becoming convinced that we are lacking in our spiritual lives, first, because we fail to pray (Luke 18:1) and, second, because we fail to pray God's Will (Ezekiel 36:36b-37). First, let everything be done, and while you are doing it, do it decently and in order. Pray always, and pray in the proper way, which is God's Will.

It is vitally important to always pray (Luke 18:1; 1 Thessalonians 5:17; Ephesians 6:18; Luke 21:36; Colossians 4:12). We fail to pray for many, many reasons, which might be categorized in four different areas: lust, apathy, materialism, and pride. These four categories might together be called our darkened L.A.M.P.

Our thoughts may be on any of numerous carnal lusts. We may have grown lackadaisical in our thoughts and service to God. Amos 6:1 declares a woe to those who are complacent, at ease in Zion, the church. We may be running after multiple things and have no time or energy to run after God. Maybe we do not want to admit our need for God's Strength, His Providence, or His Sustenance. Maybe we feel we can do it on our own.

Now, in reference to The Will of God in prayer, how might we know or better understand that Will of God? As we see from any legal will and last testament of a person, a death must occur before the will takes effect. The Will of God cannot be accomplished in the spiritual realm unless someone dies. Since the Lord Jesus already gave His life, we are now the ones called to give our life for Him so that The Will of God may be revealed individually to us. We must die to the control of our time and destiny and let God determine how to best use it. The best use of our time begins with, continues with, and never ends when we pray. If we would join Jesus in His overall mission of destroying the works of the Devil, we must join God in ... Prayer, Prayer, Prayer!

Some Final Thoughts

Prayerful equals powerful. Prayerless equals powerless. An original language word for prayer is *deesis* (pronounced deh'-ay-sis), while the word for power is *dunamis*, from which we derive the word *dynamite*, so deesis is dunamis, prayer is power! The apostle Paul's prayer for the Ephesians and for all believers (since the whole of the church has the basis for the reason Paul prays, see 3:1, 14, 15 and 2:15–22) includes for them to be empowered with "dunamis" by His Spirit in the inner person (3:16). But so we realize that even though we have positionally attained the highest level, we nonetheless must work out experientially "according to the 'dunamis' that worketh in us" (3:20b), our walk with God, Paul prays "that ye, being rooted and grounded in love, may be able to comprehend...that ye might be filled with all the fulness of God." (3:17-19). A true partnership!

Recently, I heard a sermon in which the speaker posed a question that he said others had asked, namely, "Should we pray or read the Bible first?" I wasn't sure if I understood the importance or need for the question; nevertheless, given the context of this book, of course it would be necessary to know, or read, what the Bible says in order to pray The Very Words of God. However, since God always honors sincere hearts, prayer can naturally flow from the heart of any person without any knowledge of The Words of God in the Scripture, but that does not eliminate the need for any pray-er to seek out The Living God through the only book that He wrote, the Holy Bible.

It may be that a choice between the priority of praying or reading the Bible is much like asking oneself, "Do I eat or drink first, or if I have to give up something, should I give up eating or drinking or even sleeping?" One cannot, of course, give up any of these, as they are all necessary to survival. Likewise, knowing God's Word and praying are both necessary for the survival of the spirit of the person. As the apostle Paul wrote in 2 Timothy 3:16, "All Scripture is given by inspiration of God ..." The word *inspiration* indicates the breathing of God, so the Bible is the very breathing of God and is vital for our spiritual lives, as the remainder of that verse and the previous and the following indicates.

In the same way, our praying is our breathing toward God, and if our speaking is the same Very Words that God breathed, or spoke, to us, we cannot improve on that. Psalm 33:6 informs, "By The Word of The Lord were the heavens made; and all the host of them by The Breath of His Mouth." And when God created mankind, the Scripture tells us that He "breathed" into us and mankind "became a living soul." This "breathing" is definitely a life-giving, creation force; likewise, quoting God's Holy Word in our prayers becomes a life-giving, healing, relieving, saving, rescuing, and much more force! In John 8:47a, Jesus says, "He that is of God heareth God's Words ..." and 14:12b, "the works that I do ... greater works than these shall he do." Motivating all this should be the "Greater love hath no man than this" of John 15:13a. May God and/or others hear God's Very Own Words coming from your lips in prayer!

Sometimes the Lord reveals Himself to those who do not even ask or look for Him (Isaiah 65:1). Indeed, without the Lord's prompting, none of us would even know to seek after God. As Romans 1 indicates, God has announced His presence through the creation, through our conscience, and, of course, through His Christ. At the end of Isaiah 65, verse 24, God does tell us that the day will come, in the new heavens and new earth, when "it shall come to pass, that before they call, I will answer; and while they are yet speaking, I will hear." That, though, is for that time, but until then, we must continue to verbalize our prayers, and we have the opportunity to use the Very Words that God Himself has ordained and consecrated and which Christianity has canonized to effect God's kingdom in our world and lives. And even though our Lord mentioned to us on the Sermon on the Mount that our Father in heaven "knoweth what things ye have need of, before ye ask Him," Jesus' instruction to us nonetheless in the next and previous verses was to, in fact, pray to Him (Matthew 6:5–9; 7:7, 8).

Have you ever wondered what God does when we pray? For an amazing display, read Psalm 18:6–19. See also Revelation 8:3–5, which shows the tremendous effects of our prayers, and notice in Acts 4:24 and 31 what can happen when we pray unified. In Acts 16:25–26, an earthquake even ensues after prayer!

In concluding this portion, note some of God's Quotes in the Scriptures and other quotes related to this theme of including God's Very Own Words in our own prayers:

"Neither decline from The Words of My Mouth" (Proverbs 4:5b).

"A man shall be satisfied with good by the fruit of his mouth ..." (Proverbs 12:14a).

"A man shall eat good by the fruit of his mouth ..." (Proverbs 13:2a).

"Every Word of God is pure ..." (Proverbs 30:5).

"Let me see thy countenance, let me hear thy voice; for sweet is thy voice, and thy countenance is comely" (Song of Songs 2:14b) spoken by The Lover (The Lord).

"'As for Me, this is My Covenant with them,' saith the LORD; 'My Spirit that is upon thee, and My Words which I have put in thy mouth, shall not depart out of thy mouth ...' " (Isaiah 59:21a).

"Thy Words were found, and I did eat them; and Thy Word was unto me the joy and rejoicing of mine heart: for I am called by Thy Name, O LORD God of Hosts" (Jeremiah 15:16).

"Who is he that saith, and it cometh to pass, when the Lord commandeth it not?" (Lamentations 3:37).

"And I sought for a man among them, that should make up the hedge, and stand in the gap before Me for the land, that I should not destroy it: but I found none" (Ezekiel 22:30).

"Wait on Thy God continually" (Hosea 12:6b).

"For I have not spoken of Myself; but The Father which sent Me, He gave Me a commandment, what I should say, and what I should speak" (John 12:49).

"Take with you words, and turn to the Lord ..." (Hosea 14:2). What words? See the rest of the verse along with verse 3.

"The prayer that is born of meditation upon the Word of God is the prayer that soars upward most easily to God's listening ear."[26] R. A. Torrey

"The mightiest prayers are often those drenched with the Word of God."[27] Herbert Lockyer

"You will never pray a higher or more effective prayer than when, guided by the Holy Spirit, you go to the Word, find the promise that relates to you and your situation and say, 'Lord, You said it, You do it.' "[28]

Derek Prince

"God detests the prayers of a man who has no delight in His Word. When we live with a closed Bible, we live with a closed heaven; God will not answer our prayers."[29]

Charles Stanley

"In prayer man rises to heaven to dwell with God: in the Word God comes to dwell with man. In prayer man gives himself to God: in the Word God gives himself to man."[30]

Andrew Murray

"For He whom God hath sent speaketh The Words of God ..." (John 3:34a). These words were written of Jesus; however, we can also apply them to ourselves. If you want to be known as someone God has sent, you too must speak The Very Words of God, and, of course, you can do this in prayer as well!

How to Read the Lists in This Book

In the *God's Book of Prayers* edition of this project, all Bible prayers
are divided by category (the categories are in alphabetical sequence,
i.e., blessings first, confession second, etc., with worship last). Each
category of prayer has two parts. The first part contains *full* prayers
of that particular category; the second part lists only *verses* that fit the
definition of that category from all the other biblical prayers (i.e., part
two typically does not have full prayers). These two parts of each
category are divided by a row, indicating the division. Within each
part, the prayers are listed in biblical sequence. For example, near the
middle of the category "Prayers of Thanks," you will find:

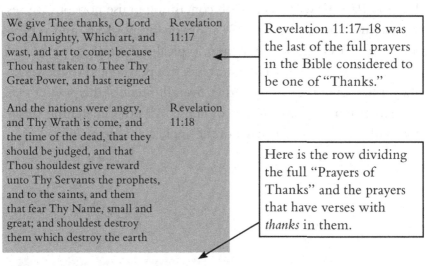

We give Thee thanks, O Lord God Almighty, Which art, and wast, and art to come; because Thou hast taken to Thee Thy Great Power, and hast reigned	Revelation 11:17

Revelation 11:17–18 was the last of the full prayers in the Bible considered to be one of "Thanks."

And the nations were angry, and Thy Wrath is come, and the time of the dead, that they should be judged, and that Thou shouldest give reward unto Thy Servants the prophets, and to the saints, and them that fear Thy Name, small and great; and shouldest destroy them which destroy the earth	Revelation 11:18

Here is the row dividing the full "Prayers of Thanks" and the prayers that have verses with *thanks* in them.

Prayer portions that contain Thanks in them

See next page for continuance of the list with the prayers that
contain verses with *thanks* in them.

2 Samuel
22:48–50
[Psalm 18]

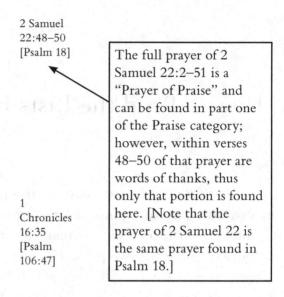

The full prayer of 2 Samuel 22:2–51 is a "Prayer of Praise" and can be found in part one of the Praise category; however, within verses 48–50 of that prayer are words of thanks, thus only that portion is found here. [Note that the prayer of 2 Samuel 22 is the same prayer found in Psalm 18.]

1 Chronicles 16:35 [Psalm 106:47]

In *The Lord's Prayers* edition, the prayers are listed only once, and that in biblical sequence, with all applicable categories spelled out beside each one. Overall, Psalm 3 (see table next) was considered to be a "Petition Prayer" with verses 3–8 containing praise portions, verses 1–7 statement portions, verses 3–4, 8 worship portions, and verse 8 a blessing. (In *God's Book of Prayers*, typically the full prayer would only be in part one of the closest category of prayer next to the verses unless I felt, as in this case, another overall intent of the pray-er was for another purpose, as here one of praise. All other matching verses only will be found in part two of the applicable categories.)

LORD, how are they increased that trouble me! Many are they that rise up against me. Many there be which say of my soul, There is no help for him in God	Psalm 3:1–2			
But Thou, O LORD, art a shield for me; my glory, and the lifter up of mine head. I cried unto the LORD with my voice, and He heard me out of His Holy Hill	Psalm 3:3–4		STATEMENT	WORSHIP
I laid me down and slept; I awaked; for the LORD sustained me	Psalm 3:5	PETITION		
I will not be afraid of ten thousands of people, that have set themselves against me round about	Psalm 3:6	PRAISE		
Arise, O LORD; save me, O my God: for Thou hast smitten all mine enemies upon the cheek bone; Thou hast broken the teeth of the ungodly	Psalm 3:7			
Salvation belongeth unto the LORD: Thy blessing is upon Thy People	Psalm 3:8		BLESSING	WORSHIP

Only *The Lord's Prayers* edition contains the concordance of words and phrases. Next to each Scriptural location of this concordance are upper- and lowercase letters. These letters specify what category of prayer that particular verse(s) belongs to. Uppercase beginning letters indicate full primary prayers of the category, and lowercase letters reveal that the verse(s) is only a portion of a full prayer that contains the indicated category of the lowercased letter. The complete codes for the nine categories of prayer are: B = Blessing; C = Confession; I = Insight; Pr = Praise; Pt = Petition; R = Response; S = Statement; T = Thanks; W = Worship.

As an example, the singular word *rain* appears in the following prayers:

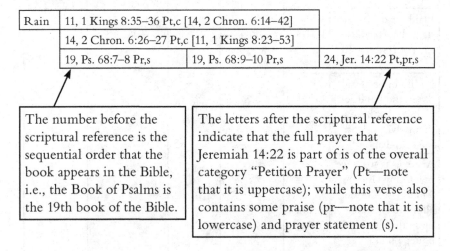

Rain	11, 1 Kings 8:35–36 Pt,c [14, 2 Chron. 6:14–42]		
	14, 2 Chron. 6:26–27 Pt,c [11, 1 Kings 8:23–53]		
	19, Ps. 68:7–8 Pr,s	19, Ps. 68:9–10 Pr,s	24, Jer. 14:22 Pt,pr,s

The number before the scriptural reference is the sequential order that the book appears in the Bible, i.e., the Book of Psalms is the 19th book of the Bible.	The letters after the scriptural reference indicate that the full prayer that Jeremiah 14:22 is part of is of the overall category "Petition Prayer" (Pt—note that it is uppercase); while this verse also contains some praise (pr—note that it is lowercase) and prayer statement (s).

More than half of the prayers of the Bible are from the Book of Psalms. More fodder and analysis continues in the next section.

Cursory Fodder for
and Initial Analysis of
the Prayers of the Bible

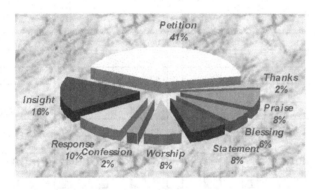

BLESSING	33	5.89%
CONFESSION	12	2.14%
INSIGHT	89	15.89%
PETITION	227	40.54%
PRAISE	46	8.21%
RESPONSE	58	10.36%
STATEMENT	43	7.68%
THANKS	9	1.61%
WORSHIP	43	7.68%
Total Prayers in the Bible	560	

I located 560 prayers in the Bible. This chart reveals the breakdown, by category.

Verses with Prayer

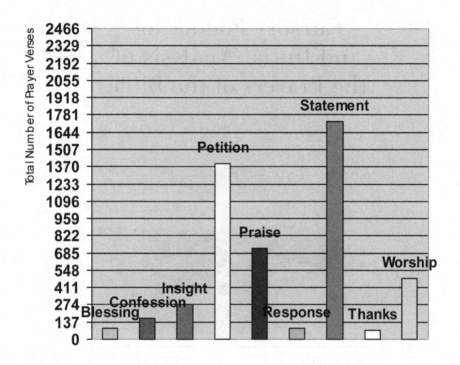

This chart shows how many verses of each prayer category are in the Bible. Many verses have more than one category per verse.

BLESSING	87
CONFESSION	167
INSIGHT	281
PETITION	1392
PRAISE	723
RESPONSE	89
STATEMENT	1732
THANKS	73
WORSHIP	483

The following is a
Prayer Words Cloud:

Much analysis can be made using this diagram. This Prayer Words Cloud shows the most common major words found in the prayers of the Bible, along with other interesting words (sixty-six in all). The larger the word appears in the cloud, the more times it is mentioned in the prayers (the quantity is beside each word). From the cover page of Herbert Lockyer's classic book, *All the Prayers of the Bible*, comes the following quote, "From the Prayers of the Bible, we know God as the One who hears and answers prayers."[31] This Prayer Words Clouds validates at a glance that The God of the Bible is, in fact, The One Who is prayed to. The second easy analysis point, which should give hope, joy, and relief to all humanity throughout history is that *I*, *my*, and *me* are the third, fourth, and fifth most common major words in the prayers of the Bible. Of course, the high incidence of *them*, *they*, *all*, *their*, *people*, and more prayed in Holy Scripture seems to indicate that many prayers were directed for others as well.

(The graphics and design of this Prayer Words Cloud is the fantastic work of San Antonio Graphic Designer Ed Garza.)

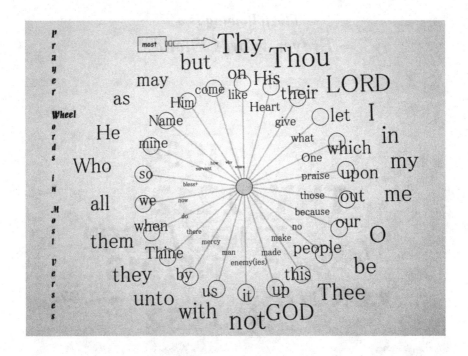

This is a Prayer Words Wheel that indicates how many prayer verses contain each particular word. The wheel itself starts at the top with the word *Thy* being in the most prayer verses, which is also indicated by the data on the next page (alphabetized, with the ranking after the comma) and appears in 831 prayer verses. The wheel continues in the clockwise direction, with each successive word getting smaller, starting over at the top and going down a little, continuing in the same circular pattern until it ends with the word *where* in the middle. Another example is the word *because*, which is the fifty-second most common word on the wheel and appears in 120 prayer verses. See each Word breakdown data on next page.

Prayer Words Wheel Data

Prayer Verses found in, by Word					
all, 17	341	LORD, 3	760	Thee, 10	464
as, 20	257	made, 55	113	their, 25	218
be, 9	485	make, 54	115	them, 16	352
because, 52	120	man, 57	111	there, 59	103
bless+, 62	97	may, 21	256	they, 15	364
but, 22	245	me, 7	648	Thine, 37	161
by, 36	169	mercy, 58	105	this, 32	194
come, 44	141	mine, 41	149	those, 51	122
do, 60	102	my, 6	701	Thou, 2	803
enemy(ies), 56	112	Name, 42	146	Thy, 1	831
give, 47	125	no, 53	118	unto, 14	384
GOD, 11	447	not, 12	420	up, 33	182
He, 19	268	now, 61	99	upon, 28	199
Heart, 46	126	O, 8	501	us, 35	179
Him, 43	145	on, 23	222	we, 39	155
His, 24	220	One, 49	124	what, 48	124
how, 64	83	our, 30	198	when, 38	161
I, 4	738	out, 29	199	where, 66	34
in, 5	734	people, 31	194	which, 27	207
it, 34	179	praise, 50	123	Who, 18	308
let, 26	212	servant, 63	97	why, 65	44
like, 45	132	so, 40	155	with, 13	403

Endnotes for the Rationale and Instructional Guide:

1. Herbert Lockyer, *All the Prayers of the Bible* (Grand Rapids: Zondervan Publishing House, 1959), 179.

2. D. Elton Trueblood. BrainyQuote.com, Xplore Inc, 2012. *http:// www.brainyquote.com/quotes/authors/d/d_elton_trueblood.html*, (accessed April 24, 2012).

3. E. M. Bounds, *The Complete Works of E. M. Bounds on Prayer* (Grand Rapids: Baker Book House Company, 1990), 19.

4. Lockyer, *All the Prayers of the Bible*, 178.

5. Lockyer, *All the Prayers of the Bible*, 124.

6. D. L. Moody, *Prevailing Prayer: What Hinders It* (Chicago: Fleming H. Revell, 1884), 107.

7. Jack Hayford, *Prayer is Invading the Impossible* (New York: Ballantine Books, 1977), 10.

8. Bounds, *The Complete Works of E. M. Bounds on Prayer*, 73.

9. Joyce Meyer, *The Power of Simple Prayer* (New York: Faith Words, 2007), 176–178.

10. "Yoido Full Gospel Church—South Korea," Worthy News, http://churches.gmttmedia.com/documents/302.html, (accessed February 7, 2012)

11. Lockyer, *All the Prayers of the Bible*, 145.

12. Lockyer, *All the Prayers of the Bible*, 219.

13. William Law, *A Serious Call to a Holy and Devout Life* (London: William Innys, 1732), 152.

14. Moody, *Prevailing Prayer: What Hinders It* (Chicago: Fleming H. Revell, 1884), 90.

15. Moody, *Prevailing Prayer: What Hinders It* (Chicago: Fleming H. Revell, 1884), 93.

16. Lockyer, *All the Prayers of the Bible*, 216.

17. Lockyer, *All the Prayers of the Bible*, 191.

18. Lockyer, *All the Prayers of the Bible*, 213.

19. Peter Lord, *The 2959 Plan* (Agape Ministries, 1976), 12.

20. Lockyer, *All the Prayers of the Bible*, 82.

21. Lockyer, *All the Prayers of the Bible*, 203.

22. Lockyer, *All the Prayers of the Bible*, 52.

23. Lockyer, *All the Prayers of the Bible*, 183.

24. Lockyer, *All the Prayers of the Bible*, 96.
25a,b. Watchman Nee, *Let Us Pray* (New York: Christian Fellowship Publishers, Inc., 1977), 7–16.
26. R. A. Torrey, *How to Pray* (chapter 7).
27. Lockyer, *All the Prayers of the Bible*, 136.
28. Derek Prince, *Secrets of a Prayer Warrior* (Grand Rapids: Chosen Books, 2009), 54.
29. Charles Stanley, *Handle with Prayer* (Colorado Springs: ChariotVictor Publishing, 1982), 71.
30. Andrew Murray, *The Inner Chamber* (New York: Fleming H. Revell Company, 1905), 25.
31. Lockyer, *All the Prayers of the Bible*, 1.

The Prayers of the Bible

Grouped into the following nine categories:

Blessing Prayers

Therefore God give thee of the dew of heaven, and the fatness of the earth, and plenty of corn and wine	Genesis 27:28
Let people serve thee, and nations bow down to thee: be lord over thy brethren, and let thy mother's sons bow down to thee: cursed be every one that curseth thee, and blessed be he that blesseth thee	Genesis 27:29
And God Almighty bless thee, and make thee fruitful, and multiply thee, that thou mayest be a multitude of people	Genesis 28:3
And give thee the blessing of Abraham, to thee, and to thy seed with thee; that thou mayest inherit the land wherein thou art a stranger, which God gave unto Abraham	Genesis 28:4
God, before Whom my fathers Abraham and Isaac did walk, The God which fed me all my life long unto this day, The Angel which redeemed me from all evil, bless the lads	Genesis 48:15–16a
And let my name be named on them, and the name of my fathers Abraham and Isaac; and let them grow into a multitude in the midst of the earth	Genesis 48:16b

In thee shall Israel bless, saying, God make thee as Ephraim and as Manasseh	Genesis 48:20b
The LORD bless thee, and keep thee: The LORD make His Face shine upon thee, and be gracious unto thee: The LORD lift up His Countenance upon thee, and give thee peace	Numbers 6:24–26
Yea, He loved the people; all His Saints are in Thy Hand: and they sat down at Thy Feet; every one shall receive of Thy Words. Moses commanded us a law, even the inheritance of the congregation of Jacob	Deuteronomy 33:3-4
Let Reuben live, and not die; and let not his men be few	Deuteronomy 33:6
Hear, LORD, the voice of Judah, and bring him unto his people: let his hands be sufficient for him; and be Thou an help to him from his enemies	Deuteronomy 33:7
Let Thy Thummim and Thy Urim be with Thy Holy One, whom Thou didst prove at Massah, and with whom Thou didst strive at the waters of Meribah; Who said unto his father and to his mother, I have not seen him; neither did he acknowledge his brethren, nor knew his own children: For they have observed Thy Word, and kept Thy Covenant. They shall teach Jacob Thy Judgments, and Israel Thy Law: they shall put incense before Thee, and whole burnt sacrifice upon Thine Altar. Bless, LORD, his substance, and accept the work of his hands; smite through the loins of them that rise against him, and of them that hate him, that they rise not again	Deuteronomy 33:8-11

The beloved of The LORD shall dwell in safety by him; and The Lord shall cover him all the day long, and he shall dwell between His Shoulders

Deuteronomy 33:12

Blessed of The LORD be his land, for the precious things of heaven, for the dew, and for the deep that coucheth beneath, And for the precious fruits brought forth by the sun, and for the precious things put forth by the moon, And for the chief things of the ancient mountains, and for the precious things of the lasting hills

Deuteronomy 33:13-17

And for the precious things of the earth and fulness thereof, and for the good will of Him that dwelt in the bush: let the blessing come upon the head of Joseph, and upon the top of the head of him that was separated from his brethren. His glory is like the firstling of his bullock, and his horns are like the horns of unicorns: with them he shall push the people together to the ends of the earth: and they are the ten thousands of Ephraim, and they are the thousands of Manasseh.

Rejoice, Zebulun, in thy going out; and, Issachar, in thy tents. They shall call the people unto the mountain; there they shall offer sacrifices of righteousness: for they shall suck of the abundance of the seas, and of treasures hid in the sand

Deuteronomy 33:18-19

Blessed be he that enlargeth Gad: he dwelleth as a lion, and teareth the arm with the crown of the head. And he provided the first part for himself, because there, in a portion of the lawgiver, was he seated; and he came with the heads of the people, he executed The Justice of The LORD, and His Judgments with Israel

Deuteronomy 33:20-21

Dan is a lion's whelp: he shall leap from Bashan	Deuteronomy 33:22
O Naphtali, satisfied with favour, and full with The Blessing of The LORD: possess thou the west and the south.	Deuteronomy 33:23
Let Asher be blessed with children; let him be acceptable to his brethren, and let him dip his foot in oil. Thy shoes shall be iron and brass; and as thy days, so shall thy strength be	Deuteronomy 33:24-25
The LORD be with you!	Ruth 2:4a
The LORD bless thee!	Ruth 2:4b
The LORD recompense thy work, and a full reward be given thee of The LORD God of Israel, under Whose Wings thou art come to trust	Ruth 2:12
Blessed be The LORD, which hath not left thee this day without a kinsman, that his name may be famous in Israel	Ruth 4:14
The LORD be with thee, as He hath been with my father	1 Samuel 20:13b
wherefore The LORD reward thee good for that thou hast done unto me this day	1 Samuel 24:19b
therefore The LORD thy God will be with thee	2 Samuel 14:17b
Now The LORD thy God add unto the people, how many soever they be, an hundredfold, and that the eyes of my lord the king may see it	2 Samuel 24:3a
The LORD thy God accept thee	2 Samuel 24:23b

Now, my son, The LORD be with thee; and prosper thou, and build the house of The LORD thy God, as He hath said of thee	1 Chronicles 22:11
Only The LORD give thee wisdom and understanding, and give thee charge concerning Israel, that thou mayest keep The Law of The LORD thy God	1 Chronicles 22:12
Then shalt thou prosper, if thou takest heed to fulfil the statutes and judgments which The LORD charged Moses with concerning Israel: be strong, and of good courage; dread not, nor be dismayed	1 Chronicles 22:13
Arise therefore, and be doing, and The LORD be with thee	1 Chronicles 22:16b
Who is there among you of all His People? The LORD his God be with him, and let him go up	2 Chronicles 36:23b [Ezra 1:3]
Who is there among you of all his people? his God be with him, and let him go up to Jerusalem, which is in Judah, and build the house of The LORD God of Israel, (He is The God,) which is in Jerusalem	Ezra 1:3 [2 Chronicles 36:23b]
The LORD hear thee in the day of trouble; the Name of The God of Jacob defend thee; Send thee help from the sanctuary, and strengthen thee out of Zion; Remember all thy offerings, and accept thy burnt sacrifice; Selah. Grant thee according to thine own heart, and fulfil all thy counsel. We will rejoice in thy salvation, and in The Name of our God we will set up our banners: The LORD fulfil all thy petitions	Psalm 20:1-5
The LORD shall increase you more and more, you and your children	Psalm 115:14

Ye are blessed of The LORD which made   Psalm 115:15
heaven and earth

The LORD shall bless thee out of Zion: and   Psalm 128:5-6
thou shalt see the good of Jerusalem all the days
of thy life. Yea, thou shalt see thy children's
children, and peace upon Israel

The Blessing of The LORD be upon you: we   Psalm 129:8b
bless you in The Name of The LORD

Prayer portions that contain Blessings in them

2 Samuel 7:29 [1 Chronicles 17:27]	Psalm 84:3-7
1 Chronicles 17:27 [2 Samuel 7:29]	Psalm 84:12
Psalm 3:8	Psalm 89:15-17
Psalm 22:26-28	Psalm 94:12-13
Psalm 32:1-2	Psalm 109:28
Psalm 41:1-3	Psalm 119:1-3
Psalm 65:4	Psalm 134:3
Psalm 72:15-17	

Confession Prayers

Oh, this people have sinned a great sin, and have made them gods of gold. Yet now, if Thou wilt forgive their sin--; and if not, blot me, I pray Thee, out of Thy Book which Thou hast written	Exodus 32:31-32
If now I have found grace in Thy Sight, O Lord, let my Lord, I pray Thee, go among us; for it is a stiffnecked people; and pardon our iniquity and our sin, and take us for Thine Inheritance	Exodus 34:9
We have sinned against Thee, both because we have forsaken our God, and also served Baalim	Judges 10:10
We have sinned: do Thou unto us whatsoever seemeth good unto Thee; deliver us only, we pray Thee, this day	Judges 10:15
We have sinned against The LORD	1 Samuel 7:6b
We have sinned, because we have forsaken The LORD, and have served Baalim and Ashtaroth: but now deliver us out of the hand of our enemies, and we will serve Thee	1 Samuel 12:10
I have sinned greatly in that I have done: and now, I beseech Thee, O LORD, take away the iniquity of Thy Servant; for I have done very foolishly	2 Samuel 24:10 [1 Chronicles 21:8]

Lo, I have sinned, and I have done wickedly: but these sheep, what have they done? let Thine Hand, I pray Thee, be against me, and against my father's house	2 Samuel 24:17 [1 Chronicles 21:17]
I have sinned greatly, because I have done this thing: but now, I beseech Thee, do away the iniquity of Thy Servant; for I have done very foolishly	1 Chronicles 21:8 [2 Samuel 24:10]
Is it not I that commanded the people to be numbered? even I it is that have sinned and done evil indeed; but as for these sheep, what have they done? let Thine Hand, I pray Thee, O LORD my God, be on me, and on my father's house; but not on Thy People, that they should be plagued	1 Chronicles 21:17 [2 Samuel 24:17]
O my God, I am ashamed and blush to lift up my face to Thee, my God: for our iniquities are increased over our head, and our trespass is grown up unto the heavens. Since the days of our fathers have we been in a great trespass unto this day; and for our iniquities have we, our kings, and our priests, been delivered into the hand of the kings of the lands, to the sword, to captivity, and to a spoil, and to confusion of face, as it is this day. And now for a little space grace hath been shown from The LORD our God, to leave us a remnant to escape, and to give us a nail in His Holy Place, that our God may lighten our eyes, and give us a little reviving in our bondage. For we were bondmen; yet our God hath not forsaken us in our bondage, but hath extended mercy unto us in the sight of the kings of Persia, to give us a reviving, to set up the house of our God, and to repair the desolations thereof, and to give us a wall in Judah and in Jerusalem	Ezra 9:6-9

And now, O our God, what shall we   Ezra 9:10–12
say after this? for we have forsaken Thy
Commandments, Which Thou hast
commanded by Thy Servants the prophets,
saying, The land, unto which ye go to possess
it, is an unclean land with the filthiness of the
people of the lands, with their abominations,
which have filled it from one end to another
with their uncleanness. Now therefore give not
your daughters unto their sons, neither take
their daughters unto your sons, nor seek their
peace or their wealth for ever: that ye may be
strong, and eat the good of the land, and leave it
for an inheritance to your children for ever

And after all that is come upon us for our   Ezra 9:13–15
evil deeds, and for our great trespass, seeing
that Thou our God hast punished us less than
our iniquities deserve, and hast given us such
deliverance as this; Should we again break Thy
Commandments, and join in affinity with
the people of these abominations? wouldest
not Thou be angry with us till Thou hadst
consumed us, so that there should be no
remnant nor escaping? O LORD God of Israel,
Thou art righteous: for we remain yet escaped,
as it is this day: behold, we are before Thee in
our trespasses: for we cannot stand before Thee
because of this

I beseech Thee, O LORD God of heaven, the great and terrible God, that keepeth covenant and mercy for them that love Him and observe His Commandments: Let Thine Ear now be attentive, and Thine Eyes open, that Thou mayest hear the prayer of Thy Servant, which I pray before Thee now, day and night, for the children of Israel Thy Servants, and confess the sins of the children of Israel, which we have sinned against Thee: both I and my father's house have sinned. We have dealt very corruptly against Thee, and have not kept the commandments, nor the statutes, nor the judgments, which Thou commandedst Thy Servant Moses

Nehemiah 1:5-7

Remember, I beseech Thee, The Word that Thou commandedst Thy Servant Moses, saying, If ye transgress, I will scatter you abroad among the nations: But if ye turn unto Me, and keep My Commandments, and do them; though there were of you cast out unto the uttermost part of the heaven, yet will I gather them from thence, and will bring them unto the place that I have chosen to set My Name there. Now these are Thy Servants and Thy People, whom Thou hast redeemed by Thy Great Power, and by Thy Strong Hand

Nehemiah 1:8-10

O LORD, I beseech Thee, let now Thine Ear be attentive to the prayer of Thy Servant, and to the prayer of Thy Servants, who desire to fear Thy Name: and prosper, I pray Thee, Thy Servant this day, and grant him mercy in the sight of this man

Nehemiah 1:11

Stand up and bless The LORD your God for ever and ever: and blessed be Thy Glorious Name, Which is exalted above all blessing and praise. Thou, even Thou, art LORD Alone; Thou hast made heaven, the heaven of heavens, with all their host, the earth, and all things that are therein, the seas, and all that is therein, and Thou preservest them all; and the host of heaven worshippeth Thee

Nehemiah 9:5b-6

Thou art The LORD The God, Who didst choose Abram, and broughtest him forth out of Ur of the Chaldees, and gavest him the name of Abraham; And foundest his heart faithful before Thee, and madest a covenant with him to give the land of the Canaanites, the Hittites, the Amorites, and the Perizzites, and the Jebusites, and the Girgashites, to give it, I say, to his seed, and hast performed Thy Words; for Thou art righteous

Nehemiah 9:7-8

And didst see the affliction of our fathers in Egypt, and heardest their cry by the Red sea; And showedst signs and wonders upon Pharaoh, and on all his servants, and on all the people of his land: for Thou knewest that they dealt proudly against them. So didst Thou get Thee a Name, as it is this day. And Thou didst divide the sea before them, so that they went through the midst of the sea on the dry land; and their persecutors thou threwest into the deeps, as a stone into the mighty waters. Moreover Thou leddest them in the day by a cloudy pillar; and in the night by a pillar of fire, to give them light in the way wherein they should go

Nehemiah 9:9-12

Thou camest down also upon mount Sinai, and spakest with them from heaven, and gavest them right judgments, and true laws, good statutes and commandments: And madest known unto them Thy Holy Sabbath, and commandedst them precepts, statutes, and laws, by the hand of Moses Thy Servant: And gavest them bread from heaven for their hunger, and broughtest forth water for them out of the rock for their thirst, and promisedst them that they should go in to possess the land which Thou hadst sworn to give them

Nehemiah 9:13-15

But they and our fathers dealt proudly, and hardened their necks, and hearkened not to Thy Commandments, And refused to obey, neither were mindful of Thy Wonders that Thou didst among them; but hardened their necks, and in their rebellion appointed a captain to return to their bondage: but Thou art a God ready to pardon, gracious and merciful, slow to anger, and of great kindness, and forsookest them not

Nehemiah 9:16-17

Yea, when they had made them a molten calf, and said, This is thy God that brought thee up out of Egypt, and had wrought great provocations; Yet Thou in Thy Manifold Mercies forsookest them not in the wilderness: the pillar of the cloud departed not from them by day, to lead them in the way; neither the pillar of fire by night, to show them light, and the way wherein they should go

Nehemiah 9:18-19

Thou gavest also Thy Good Spirit to instruct them, and withheldest not Thy Manna from their mouth, and gavest them water for their thirst. Yea, forty years didst Thou sustain them in the wilderness, so that they lacked nothing; their clothes waxed not old, and their feet swelled not

Nehemiah 9:20-21

Moreover Thou gavest them kingdoms and nations, and didst divide them into corners: so they possessed the land of Sihon, and the land of the king of Heshbon, and the land of Og king of Bashan

Nehemiah 9:22

Their children also multipliedst Thou as the stars of heaven, and broughtest them into the land, concerning which Thou hadst promised to their fathers, that they should go in to possess it. So the children went in and possessed the land, and Thou subduedst before them the inhabitants of the land, the Canaanites, and gavest them into their hands, with their kings, and the people of the land, that they might do with them as they would. And they took strong cities, and a fat land, and possessed houses full of all goods, wells digged, vineyards, and oliveyards, and fruit trees in abundance: so they did eat, and were filled, and became fat, and delighted themselves in Thy Great Goodness

Nehemiah 9:23-25

Confession Prayers

Nevertheless they were disobedient, and   Nehemiah 9:26–
rebelled against Thee, and cast Thy Law behind 27
their backs, and slew Thy prophets which
testified against them to turn them to Thee,
and they wrought great provocations. Therefore
Thou deliveredst them into the hand of their
enemies, who vexed them: and in the time of
their trouble, when they cried unto Thee, Thou
heardest them from heaven; and according
to Thy Manifold Mercies Thou gavest them
saviours, who saved them out of the hand of
their enemies

But after they had rest, they did evil again   Nehemiah 9:28–
before Thee: therefore leftest Thou them in   29
the land of their enemies, so that they had the
dominion over them: yet when they returned,
and cried unto Thee, Thou heardest them from
heaven; and many times didst Thou deliver
them according to Thy Mercies; And testifiedst
against them, that Thou mightest bring them
again unto Thy Law: yet they dealt proudly,
and hearkened not unto Thy Commandments,
but sinned against Thy Judgments, (which if a
man do, he shall live in them;) and withdrew
the shoulder, and hardened their neck, and
would not hear

Yet many years didst Thou forbear them, and   Nehemiah 9:30–
testifiedst against them by Thy Spirit in Thy   31
Prophets: yet would they not give ear: therefore
gavest Thou them into the hand of the people
of the lands. Nevertheless for Thy Great
Mercies' Sake Thou didst not utterly consume
them, nor forsake them; for Thou art a gracious
and merciful God

Now therefore, our God, The Great, The
Mighty, and The Terrible God, Who keepest
covenant and mercy, let not all the trouble seem
little before Thee, that hath come upon us, on
our kings, on our princes, and on our priests,
and on our prophets, and on our fathers, and on
all Thy People, since the time of the kings of
Assyria unto this day. Howbeit Thou art just in
all that is brought upon us; for Thou hast done
right, but we have done wickedly

Nehemiah 9:32–33

Neither have our kings, our princes, our
priests, nor our fathers, kept Thy Law, nor
hearkened unto Thy Commandments and Thy
Testimonies, wherewith Thou didst testify
against them. For they have not served Thee in
their kingdom, and in Thy Great Goodness that
Thou gavest them, and in the large and fat land
which Thou gavest before them, neither turned
they from their wicked works

Nehemiah 9:34–35

Behold, we are servants this day, and for the
land that Thou gavest unto our fathers to eat
the fruit thereof and the good thereof, behold,
we are servants in it: And it yieldeth much
increase unto the kings whom Thou hast set
over us because of our sins: also they have
dominion over our bodies, and over our cattle,
at their pleasure, and we are in great distress

Nehemiah 9:36–37

And because of all this we make a sure
covenant, and write it; and our princes, Levites,
and priests, seal unto it

Nehemiah 9:38

I know that Thou canst do every thing, and that no thought can be withholden from Thee. Who is he that hideth counsel without knowledge? therefore have I uttered that I understood not; things too wonderful for me, which I knew not. Hear, I beseech Thee, and I will speak: I will demand of Thee, and declare Thou unto me. I have heard of Thee by the hearing of the ear: but now mine eye seeth Thee. Wherefore I abhor myself, and repent in dust and ashes	Job 42:2-6

Blessed is he whose transgression is forgiven, whose sin is covered. Blessed is the man unto whom The LORD imputeth not iniquity, and in whose spirit there is no guile — Psalm 32:1-2

When I kept silence, my bones waxed old through my roaring all the day long. For day and night Thy Hand was heavy upon me: my moisture is turned into the drought of summer — Psalm 32:3-4

I acknowledged my sin unto Thee, and mine iniquity have I not hid. I said, I will confess my transgressions unto The LORD; and Thou forgavest the iniquity of my sin — Psalm 32:5

For this shall every one that is godly pray unto Thee in a time when Thou mayest be found: surely in the floods of great waters they shall not come nigh unto him — Psalm 32:6

Thou art my hiding place; Thou shalt preserve me from trouble; Thou shalt compass me about with songs of deliverance — Psalm 32:7

Have mercy upon me, O God, according   Psalm 51:1
to Thy Lovingkindness: according unto the
multitude of Thy Tender Mercies blot out my
transgressions

Wash me thoroughly from mine iniquity, and   Psalm 51:2-3
cleanse me from my sin. For I acknowledge my
transgressions: and my sin is ever before me

Against Thee, Thee only, have I sinned, and   Psalm 51:4
done this evil in Thy Sight: that Thou mightest
be justified when Thou speakest, and be clear
when Thou judgest

Behold, I was shapen in iniquity; and in sin did   Psalm 51:5
my mother conceive me

Behold, Thou desirest truth in the inward parts: Psalm 51:6
and in the hidden part Thou shalt make me to
know wisdom

Purge me with hyssop, and I shall be clean: Psalm 51:7
wash me, and I shall be whiter than snow

Make me to hear joy and gladness; that the   Psalm 51:8
bones which Thou hast broken may rejoice

Hide Thy Face from my sins, and blot out all   Psalm 51:9
mine iniquities

Create in me a clean heart, O God; and renew   Psalm 51:10
a right spirit within me

Cast me not away from Thy Presence, and take   Psalm 51:11
not Thy Holy Spirit from me

Restore unto me the joy of Thy Salvation; and   Psalm 51:12
uphold me with Thy Free Spirit

Then will I teach transgresssors Thy Ways; and sinners shall be converted unto Thee	Psalm 51:13
Deliver me from bloodguiltiness, O God, Thou God of my salvation: and my tongue shall sing aloud of Thy Righteousness	Psalm 51:14
O Lord, open Thou my lips: and My mouth shall show forth Thy Praise	Psalm 51:15
For Thou desirest not sacrifice; else would I give it: Thou delightest not in burnt offering	Psalm 51:16
The sacrifices of God are a broken spirit: a broken and a contrite heart, O God, Thou wilt not despise	Psalm 51:17
Do good in Thy Good Pleasure unto Zion: build Thou the walls of Jerusalem	Psalm 51:18
Then shalt Thou be pleased with the sacrifices of righteousness, with burnt offering and whole burnt offering: then shall they offer bullocks upon Thine Altar	Psalm 51:19
Take away all iniquity, and receive us graciously: so will we render the calves of our lips	Hosea 14:2b
Asshur shall not save us; we will not ride upon horses: neither will we say any more to the work of our hands, Ye are our gods: for in Thee the fatherless findeth mercy	Hosea 14:3
O Lord, the Great and Dreadful God, keeping the covenant and mercy to them that love Him, and to them that keep His Commandments	Daniel 9:4b

We have sinned, and have committed iniquity,
and have done wickedly, and have rebelled,
even by departing from Thy Precepts and from
Thy Judgments

Daniel 9:5

Neither have we hearkened unto Thy Servants
the prophets, which spake in Thy Name to our
kings, our princes, and our fathers, and to all
the people of the land

Daniel 9:6

O Lord, righteousness belongeth unto Thee,
but unto us confusion of faces, as at this day;
to the men of Judah, and to the inhabitants of
Jerusalem, and unto all Israel, that are near,
and that are far off, through all the countries
whither Thou hast driven them, because of
their trespass that they have trespassed against
Thee

Daniel 9:7

O Lord, to us belongeth confusion of face, to
our kings, to our princes, and to our fathers,
because we have sinned against Thee

Daniel 9:8

To The Lord our God belong mercies and
forgivenesses, though we have rebelled against
Him

Daniel 9:9

Neither have we obeyed the Voice of The
LORD our God, to walk in His Laws, which
He set before us by His Servants the prophets

Daniel 9:10

Yea, all Israel have transgressed Thy Law, even
by departing, that they might not obey Thy
Voice; therefore the curse is poured upon us,
and the oath that is written in the law of Moses
the servant of God, because we have sinned
against Him

Daniel 9:11

And He hath confirmed His Words, which He   Daniel 9:12
spake against us, and against our judges that
judged us, by bringing upon us a great evil: for
under the whole heaven hath not been done as
hath been done upon Jerusalem

As it is written in the law of Moses, all this evil   Daniel 9:13
is come upon us: yet made we not our prayer
before The LORD our God, that we might
turn from our iniquities, and understand Thy
Truth

Therefore hath The LORD watched upon the   Daniel 9:14
evil, and brought it upon us: for The LORD
our God is righteous in all His Works which
He doeth: for we obeyed not His Voice

And now, O Lord our God, that hast brought   Daniel 9:15
Thy People forth out of the land of Egypt with
a Mighty Hand, and hast gotten Thee renown,
as at this day; we have sinned, we have done
wickedly

O Lord, according to All Thy Righteousness,   Daniel 9:16
I beseech Thee, let Thine Anger and Thy Fury
be turned away from Thy City Jerusalem, Thy
Holy Mountain: because for our sins, and for
the iniquities of our fathers, Jerusalem and Thy
People are become a reproach to all that are
about us

Now therefore, O our God, hear the prayer of   Daniel 9:17
Thy Servant, and his supplications, and cause
Thy Face to shine upon Thy Sanctuary that is
desolate, for The Lord's Sake

O my God, incline Thine Ear, and hear; open Thine Eyes, and behold our desolations, and the city which is called by Thy Name: for we do not present our supplications before Thee for our righteousnesses, but for Thy Great Mercies	Daniel 9:18
O Lord, hear; O Lord, forgive; O Lord, hearken and do; defer not, for Thine Own Sake, O my God: for Thy City and Thy People are called by Thy Name	Daniel 9:19
Father, I have sinned against heaven, and [before Thee] in Thy Sight, and am no more worthy to be called Thy Son: [make me as one of Thy Hired Servants]	Luke 15:18b-19[21]
Father, I have sinned against heaven, and [before Thee] in Thy Sight, and am no more worthy to be called Thy Son[: make me as one of Thy Hired Servants]	Luke 15:21[18b-19]
God be merciful to me a sinner	Luke 18:13b

Prayer portions that contain Confessions in them

Numbers 14:19	Psalm 79:8
1 Kings 8:27-30 [2 Chronicles 6:14-42]	Psalm 79:9
1 Kings 8:33-36 [2 Chronicles 6:14-42]	Psalm 106:6-7
1 Kings 8:46-50 [2 Chronicles 6:14-42]	Psalm 130:3-4
2 Kings 5:18	Isaiah 64:5-7
2 Chronicles 6:18-21 [1 Kings 8:23-53]	Isaiah 64:9
2 Chronicles 6:24-27 [1 Kings 8:23-53]	Jeremiah 14:7

Confession Prayers

2 Chronicles 6:36-39 [1 Kings 8:23-53]

Job 7:19-21

Psalm 25:11-18

Psalm 38:18

Psalm 41:4

Psalm 69:4-5

Jeremiah 14:20

Lamentations 3:42

Lamentations 5:16

Amos 7:2b

Matthew 6:9-13; Luke 11:2-4

Luke 11:2-4; Matthew 6:9-13

Prayers for Insight

Lord GOD, what wilt Thou give me, seeing I go childless, and the steward of my house is this Eliezer of Damascus?	Genesis 15:2
Behold, to me Thou hast given no seed: and, lo, one born in my house is mine heir	Genesis 15:3
Lord GOD, whereby shall I know that I shall inherit it?	Genesis 15:8
If it be so, why am I thus?	Genesis 25:22b
Tell me, I pray Thee, Thy Name	Genesis 32:29a
Behold, when I come unto the children of Israel, and shall say unto them, The God of your fathers hath sent me unto you; and they shall say to me, What is His Name? what shall I say unto them?	Exodus 3:13
Lord, wherefore hast Thou so evil entreated this people? why is it that Thou hast sent me?	Exodus 5:22
For since I came to Pharaoh to speak in Thy Name, he hath done evil to this people; neither hast Thou delivered Thy People at all	Exodus 5:23
Behold, the children of Israel have not hearkened unto me; how then shall Pharaoh hear me, who am of uncircumcised lips?	Exodus 6:12

What shall I do unto this people? they be almost ready to stone me	Exodus 17:4
See, Thou sayest unto me, Bring up this people: and Thou hast not let me know whom Thou wilt send with me. Yet Thou hast said, I know thee by name, and thou hast also found grace in My Sight	Exodus 33:12
Now therefore, I pray Thee, if I have found grace in Thy Sight, show me now Thy Way, that I may know Thee, that I may find grace in Thy Sight: and consider that this nation is Thy People	Exodus 33:13
What shall we eat the seventh year? behold, we shall not sow, nor gather in our increase	Leviticus 25:20
O God, The God of the spirits of all flesh, shall one man sin, and wilt Thou be wroth with all the congregation?	Numbers 16:22
Alas, O Lord GOD, wherefore hast Thou at all brought this people over Jordan, to deliver us into the hand of the Amorites, to destroy us? would to God we had been content, and dwelt on the other side Jordan!	Joshua 7:7
O Lord, what shall I say, when Israel turneth their backs before their enemies!	Joshua 7:8
For the Canaanites and all the inhabitants of the land shall hear of it, and shall environ us round, and cut off our name from the earth: and what wilt Thou do unto Thy Great Name?	Joshua 7:9
Who shall go up for us against the Canaanites first, to fight against them?	Judges 1:1b

O my Lord, let the man of God which Thou didst send come again unto us, and teach us what we shall do unto the child that shall be born	Judges 13:8
Thou hast given this great deliverance into the hand of Thy Servant: and now shall I die for thirst, and fall into the hand of the uncircumcised?	Judges 15:18
Which of us shall go up first to the battle against the children of Benjamin?	Judges 20:18a
Shall I go up again to battle against the children of Benjamin my brother?	Judges 20:23a
Shall I yet again go out to battle against the children of Benjamin my brother, or shall I cease?	Judges 20:28a
O LORD God of Israel, why is this come to pass in Israel, that there should be today one tribe lacking in Israel?	Judges 21:3
if the man should yet come thither	1 Samuel 10:22a
Shall I go down after the Philistines? wilt thou deliver them into the hand of Israel?	1 Samuel 14:37a
Shall I go and smite these Philistines?	1 Samuel 23:2a
O LORD God of Israel, Thy Servant hath certainly heard that Saul seeketh to come to Keilah, to destroy the city for my sake. Will the men of Keilah deliver me up into his hand? will Saul come down, as Thy Servant hath heard? O LORD God of Israel, I beseech Thee, tell Thy Servant	1 Samuel 23:10-11a

Will the men of Keilah deliver me and my men into the hand of Saul?	1 Samuel 23:12a
Shall I pursue after this troop? shall I overtake them?	1 Samuel 30:8a
Shall I go up into any of the cities of Judah?	2 Samuel 2:1a
Shall I go up to the Philistines? wilt Thou deliver them into mine hand?	2 Samuel 5:19a [1 Chronicles 14:10a]
O LORD my God, hast Thou also brought evil upon the widow with whom I sojourn, by slaying her son?	1 Kings 17:20
By whom?...Who shall order the battle?	1 Kings 20:14
Shall I recover of this disease?	2 Kings 8:8b,9b
Shall I go up against the Philistines? And wilt Thou deliver them into mine hand?	1 Chronicles 14:10a [2 Samuel 5:19a]
Do not condemn me; show me wherefore Thou contendest with me. Is it good unto Thee that Thou shouldest oppress, that Thou shouldest despise the Work of Thine Hands, and shine upon the counsel of the wicked? Hast Thou eyes of flesh? or seest Thou as man seeth?	Job 10:2-4

Are Thy Days as the days of man? are Thy   Job 10:5-9
Years as man's days, That Thou inquirest
after mine iniquity, and searchest after my
sin? Thou knowest that I am not wicked; and
there is none that can deliver out of Thine
Hand. Thine Hands have made me and
fashioned me together round about; yet Thou
dost destroy me. Remember, I beseech Thee,
that Thou hast made me as the clay; and wilt
Thou bring me into dust again?

Hast Thou not poured me out as milk, and   Job 10:10-11
curdled me like cheese? Thou hast clothed
me with skin and flesh, and hast fenced me
with bones and sinews

Thou hast granted me life and favour, and   Job 10:12-13
Thy Visitation hath preserved my spirit. And
these things hast Thou hid in Thine Heart: I
know that this is with Thee

If I sin, then Thou markest me, and Thou   Job 10:14-17
wilt not acquit me from mine iniquity.
If I be wicked, woe unto me; and if I be
righteous, yet will I not lift up my head. I am
full of confusion; therefore see Thou mine
affliction; For it increaseth. Thou huntest
me as a fierce lion: and again Thou showest
Thyself marvellous upon me. Thou renewest
Thy Witnesses against me, and increasest
Thine Indignation upon me; changes and war
are against me

Wherefore then hast Thou brought me forth   Job 10:18-22
out of the womb? Oh that I had given up the
ghost, and no eye had seen me! I should have
been as though I had not been; I should have
been carried from the womb to the grave.
Are not my days few? cease then, and let me
alone, that I may take comfort a little, Before
I go whence I shall not return, even to the
land of darkness and the shadow of death;
A land of darkness, as darkness itself; and of
the shadow of death, without any order, and
where the light is as darkness

O LORD, rebuke me not in Thine Anger,   Psalm 6:1-3
neither chasten me in Thy Hot Displeasure.
Have mercy upon me, O LORD; for I am
weak: O LORD, heal me; for my bones are
vexed. My soul is also sore vexed: but Thou,
O LORD, how long?

My God, my God, why hast Thou forsaken   Psalm 22:1
me? why art Thou so far from helping me,   [Matthew
and from the words of my roaring?   27:46b; Mark
                                               15:34b]

O my God, I cry in the daytime, but Thou   Psalm 22:2
hearest not; and in the night season, and am
not silent

But Thou art holy, O Thou that inhabitest   Psalm 22:3-5
the praises of Israel. Our fathers trusted in
Thee: they trusted, and Thou didst deliver
them. They cried unto Thee, and were
delivered: they trusted in Thee, and were not
confounded

But I am a worm, and no man; a reproach of   Psalm 22:6-8
men, and despised of the people. All they that
see me laugh me to scorn: they shoot out the
lip, they shake the head, saying, He trusted
on The LORD that He would deliver him:
let Him deliver him, seeing He delighted in
him

But Thou art He that took me out of the   Psalm 22:9-10
womb: Thou didst make me hope when I was
upon my mother's breasts. I was cast upon
Thee from the womb: Thou art my God
from my mother's belly

Be not far from me; for trouble is near; for   Psalm 22:11
there is none to help

Many bulls have compassed me: strong bulls   Psalm 22:12-13
of Bashan have beset me round. They gaped
upon me with their mouths, as a ravening and
a roaring lion

I am poured out like water, and all my   Psalm 22:14-19
bones are out of joint: my heart is like wax;
it is melted in the midst of my bowels. My
strength is dried up like a potsherd; and my
tongue cleaveth to my jaws; and Thou hast
brought me into the dust of death. For dogs
have compassed me: the assembly of the
wicked have inclosed me: they pierced my
hands and my feet. I may tell all my bones:
they look and stare upon me. They part my
garments among them, and cast lots upon
my vesture. But be not Thou far from me, O
LORD: O my strength, haste Thee to help
me

Deliver my soul from the sword; my darling   Psalm 22:20-21
from the power of the dog. Save me from the
lion's mouth: for Thou hast heard me from
the horns of the unicorns

I will declare Thy Name unto my brethren,   Psalm 22:22
in the midst of the church [congregation]   [Hebrews 2:12]
will I [sing] praise [unto] Thee

Ye that fear The LORD, praise Him; all   Psalm 22:23-24
ye the seed of Jacob, glorify Him; and fear
Him, all ye the seed of Israel. For He hath
not despised nor abhorred the affliction of the
afflicted; neither hath He hid His Face from
him; but when he cried unto Him, He heard

My praise shall be of Thee in the great   Psalm 22:25
congregation: I will pay my vows before
them that fear Him

The meek shall eat and be satisfied: they   Psalm 22:26-28
shall praise The LORD that seek Him: your
heart shall live for ever. All the ends of the
world shall remember and turn unto The
LORD: and all the kindreds of the nations
shall worship before Thee. For the Kingdom
is The LORD's: and He is The Governor
among the nations

All they that be fat upon earth shall eat   Psalm 22:29-31
and worship: all they that go down to the
dust shall bow before Him: and none can
keep alive his own soul. A seed shall serve
him; it shall be accounted to The Lord for
a generation. They shall come, and shall
declare His Righteousness unto a people that
shall be born, that He hath done this

As the hart panteth after the water brooks, so panteth my soul after Thee, O God	Psalm 42:1
O my God, my soul is cast down within me: therefore will I remember Thee from the land of Jordan, and of the Hermonites, from the hill Mizar	Psalm 42:6
Deep calleth unto deep at the noise of Thy Waterspouts: all Thy Waves and Thy Billows are gone over me	Psalm 42:7 [Jonah 2:3]
Why hast Thou forgotten me? why go I mourning because of the oppression of the enemy?	Psalm 42:9
How long, LORD? wilt Thou hide Thyself for ever? shall Thy Wrath burn like fire?	Psalm 89:46
Remember how short my time is: wherefore hast Thou made all men in vain? What man is he that liveth, and shall not see death? shall he deliver his soul from the hand of the grave?	Psalm 89:47-48
Lord, where are Thy Former Lovingkindnesses, which Thou swarest unto David in Thy Truth?	Psalm 89:49
Remember, Lord, the reproach of Thy Servants; how I do bear in my bosom the reproach of all the mighty people; Wherefore Thine Enemies have reproached, O LORD; wherewith they have reproached the footsteps of Thine Anointed	Psalm 89:50-51
Blessed be The LORD for evermore. Amen, and Amen	Psalm 89:52

Prayers *for* Insight

Lord, how long?	Isaiah 6:11a

[Lord,] who hath believed our report? and to whom hath [is] The Arm of The Lord been revealed?

Isaiah 53:1
[John 12:38b; Romans 10:16b]

Righteous art Thou, O LORD, when I plead with Thee: yet let me talk with Thee of Thy Judgments: Wherefore doth the way of the wicked prosper? wherefore are all they happy that deal very treacherously? Thou hast planted them, yea, they have taken root: they grow, yea, they bring forth fruit: Thou art near in their mouth, and far from their reins

Jeremiah 12:1-2

But Thou, O LORD, knowest me: Thou hast seen me, and tried mine heart toward Thee: pull them out like sheep for the slaughter, and prepare them for the day of slaughter

Jeremiah 12:3

How long shall the land mourn, and the herbs of every field wither, for the wickedness of them that dwell therein? the beasts are consumed, and the birds; because they said, He shall not see our last end

Jeremiah 12:4

Ah Lord GOD! behold, Thou hast made the heaven and the earth by Thy Great Power and Stretched Out Arm, and there is nothing too hard for Thee:

Jeremiah 32:17

Thou showest lovingkindness unto thousands, and recompensest the iniquity of the fathers into the bosom of their children after them: The Great, The Mighty God, The LORD of Hosts, is His Name,

Jeremiah 32:18

Great in counsel, and mighty in work: for Thine Eyes are open upon all the ways of the sons of men: to give every one according to his ways, and according to the fruit of his doings:	Jeremiah 32:19; 17:10b [Revelation 2:23b]
Which hast set signs and wonders in the land of Egypt, even unto this day, and in Israel, and among other men; and hast made Thee a Name, as at this day;	Jeremiah 32:20
And hast brought forth Thy People Israel out of the land of Egypt with signs, and with wonders, and with a strong hand, and with a stretched out arm, and with great terror;	Jeremiah 32:21
And hast given them this land, which Thou didst swear to their fathers to give them, a land flowing with milk and honey;	Jeremiah 32:22
And they came in, and possessed it; but they obeyed not Thy Voice, neither walked in Thy Law; they have done nothing of all that Thou commandedst them to do: therefore Thou hast caused all this evil to come upon them:	Jeremiah 32:23
Behold the mounts, they are come unto the city to take it; and the city is given into the hand of the Chaldeans, that fight against it, because of the sword, and of the famine, and of the pestilence: and what Thou hast spoken is come to pass; and, behold, Thou seest it	Jeremiah 32:24
And Thou hast said unto me, O Lord GOD, Buy thee the field for money, and take witnesses; for the city is given into the hand of the Chaldeans	Jeremiah 32:25

O Thou Sword of The LORD, how long will it be ere Thou be quiet? put up Thyself into Thy Scabbard, rest, and be still	Jeremiah 47:6
Ah Lord GOD! wilt Thou destroy all the residue of Israel in Thy Pouring Out of Thy Fury upon Jerusalem?	Ezekiel 9:8b
O my Lord, what shall be the end of these things?	Daniel 12:8b
O LORD, how long shall I cry, and Thou wilt not hear! even cry out unto Thee of violence, and Thou wilt not save!	Habakkuk 1:2
Why dost Thou show me iniquity, and cause me to behold grievance? for spoiling and violence are before me: and there are that raise up strife and contention	Habakkuk 1:3
Therefore the law is slacked, and judgment doth never go forth: for the wicked doth compass about the righteous; therefore wrong judgment proceedeth	Habakkuk 1:4
Art Thou not from everlasting, O LORD my God, mine Holy One? we shall not die. O LORD, Thou hast ordained them for judgment; and, O Mighty God, Thou hast established them for correction	Habakkuk 1:12
Thou art of purer eyes than to behold evil, and canst not look on iniquity: wherefore lookest Thou upon them that deal treacherously, and holdest Thy Tongue when the wicked devoureth the man that is more righteous than he?	Habakkuk 1:13

And makest men as the fishes of the sea, as the creeping things, that have no ruler over them? They take up all of them with the angle, they catch them in their net, and gather them in their drag: therefore they rejoice and are glad	Habakkuk 1:14-15
Therefore they sacrifice unto their net, and burn incense unto their drag; because by them their portion is fat, and their meat plenteous. Shall they therefore empty their net, and not spare continually to slay the nations?	Habakkuk 1:16-17
I will stand upon my watch, and set me upon the tower, and will watch to see what he will say unto me, and what I shall answer when I am reproved	Habakkuk 2:1
Art Thou He that should come{?,} or {do} we look for another?	Matthew 11:3; Luke 7:20b
Why speakest Thou unto them in parables?	Matthew 13:10b
Declare unto us this parable	Matthew 15:15b
Why could not we cast him out?	Matthew 17:19b; Mark 9:28b
Who is the greatest in the kingdom of heaven?	Matthew 18:1
Lord, how oft shall my brother sin against me, and I forgive him? till seven times?	Matthew 18:21

Good Master, what [good thing] shall I do, [to] that I may [have] inherit eternal life?	Matthew 19:16; Mark 10:17b; Luke 18:18
Which?	Matthew 19:18a
All these things have I kept from my youth up: what lack I yet?	Matthew 19:20
Who then can be saved?	Matthew 19:25b; Mark 10:26; Luke 18:26
Behold, we have forsaken all, and followed Thee; what shall we have therefore?	Matthew 19:27
[Master, but] Tell us, when shall these things be? and what shall be the sign [of Thy Coming] [when {all} these things shall {come to pass} be fulfilled?], and of the end of the world?	Matthew 24:3b; Mark 13:4; Luke 21:7
Eli, Eli, lama sabachthani?	Matthew 27:46b; Mark 15:34b
My God, My God, why hast Thou forsaken me?	Matthew 27:46b; Mark 15:34b [Psalm 22:1a]
Why could not we cast him out?	Mark 9:28b; Matthew 17:19b
Good Master, what [good thing] shall I do, [to] that I may [have] inherit eternal life?	Mark 10:17b; Matthew 19:16; Luke 18:18

Who then can be saved?	Mark 10:26; Matthew 19:25b; Luke 18:26
Which is the first commandment of all?	Mark 12:28b
[Master, but] Tell us, when shall these things be? and what shall be the sign [of Thy Coming] [when {all} these things shall {come to pass} be fulfilled?], and of the end of the world?	Mark 13:4; Matthew 24:3b; Luke 21:7
Is it I?	Mark 14:19b; John 13:25; 21:20b
Eloi, Eloi, lama sabachthani?	Mark 15:34b; Matthew 27:46b
My God, My God, why hast Thou forsaken me?	Mark 15:34b; Matthew 27:46b [Psalm 22:1a]
Art Thou He that should come{?,} or {do} we look for another?	Luke 7:20b; Matthew 11:3
What might this parable be?	Luke 8:9
Lord, speakest Thou this parable unto us, or even to all?	Luke 12:41
Lord, are there few that be saved?	Luke 13:23a
Where, Lord?	Luke 17:37a

Good Master, what [good thing] shall I do, [to] that I may [have] inherit eternal life?	Luke 18:18; Matthew 19:16; Mark 10:17b
Who then can be saved?	Luke 18:26; Matthew 19:25b; Mark 10:26
[Master, but] Tell us, when shall these things be? and what shall be the sign [of Thy Coming] [when {all} these things shall {come to pass} be fulfilled?], and of the end of the world?	Luke 21:7; Matthew 24:3b; Mark 13:4
How can a man be born when he is old? can he enter the second time into his mother's womb, and be born?	John 3:4
How can these things be?	John 3:9
Sir, Thou hast nothing to draw with, and the well is deep: from whence then hast Thou that Living Water?	John 4:11
Art Thou greater than our father Jacob, which gave us the well, and drank thereof himself, and his children, and his cattle?	John 4:12
Rabbi, when camest Thou hither?	John 6:25b
What shall we do, that we might work the Works of God?	John 6:28
We be Abraham's seed, and were never in bondage to any man: how sayest Thou, Ye shall be made free?	John 8:33

Who is He, Lord, that I might believe on Him?	John 9:36
Lord, who hath believed our report? and to whom hath [is] The Arm of The Lord been revealed?	John 12:38b [Isaiah 53:1; Romans 10:16b]
Lord, who is it?	John 13:25; 21:20b; Mark 14:19b
Lord, whither goest Thou?	John 13:36a
Lord, why cannot I follow Thee now? I will lay down my life for Thy Sake	John 13:37
Lord, we know not whither Thou goest; and how can we know the way?	John 14:5
Lord, how is it that Thou wilt manifest Thyself unto us, and not unto the world?	John 14:22
What is truth?	John 18:38a
Lord, which is he that betrayeth Thee?	John 21:20b; 13:25; Mark 14:19b
Lord, and what shall this man do?	John 21:21
Lord, wilt Thou at this time restore again the kingdom to Israel?	Acts 1:6b

Thou, Lord, Which knowest the hearts of all men, show whether of these two Thou hast chosen, that he may take part of this ministry and apostleship, from which Judas by transgression fell, that he might go to his own place	Acts 1:24–25
Who art Thou, Lord?	Acts 9:5a; 22:8a; 26:15a
Lord, what wilt Thou have me to do?	Acts 9:6a; 22:10a
Who art Thou, Lord?	Acts 22:8a; 9:5a; 26:15a
What shall I do, Lord?	Acts 22:10a; 9:6a
Who art Thou, Lord?	Acts 26:15a; 9:5a; 22:8a
Lord, who hath believed our report?	Romans 10:16b [Isaiah 53:1; John 12:38b]
How long, O Lord, holy and true, dost Thou not judge and avenge our blood on them that dwell on the earth?	Revelation 6:10

Prayer portions that contain Insight Requests in them

Genesis 18:23	Psalm 56:12-13
Genesis 20:4-5	Psalm 73:15-19
Exodus 3:11	Psalm 74:1-2
Exodus 6:30	Psalm 74:9-11
Exodus 32:11	Psalm 77:6-9
Exodus 33:16	Psalm 79:5
Exodus 33:18	Psalm 80:4-6
Numbers 11:11-13	Psalm 80:12-15
2 Samuel 7:18 [1 Chronicles 17:16]	Psalm 85:4-6
2 Samuel 7:19 [1 Chronicles 17:17]	Psalm 88:14
1 Kings 3:6-9 [2 Chronicles 1:8-10]	Psalm 90:13-14
1 Chron 17:16 [2 Samuel 7:18]	Psalm 94:3-4
1 Chron 17:17 [2 Samuel 7:19]	Psalm 94:14-16
2 Chron 1:8-10 [1 Kings 3:6-9]	Psalm 101:2
Job 7:17-21	Psalm 119:81-84
Psalm 8:3-5 [Hebrews 2:6b-7a]	Psalm 144:3
Psalm 8:6-8 [Hebrews 2:7b-8a]	Isaiah 63:17
Psalm 10:1 (2-11)	Isaiah 64:12
Psalm 10:13-14	Jeremiah 14:8
Psalm 13:1-2	Jeremiah 14:19
Psalm 16:11	Jeremiah 15:18
Psalm 25:4-5	Lamentations 2:20-22
Psalm 25:14-16	Lamentations 5:20
Psalm 35:15-17	Amos 7:2b
Psalm 39:1-5	Amos 7:5
Psalm 43:2	John 14:8
Psalm 44:23-24	Hebrews 2:6b-7 [Psalm 8:4-6a]

Petition Prayers

O that Ishmael might live before Thee!	Genesis 17:18
Wilt Thou also destroy the righteous with the wicked?	Genesis 18:23
Peradventure there be fifty righteous within the city: wilt Thou also destroy and not spare the place for the fifty righteous that are therein?	Genesis 18:24
That be far from Thee to do after this manner, to slay the righteous with the wicked: and that the righteous should be as the wicked, that be far from Thee: Shall not the Judge of all the earth do right?	Genesis 18:25
Behold now, I have taken upon me to speak unto The Lord, which am but dust and ashes: Peradventure there shall lack five of the fifty righteous: wilt Thou destroy all the city for lack of five?	Genesis 18:27–28a
Peradventure there shall be forty found there	Genesis 18:29a
Oh let not The Lord be angry, and I will speak: Peradventure there shall thirty be found there	Genesis 18:30a
Behold now, I have taken upon me to speak unto The Lord: Peradventure there shall be twenty found there	Genesis 18:31a

Oh let not The Lord be angry, and I will speak yet but this once: Peradventure ten shall be found there
Genesis 18:32a

Lord, wilt Thou slay also a righteous nation? Said he not unto me, She is my sister? and she, even she herself said, He is my brother: in the integrity of my heart and innocency of my hands have I done this
Genesis 20:4-5

O LORD God of my master Abraham, I pray Thee, send me good speed this day, and show kindness unto my master Abraham. Behold, I stand here by the well of water; and the daughters of the men of the city come out to draw water: And let it come to pass, that the damsel to whom I shall say, Let down thy pitcher, I pray thee, that I may drink; and she shall say, Drink, and I will give thy camels drink also: let the same be she that Thou hast appointed for Thy Servant Isaac; and thereby shall I know that Thou hast shown kindness unto my master
Genesis 24:12-14

O LORD God of my master Abraham, if now Thou do prosper my way which I go: Behold, I stand by the well of water; and it shall come to pass, that when the virgin cometh forth to draw water, and I say to her, Give me, I pray thee, a little water of thy pitcher to drink; And she say to me, Both drink thou, and I will also draw for thy camels: let the same be the woman whom The LORD hath appointed out for my master's son
Genesis 24:42-44

If God will be with me, and will keep me in this way that I go, and will give me bread to eat, and raiment to put on, So that I come again to my father's house in peace; then shall The LORD be my God
Genesis 28:20-21

And this stone, which I have set for a pillar, shall be God's House: and of all that Thou shalt give me I will surely give the tenth unto Thee	Genesis 28:22
The LORD watch between me and thee, when we are absent one from another…see, God is witness betwixt me and thee	Genesis 31:49b–50
The God of Abraham, and The God of Nahor, The God of their father, judge betwixt us	Genesis 31:53
O God of my father Abraham, and God of my father Isaac, The LORD Which saidst unto me, Return unto thy country, and to thy kindred, and I will deal well with thee	Genesis 32:9
I am not worthy of the least of all the mercies, and of all the truth, which Thou hast shown unto Thy Servant; for with my staff I passed over this Jordan; and now I am become two bands	Genesis 32:10
Deliver me, I pray Thee, from the hand of my brother, from the hand of Esau: for I fear him, lest he will come and smite me, and the mother with the children	Genesis 32:11
And Thou saidst, I will surely do thee good, and make thy seed as the sand of the sea, which cannot be numbered for multitude	Genesis 32:12
I will not let Thee go, except Thou bless me	Genesis 32:26b
And God Almighty give you mercy before the man, that he may send away your other brother, and Benjamin	Genesis 43:14a

God, before Whom my fathers Abraham and Isaac did walk, The God which fed me all my life long unto this day, The Angel which redeemed me from all evil, bless the lads	Genesis 48:15–16a
And let my name be named on them, and the name of my fathers Abraham and Isaac; and let them grow into a multitude in the midst of the earth	Genesis 48:16b
O my Lord, send, I pray Thee, by the hand of him whom Thou wilt send	Exodus 4:13
LORD, why doth Thy Wrath wax hot against Thy People, which Thou hast brought forth out of the land of Egypt with great power, and with a mighty hand?	Exodus 32:11
Wherefore should the Egyptians speak, and say, For mischief did He bring them out, to slay them in the mountains, and to consume them from the face of the earth? Turn from Thy Fierce Wrath, and repent of this evil against Thy People	Exodus 32:12
Remember Abraham, Isaac, and Israel, Thy Servants, to whom Thou swarest by Thine Own Self, and saidst unto them, I will multiply your seed as the stars of heaven, and all this land that I have spoken of will I give unto your seed, and they shall inherit it for ever	Exodus 32:13
Oh, this people have sinned a great sin, and have made them gods of gold. Yet now, if Thou wilt forgive their sin--; and if not, blot me, I pray Thee, out of Thy Book which Thou hast written	Exodus 32:31–32

See, Thou sayest unto me, Bring up this people: and Thou hast not let me know whom Thou wilt send with me. Yet Thou hast said, I know thee by name, and thou hast also found grace in My Sight	Exodus 33:12
Now therefore, I pray Thee, if I have found grace in Thy Sight, show me now Thy Way, that I may know Thee, that I may find grace in Thy Sight: and consider that this nation is Thy People	Exodus 33:13
If Thy Presence go not with me, carry us not up hence	Exodus 33:15
For wherein shall it be known here that I and Thy People have found grace in Thy Sight? is it not in that Thou goest with us? so shall we be separated, I and Thy People, from all the people that are upon the face of the earth	Exodus 33:16
I beseech Thee, show me Thy Glory	Exodus 33:18
If now I have found grace in Thy Sight, O Lord, let my Lord, I pray Thee, go among us; for it is a stiffnecked people; and pardon our iniquity and our sin, and take us for Thine Inheritance	Exodus 34:9
Rise up, LORD, and let Thine Enemies be scattered; and let them that hate Thee flee before Thee	Numbers 10:35b
Return, O LORD, unto the many thousands of Israel	Numbers 10:36b
Wherefore hast Thou afflicted Thy Servant? and wherefore have I not found favour in Thy Sight, that Thou layest the burden of all this people upon me?	Numbers 11:11

Have I conceived all this people? have I begotten them, that Thou shouldest say unto me, Carry them in thy bosom, as a nursing father beareth the sucking child, unto the land which Thou swarest unto their fathers?	Numbers 11:12
Whence should I have flesh to give unto all this people? for they weep unto me, saying, Give us flesh, that we may eat	Numbers 11:13
I am not able to bear all this people alone, because it is too heavy for me	Numbers 11:14
And if Thou deal thus with me, kill me, I pray Thee, out of hand, if I have found favour in Thy Sight; and let me not see my wretchedness	Numbers 11:15
Heal her now, O God, I beseech Thee	Numbers 12:13
Respect not Thou their offering: I have not taken one ass from them, neither have I hurt one of them	Numbers 16:15
O God, The God of the spirits of all flesh, shall one man sin, and wilt Thou be wroth with all the congregation?	Numbers 16:22
If Thou wilt indeed deliver this people into my hand, then I will utterly destroy their cities	Numbers 21:2
Let The LORD, The God of the spirits of all flesh, set a man over the congregation, Which may go out before them, and which may go in before them, and which may lead them out, and which may bring them in; that the congregation of The LORD be not as sheep which have no shepherd	Numbers 27:16-17

O Lord GOD, Thou hast begun to show Thy   Deuteronomy
Servant Thy Greatness, and Thy Mighty Hand: 3:24-25
for what God is there in heaven or in earth, that
can do according to Thy Works, and according
to Thy Might?

I pray Thee, let me go over, and see the
good land that is beyond Jordan, that goodly
mountain, and Lebanon

O Lord GOD, destroy not Thy People and   Deuteronomy
Thine Inheritance, which Thou hast redeemed   9:26
through Thy Greatness, which Thou hast
brought forth out of Egypt with A Mighty Hand

Remember Thy Servants, Abraham, Isaac, and   Deuteronomy
Jacob; look not unto the stubbornness of this   9:27-28
people, nor to their wickedness, nor to their
sin: Lest the land whence Thou broughtest us
out say, Because The LORD was not able to
bring them into the land which He promised
them, and because He hated them, He hath
brought them out to slay them in the wilderness

Yet they are Thy People and Thine Inheritance,   Deuteronomy
which Thou broughtest out by Thy Mighty   9:29
Power and by Thy Stretched Out Arm

Our hands have not shed this blood, neither   Deuteronomy
have our eyes seen it. Be merciful, O LORD,   21:7-8a
unto Thy People Israel, whom Thou hast
redeemed, and lay not innocent blood unto
Thy People of Israel's charge

I have brought away the hallowed things out of mine house, and also have given them unto the Levite, and unto the stranger, to the fatherless, and to the widow, according to all Thy Commandments which Thou hast commanded me: I have not transgressed Thy Commandments, neither have I forgotten them	Deuteronomy 26:13
I have not eaten thereof in my mourning, neither have I taken away aught thereof for any unclean use, nor given aught thereof for the dead: but I have hearkened to The Voice of The LORD my God, and have done according to all that Thou hast commanded me	Deuteronomy 26:14
Look down from Thy Holy Habitation, from heaven, and bless Thy People Israel, and the land which Thou hast given us, as Thou swarest unto our fathers, a land that floweth with milk and honey	Deuteronomy 26:15
So let all Thine Enemies perish, O LORD: but let them that love Him be as the sun when he goeth forth in his might	Judges 5:31
If Thou wilt save Israel by mine hand, as Thou hast said, Behold, I will put a fleece of wool in the floor; and if the dew be on the fleece only, and it be dry upon all the earth beside, then shall I know that Thou wilt save Israel by mine hand, as Thou hast said	Judges 6:36-37
Let not Thine Anger be hot against me, and I will speak but this once: let me prove, I pray Thee, but this once with the fleece; let it now be dry only upon the fleece, and upon all the ground let there be dew	Judges 6:39

We have sinned: do Thou unto us whatsoever seemeth good unto Thee; deliver us only, we pray Thee, this day	Judges 10:15

O my Lord, let the man of God which Thou didst send come again unto us, and teach us what we shall do unto the child that shall be born	Judges 13:8

O Lord GOD, remember me, I pray Thee, and strengthen me, I pray Thee, only this once, O God, that I may be at once avenged of the Philistines for my two eyes	Judges 16:28

O LORD of hosts, if Thou wilt indeed look on the affliction of Thine Handmaid, and remember me, and not forget Thine Handmaid, but wilt give unto Thine Handmaid a man child, then I will give him unto The LORD all the days of his life, and there shall no razor come upon his head	1 Samuel 1:11

Speak; for Thy Servant heareth	1 Samuel 3:10b

We have sinned, because we have forsaken The LORD, and have served Baalim and Ashtaroth: but now deliver us out of the hand of our enemies, and we will serve Thee	1 Samuel 12:10

Let The LORD even require it at the hand of David's enemies	1 Samuel 20:16b

The LORD judge between me and thee, and The LORD avenge me of thee: but mine hand shall not be upon thee	1 Samuel 24:12

The LORD therefore be judge, and judge between me and thee, and see, and plead my cause, and deliver me out of thine hand	1 Samuel 24:15

And, behold, as thy life was much set by this
day in mine eyes, so let my life be much set by
in the eyes of The LORD, and let Him deliver
me out of all tribulation

1 Samuel 26:24

O LORD, I pray Thee, turn the counsel of
Ahithophel into foolishness

2 Samuel 15:31b

I have sinned greatly in that I have done: and
now, I beseech Thee, O LORD, take away the
iniquity of Thy Servant; for I have done very
foolishly

2 Samuel 24:10
[1 Chronicles
21:8]

Lo, I have sinned, and I have done wickedly:
but these sheep, what have they done? let Thine
Hand, I pray Thee, be against me, and against
my father's house

2 Samuel 24:17
[1 Chronicles
21:17]

God make the name of Solomon better than
thy name, and make his throne greater than thy
throne

1 Kings 1:47a

Thou hast shown unto Thy Servant David my
father great mercy, according as he walked
before Thee in truth, and in righteousness,
and in uprightness of heart with Thee; and
Thou hast kept for him this great kindness,
that Thou hast given him a son to sit on his
throne, as it is this day. And now, O LORD
my God, Thou hast made Thy Servant king
instead of David my father: and I am but a little
child: I know not how to go out or come in.
And Thy Servant is in the midst of Thy People
which Thou hast chosen, a great people, that
cannot be numbered nor counted for multitude.
Give therefore Thy Servant an understanding
heart to judge Thy People, that I may discern
between good and bad: for who is able to judge
this Thy So Great a People?

1 Kings 3:6-9
[2 Chronicles
1:8-10]

LORD God of Israel, there is no God like
Thee, in heaven above, or on earth beneath,
Who keepest covenant and mercy with Thy
Servants that walk before Thee with all their
heart: Who hast kept with Thy Servant David
my father that Thou promisedst him: Thou
spakest also with Thy Mouth, and hast fulfilled
it with Thine Hand, as it is this day. Therefore
now, LORD God of Israel, keep with Thy
Servant David my father that Thou promisedst
him, saying, There shall not fail thee a man in
My Sight to sit on the throne of Israel; so that
thy children take heed to their way, that they
walk before Me as thou hast walked before Me

1 Kings 8:23-25
[2 Chronicles
6:14-42]

And now, O God of Israel, let Thy Word, I
pray Thee, be verified, Which Thou spakest
unto Thy Servant David my father

1 Kings 8:26
[2 Chronicles
6:14-42]

But will God indeed dwell on the earth?
behold, the heaven and heaven of heavens
cannot contain Thee; how much less this
house that I have builded? Yet have Thou
respect unto the prayer of Thy Servant, and
to his supplication, O LORD my God, to
hearken unto the cry and to the prayer, which
Thy Servant prayeth before Thee today: That
Thine Eyes may be open toward this house
night and day, even toward the place of which
Thou hast said, My Name shall be there: that
Thou mayest hearken unto the prayer which
Thy Servant shall make toward this place.
And hearken Thou to the supplication of Thy
Servant, and of Thy People Israel, when they
shall pray toward this place: and hear Thou in
heaven Thy Dwellingplace: and when Thou
hearest, forgive

1 Kings 8:27-30
[2 Chronicles
6:14-42]

If any man trespass against his neighbour, and an oath be laid upon him to cause him to swear, and the oath come before Thine Altar in this house: Then hear Thou in heaven, and do, and judge Thy Servants, condemning the wicked, to bring his way upon his head; and justifying the righteous, to give him according to his righteousness	1 Kings 8:31-32 [2 Chronicles 6:14-42]
When Thy People Israel be smitten down before the enemy, because they have sinned against Thee, and shall turn again to Thee, and confess Thy Name, and pray, and make supplication unto Thee in this house: Then hear Thou in heaven, and forgive the sin of Thy People Israel, and bring them again unto the land which Thou gavest unto their fathers	1 Kings 8:33-34 [2 Chronicles 6:14-42]
When heaven is shut up, and there is no rain, because they have sinned against Thee; if they pray toward this place, and confess Thy Name, and turn from their sin, when Thou afflictest them: Then hear Thou in heaven, and forgive the sin of Thy Servants, and of Thy People Israel, that Thou teach them the good way wherein they should walk, and give rain upon Thy Land, which Thou hast given to Thy People for an inheritance	1 Kings 8:35-36 [2 Chronicles 6:14-42]

If there be in the land famine, if there be
pestilence, blasting, mildew, locust, or if there
be caterpillar; if their enemy besiege them in
the land of their cities; whatsoever plague,
whatsoever sickness there be; What prayer
and supplication soever be made by any man,
or by all Thy People Israel, which shall know
every man the plague of his own heart, and
spread forth his hands toward this house: Then
hear Thou in heaven Thy Dwellingplace,
and forgive, and do, and give to every man
according to his ways, whose heart Thou
knowest; (for Thou, even Thou Only, knowest
the hearts of all the children of men;) That they
may fear Thee all the days that they live in the
land which Thou gavest unto our fathers

1 Kings 8:37-40
[2 Chronicles
6:14-42]

Moreover concerning a stranger, that is not
of Thy People Israel, but cometh out of a far
country for Thy Name's Sake; (For they shall
hear of Thy Great Name, and of Thy Strong
Hand, and of Thy Stretched Out Arm;) when
he shall come and pray toward this house;
Hear Thou in heaven Thy Dwellingplace, and
do according to all that the stranger calleth to
Thee for: that all people of the earth may know
Thy Name, to fear Thee, as do Thy People
Israel; and that they may know that this house,
which I have builded, is called by Thy Name

1 Kings 8:41-43
[2 Chronicles
6:14-42]

If Thy People go out to battle against their
enemy, whithersoever Thou shalt send them,
and shall pray unto The LORD toward the
city which Thou hast chosen, and toward the
house that I have built for Thy Name: Then
hear Thou in heaven their prayer and their
supplication, and maintain their cause

1 Kings 8:44-45
[2 Chronicles
6:14-42]

If they sin against Thee, (for there is no man
that sinneth not,) and Thou be angry with
them, and deliver them to the enemy, so that
they carry them away captives unto the land
of the enemy, far or near; Yet if they shall
bethink themselves in the land whither they
were carried captives, and repent, and make
supplication unto Thee in the land of them that
carried them captives, saying, We have sinned,
and have done perversely, we have committed
wickedness; And so return unto Thee with all
their heart, and with all their soul, in the land
of their enemies, which led them away captive,
and pray unto Thee toward their land, which
Thou gavest unto their fathers, the city which
Thou hast chosen, and the house which I have
built for Thy Name: Then hear Thou their
prayer and their supplication in heaven Thy
Dwellingplace, and maintain their cause, And
forgive Thy People that have sinned against
Thee, and all their transgressions wherein they
have transgresssed against Thee, and give them
compassion before them who carried them
captive, that they may have compassion on them

1 Kings 8:46-50
[2 Chronicles
6:14-42]

For they be Thy People, and Thine Inheritance,
which Thou broughtest forth out of Egypt, from
the midst of the furnace of iron: That Thine
Eyes may be open unto the supplication of Thy
Servant, and unto the supplication of Thy People
Israel, to hearken unto them in all that they call
for unto Thee. For Thou didst separate them
from among all the people of the earth, to be
Thine Inheritance, as Thou spakest by the hand
of Moses Thy Servant, when Thou broughtest
our fathers out of Egypt, O LORD God

1 Kings 8:51-53
[2 Chronicles
6:14-42]

Blessed be The LORD, that hath given rest   1 Kings 8:56
unto His People Israel, according to all that He
promised: there hath not failed One Word of all
His Good Promise, which He promised by the
hand of Moses His Servant

The LORD our God be with us, as He was   1 Kings 8:57-58
with our fathers: let Him not leave us, nor
forsake us: That He may incline our hearts unto
Him, to walk in all His Ways, and to keep His
Commandments, and His Statutes, and His
Judgments, which He commanded our fathers

And let these my words, wherewith I have   1 Kings 8:59-60
made supplication before The LORD, be nigh
unto The LORD our God day and night, that
he maintain the cause of His Servant, and the
cause of His People Israel at all times, as the
matter shall require: That all the people of the
earth may know that The LORD is God, and
that there is none else

Let your heart therefore be perfect with The   1 Kings 8:61
LORD our God, to walk in His Statutes, and
to keep His Commandments, as at this day

O LORD my God, I pray Thee, let this child's   1 Kings 17:21b
soul come into him again

LORD God of Abraham, Isaac, and of Israel,   1 Kings 18:36b
let it be known this day that Thou art God in
Israel, and that I am Thy Servant, and that I
have done all these things at Thy Word

Hear me, O LORD, hear me, that this people   1 Kings 18:37
may know that Thou art The LORD God, and
that Thou hast turned their heart back again

In this thing The LORD pardon thy servant, that when my master goeth into the house of Rimmon to worship there, and he leaneth on my hand, and I bow myself in the house of Rimmon: when I bow down myself in the house of Rimmon, The LORD pardon thy servant in this thing	2 Kings 5:18
LORD, I pray Thee, open his eyes, that he may see	2 Kings 6:17a
Smite this people, I pray Thee, with blindness	2 Kings 6:18a
LORD, open the eyes of these men, that they may see	2 Kings 6:20a
O LORD GOD of Israel, Which dwellest between the cherubims, Thou art The God, even Thou Alone, of all the kingdoms of the earth; Thou hast made heaven and earth.	2 Kings 19:15 [Isaiah 37:16]
LORD, bow down Thine Ear, and hear: open, LORD, Thine Eyes, and see: and hear the words of Sennacherib, which hath sent him to reproach The Living God	2 Kings 19:16 [Isaiah 37:17]
Of a truth, LORD, the kings of Assyria have destroyed the nations and their lands, And have cast their gods into the fire: for they were no gods, but the work of men's hands, wood and stone: therefore they have destroyed them. Now therefore, O LORD our God, I beseech Thee, save Thou us out of his hand, that all the kingdoms of the earth may know that Thou art The LORD God, even Thou Only	2 Kings 19:17-19 [Isaiah 37:18-20]

I beseech Thee, O LORD, remember now how I have walked before Thee in truth and with a perfect heart, and have done that which is good in Thy Sight	2 Kings 20:3a [Isaiah 38:3a]
Oh that Thou wouldest bless me indeed, and enlarge my coast, and that Thine Hand might be with me, and that Thou wouldest keep me from evil, that it may not grieve me!	1 Chronicles 4:10a
… but if ye be come to betray me to mine enemies, seeing there is no wrong in mine hands, The God of our fathers look thereon, and rebuke it	1 Chronicles 12:17b
Save us, O God of our salvation, and gather us together, and deliver us from the heathen, that we may give thanks to Thy Holy Name, and glory in Thy Praise	1 Chronicles 16:35 [Psalm 106:47]
I have sinned greatly, because I have done this thing: but now, I beseech Thee, do away the iniquity of Thy Servant; for I have done very foolishly	1 Chronicles 21:8 [2 Samuel 24:10]
Is it not I that commanded the people to be numbered? even I it is that have sinned and done evil indeed; but as for these sheep, what have they done? let Thine Hand, I pray Thee, O LORD my God, be on me, and on my father's house; but not on Thy People, that they should be plagued	1 Chronicles 21:17 [2 Samuel 24:17]
And give unto Solomon my son a perfect heart, to keep Thy Commandments, Thy Testimonies, and Thy Statutes, and to do all these things, and to build the palace, for the which I have made provision	1 Chronicles 29:19

Thou hast shown great mercy unto David my
father, and hast made me to reign in his stead.
Now, O LORD God, let Thy Promise unto
David my father be established: for Thou hast
made me king over a people like the dust of
the earth in multitude. Give me now wisdom
and knowledge, that I may go out and come in
before this people: for who can judge this Thy
People, that is so great?

2 Chronicles
1:8-10 [1 Kings
3:6-9]

O LORD God of Israel, there is no God like
Thee in the heaven, nor in the earth; Which
keepest covenant, and showest mercy unto
Thy Servants, that walk before Thee with all
their hearts: Thou which hast kept with Thy
Servant David my father that which Thou hast
promised him; and spakest with Thy Mouth,
and hast fulfilled it with Thine Hand, as it is
this day. Now therefore, O LORD God of
Israel, keep with Thy Servant David my father
that which Thou hast promised him, saying,
There shall not fail thee a man in My Sight
to sit upon the throne of Israel; yet so that thy
children take heed to their way to walk in My
Law, as thou hast walked before Me

2 Chronicles
6:14-16 [1 Kings
8:23-53]

Now then, O LORD God of Israel, let Thy
Word be verified, which Thou hast spoken
unto Thy Servant David

2 Chronicles
6:17 [1 Kings
8:23-53]

But will God in very deed dwell with men on the earth? behold, heaven and the heaven of heavens cannot contain Thee; how much less this house which I have built! Have respect therefore to the prayer of Thy Servant, and to his supplication, O LORD my God, to hearken unto the cry and the prayer which Thy Servant prayeth before Thee: That Thine Eyes may be open upon this house day and night, upon the place whereof Thou hast said that Thou wouldest put Thy Name there; to hearken unto the prayer which Thy Servant prayeth toward this place. Hearken therefore unto the supplications of Thy Servant, and of Thy People Israel, which they shall make toward this place: hear Thou from Thy Dwelling Place, even from heaven; and when Thou hearest, forgive	2 Chronicles 6:18-21 [1 Kings 8:23-53]
If a man sin against his neighbour, and an oath be laid upon him to make him swear, and the oath come before Thine Altar in this house; Then hear Thou from heaven, and do, and judge Thy Servants, by requiting the wicked, by recompensing his way upon his own head; and by justifying the righteous, by giving him according to his righteousness	2 Chronicles 6:22-23 [1 Kings 8:23-53]
And if Thy People Israel be put to the worse before the enemy, because they have sinned against Thee; and shall return and confess Thy Name, and pray and make supplication before Thee in this house; Then hear Thou from the heavens, and forgive the sin of Thy People Israel, and bring them again unto the land which Thou gavest to them and to their fathers	2 Chronicles 6:24-25 [1 Kings 8:23-53]

When the heaven is shut up, and there is no rain, because they have sinned against Thee; yet if they pray toward this place, and confess Thy Name, and turn from their sin, when Thou dost afflict them; Then hear Thou from heaven, and forgive the sin of Thy Servants, and of Thy People Israel, when Thou hast taught them the good way, wherein they should walk; and send rain upon Thy Land, which Thou hast given unto Thy People for an inheritance

2 Chronicles 6:26-27 [1 Kings 8:23-53]

If there be dearth in the land, if there be pestilence, if there be blasting, or mildew, locusts, or caterpillars; if their enemies besiege them in the cities of their land; whatsoever sore or whatsoever sickness there be: Then what prayer or what supplication soever shall be made of any man, or of all Thy People Israel, when every one shall know his own sore and his own grief, and shall spread forth his hands in this house: Then hear Thou from heaven Thy Dwellingplace, and forgive, and render unto every man according unto all his ways, whose heart Thou knowest; (for Thou Only knowest the hearts of the children of men:) That they may fear Thee, to walk in Thy Ways, so long as they live in the land which Thou gavest unto our fathers

2 Chronicles 6:28-31 [1 Kings 8:23-53]

Moreover concerning the stranger, which is not of Thy People Israel, but is come from a far country for Thy Great Name's Sake, and Thy Mighty Hand, and Thy Stretched Out Arm; if they come and pray in this house; Then hear Thou from the heavens, even from Thy Dwellingplace, and do according to all that the stranger calleth to Thee for; that all people of the earth may know Thy Name, and fear Thee, as doth Thy People Israel, and may know that this house which I have built is called by Thy Name

2 Chronicles 6:32-33 [1 Kings 8:23-53]

If Thy People go out to war against their enemies by the way that Thou shalt send them, and they pray unto Thee toward this city which Thou hast chosen, and the house which I have built for Thy Name; Then hear Thou from the heavens their prayer and their supplication, and maintain their cause	2 Chronicles 6:34-35 [1 Kings 8:23-53]
If they sin against Thee, (for there is no man which sinneth not,) and Thou be angry with them, and deliver them over before their enemies, and they carry them away captives unto a land far off or near; Yet if they bethink themselves in the land whither they are carried captive, and turn and pray unto Thee in the land of their captivity, saying, We have sinned, we have done amiss, and have dealt wickedly; If they return to Thee with all their heart and with all their soul in the land of their captivity, whither they have carried them captives, and pray toward their land, which Thou gavest unto their fathers, and toward the city which Thou hast chosen, and toward the house which I have built for Thy Name: Then hear Thou from the heavens, even from Thy Dwellingplace, their prayer and their supplications, and maintain their cause, and forgive Thy People which have sinned against Thee	2 Chronicles 6:36-39 [1 Kings 8:23-53]
Now, my God, let, I beseech Thee, Thine Eyes be open, and let Thine Ears be attent unto the prayer that is made in this place. Now therefore arise, O LORD God, into Thy Resting Place, Thou, and the ark of Thy Strength: let Thy Priests, O LORD God, be clothed with salvation, and let Thy Saints rejoice in goodness. O LORD God, turn not away the face of Thine Anointed: remember the mercies of David Thy Servant	2 Chronicles 6:40-42 [1 Kings 8:23-53]

LORD, it is nothing with Thee to help, whether with many, or with them that have no power: help us, O LORD our God; for we rest on Thee, and in Thy Name we go against this multitude. O LORD, Thou art our God; let no man prevail against Thee	2 Chronicles 14:11
O LORD God of our fathers, art not Thou God in heaven? and rulest not Thou over all the kingdoms of the heathen? and in Thine Hand is there not power and might, so that none is able to withstand Thee?	2 Chronicles 20:6
Art not Thou our God, Who didst drive out the inhabitants of this land before Thy People Israel, and gavest it to the seed of Abraham Thy Friend for ever? And they dwelt therein, and have built Thee a sanctuary therein for Thy Name, saying, If, when evil cometh upon us, as the sword, judgment, or pestilence, or famine, we stand before this house, and in Thy Presence, (for Thy Name is in this house,) and cry unto Thee in our affliction, then Thou wilt hear and help	2 Chronicles 20:7-9
And now, behold, the children of Ammon and Moab and mount Seir, whom Thou wouldest not let Israel invade, when they came out of the land of Egypt, but they turned from them, and destroyed them not; Behold, I say, how they reward us, to come to cast us out of Thy Possession, which Thou hast given us to inherit	2 Chronicles 20:10-11
O our God, wilt Thou not judge them? for we have no might against this great company that cometh against us; neither know we what to do: but our eyes are upon Thee	2 Chronicles 20:12

The good LORD pardon every one That prepareth his heart to seek God, The LORD God of his fathers, though he be not cleansed according to the purification of the sanctuary

2 Chronicles 30:18b-19

I beseech Thee, O LORD God of heaven, the great and terrible God, that keepeth covenant and mercy for them that love Him and observe His Commandments: Let Thine Ear now be attentive, and Thine Eyes open, that Thou mayest hear the prayer of Thy Servant, which I pray before Thee now, day and night, for the children of Israel Thy Servants, and confess the sins of the children of Israel, which we have sinned against Thee: both I and my father's house have sinned. We have dealt very corruptly against Thee, and have not kept the commandments, nor the statutes, nor the judgments, which Thou commandedst Thy Servant Moses

Nehemiah 1:5-7

Remember, I beseech Thee, The Word that Thou commandedst Thy Servant Moses, saying, If ye transgress, I will scatter you abroad among the nations: But if ye turn unto Me, and keep My Commandments, and do them; though there were of you cast out unto the uttermost part of the heaven, yet will I gather them from thence, and will bring them unto the place that I have chosen to set My Name there. Now these are Thy Servants and Thy People, whom Thou hast redeemed by Thy Great Power, and by Thy Strong Hand

Nehemiah 1:8-10

O LORD, I beseech Thee, let now Thine Ear be attentive to the prayer of Thy Servant, and to the prayer of Thy Servants, who desire to fear Thy Name: and prosper, I pray Thee, Thy Servant this day, and grant him mercy in the sight of this man

Nehemiah 1:11

Hear, O our God; for we are despised: and turn their reproach upon their own head, and give them for a prey in the land of captivity: And cover not their iniquity, and let not their sin be blotted out from before Thee: for they have provoked Thee to anger before the builders — Nehemiah 4:4-5

Think upon me, my God, for good, according to all that I have done for this people — Nehemiah 5:19

Now therefore, O God, strengthen my hands — Nehemiah 6:9b

My God, think Thou upon Tobiah and Sanballat according to these their works, and on the prophetess Noadiah, and the rest of the prophets, that would have put me in fear — Nehemiah 6:14

Remember me, O my God, concerning this, and wipe not out my good deeds that I have done for the house of my God, and for the offices thereof — Nehemiah 13:14

Remember me, O my God, concerning this also, and spare me according to the Greatness of Thy Mercy — Nehemiah 13:22b

Remember them, O my God, because they have defiled the priesthood, and the covenant of the priesthood, and of the Levites — Nehemiah 13:29

Remember me, O my God, for good — Nehemiah 13:31b

Only do not two things unto me: then will I not hide myself from Thee. Withdraw Thine Hand far from me: and let not Thy Dread make me afraid — Job 13:20-21

Then call Thou, and I will answer: or let me   Job 13:22-23
speak, and answer Thou me. How many are
mine iniquities and sins? make me to know my
transgression and my sin

Lay down now, put me in a surety with Thee;   Job 17:3-5
who is he that will strike hands with me? For
Thou hast hid their heart from understanding:
therefore shalt Thou not exalt them. He that
speaketh flattery to his friends, even the eyes of
his children shall fail

LORD, how are they increased that trouble   Psalm 3:1-2
me! many are they that rise up against me.
Many there be which say of my soul, There is
no help for him in God

But Thou, O LORD, art a shield for me; my   Psalm 3:3-4
glory, and the lifter up of mine head. I cried
unto The LORD with my voice, and He heard
me out of His Holy Hill

I laid me down and slept; I awaked; for The   Psalm 3:5
LORD sustained me

I will not be afraid of ten thousands of people,   Psalm 3:6
that have set themselves against me round about

Arise, O LORD; save me, O my God: for   Psalm 3:7
Thou hast smitten all mine enemies upon the
cheek bone; Thou hast broken the teeth of the
ungodly

Salvation belongeth unto The LORD: Thy   Psalm 3:8
Blessing is upon Thy People

Hear me when I call, O God of my
righteousness: Thou hast enlarged me when I
was in distress; have mercy upon me, and hear
my prayer

Psalm 4:1

There be many that say, Who will show us any
good? LORD, lift Thou up the Light of Thy
Countenance upon us

Psalm 4:6

Thou hast put gladness in my heart, more
than in the time that their corn and their wine
increased

Psalm 4:7

I will both lay me down in peace, and sleep: for
Thou, LORD, only makest me dwell in safety

Psalm 4:8

Give ear to my words, O LORD, consider my
meditation. Hearken unto the voice of my cry,
my King, and my God: for unto Thee will I
pray. My voice shalt Thou hear in the morning,
O LORD; in the morning will I direct my
prayer unto Thee, and will look up

Psalm 5:1-3

For Thou art not a God that hath pleasure
in wickedness: neither shall evil dwell with
Thee. The foolish shall not stand in Thy Sight:
Thou hatest all workers of iniquity. Thou shalt
destroy them that speak leasing: The LORD
will abhor the bloody and deceitful man

Psalm 5:4-6

But as for me, I will come into Thy House in
the multitude of Thy Mercy: and in Thy Fear
will I worship toward Thy Holy Temple

Psalm 5:7

Lead me, O LORD, in Thy Righteousness   Psalm 5:8-10
because of mine enemies; make Thy Way
straight before my face. For there is no
faithfulness in their mouth; their inward part
is very wickedness; their throat is an open
sepulchre; they flatter with their tongue.
Destroy Thou them, O God; let them fall
by their own counsels; cast them out in the
multitude of their transgressions; for they have
rebelled against Thee

But let all those that put their trust in Thee   Psalm 5:11-12
rejoice: let them ever shout for joy, because
Thou defendest them: let them also that love
Thy Name be joyful in Thee. For Thou,
LORD, wilt bless the righteous; with favour
wilt Thou compass him as with a shield

O LORD, rebuke me not in Thine Anger,   Psalm 6:1-3
neither chasten me in Thy Hot Displeasure.
Have mercy upon me, O LORD; for I am
weak: O LORD, heal me; for my bones are
vexed. My soul is also sore vexed: but Thou, O
LORD, how long?

Return, O LORD, deliver my soul: oh save me   Psalm 6:4-5
for Thy Mercies' Sake. For in death there is no
remembrance of Thee: in the grave who shall
give Thee thanks?

I am weary with my groaning; all the night   Psalm 6:6-7
make I my bed to swim; I water my couch with
my tears. Mine eye is consumed because of
grief; it waxeth old because of all mine enemies

Depart from me, all ye workers of iniquity;   Psalm 6:8-9
for The LORD hath heard the voice of
my weeping. The LORD hath heard my
supplication; The LORD will receive my
prayer

Let all mine enemies be ashamed and sore   Psalm 6:10
vexed: let them return and be ashamed
suddenly

O LORD my God, in Thee do I put my trust: Psalm 7:1-2
save me from all them that persecute me, and
deliver me: Lest he tear my soul like a lion,
rending it in pieces, while there is none to
deliver

O LORD my God, If I have done this; if there   Psalm 7:3-5
be iniquity in my hands; If I have rewarded
evil unto him that was at peace with me; (yea,
I have delivered him that without cause is mine
enemy:) Let the enemy persecute my soul, and
take it; yea, let him tread down my life upon
the earth, and lay mine honour in the dust

Arise, O LORD, in Thine Anger, lift up   Psalm 7:6
Thyself because of the rage of mine enemies:
and awake for me to the judgment that Thou
hast commanded

So shall the congregation of the people compass   Psalm 7:7-8
Thee about: for their sakes therefore return
Thou on high. The LORD shall judge the
people: judge me, O LORD, according to my
righteousness, and according to mine integrity
that is in me

Oh let the wickedness of the wicked come to   Psalm 7:9
an end; but establish the just: for the righteous
God trieth the hearts and reins

Why standest Thou afar off, O LORD? why hidest Thou Thyself in times of trouble?	Psalm 10:1 (2-11)
Arise, O LORD; O God, lift up Thine Hand: forget not the humble	Psalm 10:12
Wherefore doth the wicked contemn God? he hath said in his heart, Thou wilt not require it. Thou hast seen it; for Thou beholdest mischief and spite, to requite it with Thy Hand: the poor committeth himself unto Thee; Thou art the helper of the fatherless	Psalm 10:13-14
Break Thou the arm of the wicked and the evil man: seek out his wickedness till Thou find none	Psalm 10:15
The LORD is King for ever and ever: the heathen are perished out of His Land	Psalm 10:16
LORD, Thou hast heard the desire of the humble: Thou wilt prepare their heart, Thou wilt cause Thine Ear to hear: To judge the fatherless and the oppressed, that the man of the earth may no more oppress	Psalm 10:17-18
Help, LORD; for the godly man ceaseth; for the faithful fail from among the children of men. They speak vanity every one with his neighbour: with flattering lips and with a double heart do they speak	Psalm 12:1-2
The LORD shall cut off all flattering lips, and the tongue that speaketh proud things: Who have said, With our tongue will we prevail; our lips are our own: who is lord over us?	Psalm 12:3-4

For the oppression of the poor, for the sighing   Psalm 12:5-8
of the needy, now will I arise, saith The
LORD; I will set him in safety from him that
puffeth at him. The Words of The LORD are
Pure Words: as silver tried in a furnace of earth,
purified seven times. Thou shalt keep them,
O LORD, Thou shalt preserve them from this
generation for ever. The wicked walk on every
side, when the vilest men are exalted

How long wilt Thou forget me, O LORD? for   Psalm 13:1-2
ever? how long wilt Thou hide Thy Face from
me? How long shall I take counsel in my soul,
having sorrow in my heart daily? how long
shall mine enemy be exalted over me?

Consider and hear me, O LORD my God: Psalm 13:3-5
lighten mine eyes, lest I sleep the sleep of death;
Lest mine enemy say, I have prevailed against
him; and those that trouble me rejoice when I
am moved. But I have trusted in Thy Mercy;
my heart shall rejoice in Thy Salvation

I will sing unto The LORD, because He hath   Psalm 13:6
dealt bountifully with me

Preserve me, O God: for in Thee do I put my   Psalm 16:1
trust

O my soul, thou hast said unto The LORD,   Psalm 16:2-3
Thou art my Lord: my goodness extendeth not
to Thee; But to the saints that are in the earth,
and to the excellent, in whom is all my delight

Their sorrows shall be multiplied that hasten   Psalm 16:4–6
after another god: their drink offerings of blood
will I not offer, nor take up their names into
my lips. The LORD is the portion of mine
inheritance and of my cup: Thou maintainest
my lot. The lines are fallen unto me in pleasant
places; yea, I have a goodly heritage

I will bless The LORD, Who hath given me   Psalm 16:7–8
counsel: my reins also instruct me in the night
seasons. I have set The LORD always before
me: because He is at my right hand, I shall not
be moved

Therefore my heart is glad, and my glory   Psalm 16:9–10
rejoiceth: my flesh also shall rest in hope. For
Thou wilt not leave my soul in hell; neither
wilt Thou suffer Thine Holy One to see
corruption

Thou wilt show me the path of life: in Thy   Psalm 16:11
Presence is fulness of joy; at Thy Right Hand
there are pleasures for evermore

Hear the right, O LORD, attend unto my cry,   Psalm 17:1–3
give ear unto my prayer, that goeth not out of
feigned lips. Let my sentence come forth from
Thy Presence; let Thine Eyes behold the things
that are equal. Thou hast proved mine heart;
Thou hast visited me in the night; Thou hast
tried me, and shalt find nothing; I am purposed
that my mouth shall not transgress

Concerning the works of men, by the Word of   Psalm 17:4–5
Thy Lips I have kept me from the paths of the
destroyer. Hold up my goings in Thy Paths,
that my footsteps slip not

I have called upon Thee, for Thou wilt hear
me, O God: incline Thine Ear unto me, and
hear my speech

Psalm 17:6

Show Thy Marvellous Lovingkindness, O
Thou that savest by Thy Right Hand them
which put their trust in Thee from those that
rise up against them

Psalm 17:7

Keep me as the apple of the eye, hide me under
the Shadow of Thy Wings, From the wicked
that oppress me, from my deadly enemies, who
compass me about. They are inclosed in their
own fat: with their mouth they speak proudly.
They have now compassed us in our steps: they
have set their eyes bowing down to the earth;
Like as a lion that is greedy of his prey, and as it
were a young lion lurking in secret places

Psalm 17:8–12

Arise, O LORD, disappoint him, cast him
down: deliver my soul from the wicked, which
is Thy Sword: From men which are Thy Hand,
O LORD, from men of the world, which have
their portion in this life, and whose belly Thou
fillest with Thy Hid Treasure: they are full of
children, and leave the rest of their substance to
their babes. As for me, I will behold Thy Face
in righteousness: I shall be satisfied, when I
awake, with Thy Likeness

Psalm 17:13–15

The Law of the LORD is perfect, converting   Psalm 19:7-13
the soul: the Testimony of The LORD is
sure, making wise the simple. The Statutes
of The LORD are right, rejoicing the heart:
the Commandment of The LORD is pure,
enlightening the eyes. The fear of The LORD
is clean, enduring for ever: the Judgments of
The LORD are true and righteous altogether.
More to be desired are They than gold, yea,
than much fine gold: sweeter also than honey
and the honeycomb. Moreover by Them is Thy
Servant warned: and in keeping of Them there
is great reward. Who can understand his errors?
cleanse Thou me from secret faults. Keep back
Thy Servant also from presumptuous sins; let
them not have dominion over me: then shall
I be upright, and I shall be innocent from the
great transgression

Let the words of my mouth, and the meditation   Psalm 19:14
of my heart, be acceptable in Thy Sight, O
LORD, my strength, and my redeemer

The LORD hear thee in the day of trouble; the   Psalm 20:1-5
Name of The God of Jacob defend thee; Send
thee help from the sanctuary, and strengthen
thee out of Zion; Remember all thy offerings,
and accept thy burnt sacrifice; Selah. Grant thee
according to thine own heart, and fulfil all thy
counsel. We will rejoice in thy salvation, and
in The Name of our God we will set up our
banners: The LORD fulfil all thy petitions

Save, LORD: let the King hear us when we call   Psalm 20:9

Unto Thee, O LORD, do I lift up my soul.   Psalm 25:1-3
O my God, I trust in Thee: let me not be
ashamed, let not mine enemies triumph
over me. Yea, let none that wait on Thee be
ashamed: let them be ashamed which transgress
without cause

Show me Thy Ways, O LORD; teach me Thy   Psalm 25:4-5
Paths. Lead me in Thy Truth, and teach me: for
Thou art The God of my salvation; on Thee do
I wait all the day

Remember, O LORD, Thy Tender Mercies   Psalm 25:6-7
and Thy Lovingkindnesses; for they have been
ever of old. Remember not the sins of my
youth, nor my transgressions: according to Thy
Mercy remember Thou me for Thy Goodness'
Sake, O LORD

Good and upright is The LORD: therefore will   Psalm 25:8-9
He teach sinners in The Way. The meek will
He guide in judgment: and the meek will He
teach His Way

All the Paths of The LORD are mercy and   Psalm 25:10
truth unto such as keep His Covenant and His
Testimonies

For Thy Name's Sake, O LORD, pardon mine   Psalm 25:11-13
iniquity; for it is great. What man is he that
feareth The LORD? him shall He teach in the
way that he shall choose. His soul shall dwell at
ease; and his seed shall inherit the earth

The Secret of The LORD is with them
that fear Him; and He will show them His
Covenant. Mine eyes are ever toward The
LORD; for He shall pluck my feet out of the
net. Turn Thee unto me, and have mercy upon
me; for I am desolate and afflicted

Psalm 25:14-16

The troubles of my heart are enlarged: O bring
Thou me out of my distresses. Look upon mine
affliction and my pain; and forgive all my sins

Psalm 25:17-18

Consider mine enemies; for they are many; and
they hate me with cruel hatred. O keep my
soul, and deliver me: let me not be ashamed;
for I put my trust in Thee. Let integrity and
uprightness preserve me; for I wait on Thee.
Redeem Israel, O God, out of all his troubles

Psalm 25:19-22

Judge me, O LORD; for I have walked in mine
integrity: I have trusted also in The LORD;
therefore I shall not slide. Examine me, O
LORD, and prove me; try my reins and my
heart. For Thy Lovingkindness is before mine
eyes: and I have walked in Thy Truth. I have
not sat with vain persons, neither will I go in
with dissemblers. I have hated the congregation
of evil doers; and will not sit with the wicked.
I will wash mine hands in innocency: so will
I compass Thine Altar, O LORD: That I may
publish with the voice of thanksgiving, and tell
of all Thy Wondrous Works

Psalm 26:1-7

LORD, I have loved the Habitation of Thy
House, and the place where Thine Honour
dwelleth

Psalm 26:8

Gather not my soul with sinners, nor my life   Psalm 26:9-12
with bloody men: In whose hands is mischief,
and their right hand is full of bribes. But as for
me, I will walk in mine integrity: redeem me,
and be merciful unto me. My foot standeth in
an even place: in the congregations will I bless
The LORD

Hear, O LORD, when I cry with my voice: Psalm 27:7
have mercy also upon me, and answer me

When Thou saidst, Seek ye My Face; my heart   Psalm 27:8
said unto Thee, Thy Face, LORD, will I seek

Hide not Thy Face far from me; put not Thy   Psalm 27:9
Servant away in anger: Thou hast been my
help; leave me not, neither forsake me, O God
of my salvation

When my father and my mother forsake me,   Psalm 27:10
then The LORD will take me up

Teach me Thy Way, O LORD, and lead me in   Psalm 27:11
a plain path, because of mine enemies

Deliver me not over unto the will of mine   Psalm 27:12-14
enemies: for false witnesses are risen up
against me, and such as breathe out cruelty.
I had fainted, unless I had believed to see
the Goodness of The LORD in the land of
the living. Wait on The LORD: be of good
courage, and He shall strengthen thine heart:
wait, I say, on The LORD

Unto Thee will I cry, O LORD my rock; be   Psalm 28:1
not silent to me: lest, if Thou be silent to me, I
become like them that go down into the pit

Hear the voice of my supplications, when I cry   Psalm 28:2
unto Thee, when I lift up my hands toward
Thy Holy Oracle

Draw me not away with the wicked, and with   Psalm 28:3-5
the workers of iniquity, which speak peace
to their neighbours, but mischief is in their
hearts. Give them according to their deeds,
and according to the wickedness of their
endeavours: give them after the work of their
hands; render to them their desert. Because
they regard not the Works of The LORD, nor
the operation of His Hands, He shall destroy
them, and not build them up

Blessed be The LORD, because He hath heard   Psalm 28:6
the voice of my supplications

Save Thy People, and bless Thine Inheritance: Psalm 28:9
feed them also, and lift them up for ever

In Thee, O LORD, do I put my trust; let   Psalm 31:1
me never be ashamed: deliver me in Thy
Righteousness

Bow down Thine Ear to me; deliver me   Psalm 31:2-3
speedily: be Thou my strong rock, for an house
of defence to save me. For Thou art my rock
and my fortress; therefore for Thy Name's Sake
lead me, and guide me

Pull me out of the net that they have laid   Psalm 31:4-5
privily for me: for Thou art my strength. Into   [Luke 23:46]
Thine Hand I commit my spirit: Thou hast
redeemed me, O LORD God of truth

I have hated them that regard lying vanities: but   Psalm 31:6
I trust in The LORD

I will be glad and rejoice in Thy Mercy: for Psalm 31:7-8
Thou hast considered my trouble; Thou hast
known my soul in adversities; And hast not shut
me up into the hand of the enemy: Thou hast
set my feet in a large room

Have mercy upon me, O LORD, for I am in Psalm 31:9-14
trouble: mine eye is consumed with grief, yea,
my soul and my belly. For my life is spent with
grief, and my years with sighing: my strength
faileth because of mine iniquity, and my bones
are consumed. I was a reproach among all mine
enemies, but especially among my neighbours,
and a fear to mine acquaintance: they that did
see me without fled from me. I am forgotten
as a dead man out of mind: I am like a broken
vessel. For I have heard the slander of many:
fear was on every side: while they took counsel
together against me, they devised to take away
my life. But I trusted in Thee, O LORD: I
said, Thou art my God

My times are in Thy Hand: deliver me from Psalm 31:15
the hand of mine enemies, and from them that
persecute me

Make Thy Face to shine upon Thy Servant: Psalm 31:16
save me for Thy Mercies' Sake

Let me not be ashamed, O LORD; for I have Psalm 31:17
called upon Thee: let the wicked be ashamed,
and let them be silent in the grave

Let the lying lips be put to silence; which speak Psalm 31:18
grievous things proudly and contemptuously
against the righteous

Oh how great is Thy Goodness, which Thou   Psalm 31:19
hast laid up for them that fear Thee; which
Thou hast wrought for them that trust in Thee
before the sons of men!

Thou shalt hide them in the secret of Thy   Psalm 31:20
Presence from the pride of man: Thou shalt
keep them secretly in a pavilion from the strife
of tongues

Blessed be The LORD: for He hath shown   Psalm 31:21-22
me His Marvellous Kindness in a strong city.
For I said in my haste, I am cut off from before
Thine Eyes: nevertheless Thou heardest the
voice of my supplications when I cried unto
Thee

O love the LORD, all ye His Saints: for The   Psalm 31:23-24
LORD preserveth the faithful, and plentifully
rewardeth the proud doer. Be of good courage,
and He shall strengthen your heart, all ye that
hope in The LORD

Let Thy Mercy, O LORD, be upon us,   Psalm 33:22
according as we hope in Thee

Plead my cause, O LORD, with them that   Psalm 35:1-3
strive with me: fight against them that fight
against me. Take hold of shield and buckler, and
stand up for mine help. Draw out also the spear,
and stop the way against them that persecute
me: say unto my soul, I am Thy Salvation

Let them be confounded and put to shame that   Psalm 35:4–8
seek after my soul: let them be turned back
and brought to confusion that devise my hurt.
Let them be as chaff before the wind: and let
the angel of The LORD chase them. Let their
way be dark and slippery: and let the angel of
The LORD persecute them. For without cause
have they hid for me their net in a pit, which
without cause they have digged for my soul. Let
destruction come upon him at unawares; and
let his net that he hath hid catch himself: into
that very destruction let him fall

And my soul shall be joyful in The LORD: it   Psalm 35:9
shall rejoice in His Salvation

All my bones shall say, LORD, who is like unto   Psalm 35:10
Thee, Which deliverest the poor from him that
is too strong for him, yea, the poor and the
needy from him that spoileth him?

False witnesses did rise up; they laid to my   Psalm 35:11–14
charge things that I knew not. They rewarded
me evil for good to the spoiling of my soul. But
as for me, when they were sick, my clothing
was sackcloth: I humbled my soul with fasting;
and my prayer returned into mine own bosom.
I behaved myself as though he had been my
friend or brother: I bowed down heavily, as one
that mourneth for his mother

But in mine adversity they rejoiced, and   Psalm 35:15–17
gathered themselves together: yea, the abjects
gathered themselves together against me, and
I knew it not; they did tear me, and ceased
not: With hypocritical mockers in feasts, they
gnashed upon me with their teeth. Lord, how
long wilt Thou look on? rescue my soul from
their destructions, my darling from the lions

I will give Thee thanks in the great   Psalm 35:18
congregation: I will praise Thee among much
people

Let not them that are mine enemies wrongfully   Psalm 35:19-23
rejoice over me: neither let them wink with
the eye that hate me without a cause. For they
speak not peace: but they devise deceitful
matters against them that are quiet in the land.
Yea, they opened their mouth wide against me,
and said, Aha, aha, our eye hath seen it. This
Thou hast seen, O LORD: keep not silence: O
Lord, be not far from me. Stir up Thyself, and
awake to my judgment, even unto my cause,
my God and my Lord

Judge me, O LORD my God, according to   Psalm 35:24-26
Thy Righteousness; and let them not rejoice
over me. Let them not say in their hearts, Ah,
so would we have it: let them not say, We have
swallowed him up. Let them be ashamed and
brought to confusion together that rejoice at
mine hurt: let them be clothed with shame and
dishonour that magnify themselves against me

Let them shout for joy, and be glad, that   Psalm 35:27-28
favour my righteous cause: yea, let them say
continually, Let The LORD be magnified,
Which hath pleasure in the prosperity of His
Servant. And my tongue shall speak of Thy
Righteousness and of Thy Praise all the day
long

O LORD, rebuke me not in Thy Wrath: Psalm 38:1-5
neither chasten me in Thy Hot Displeasure. For
Thine Arrows stick fast in me, and Thy Hand
presseth me sore. There is no soundness in my
flesh because of Thine Anger; neither is there
any rest in my bones because of my sin. For
mine iniquities are gone over mine head: as an
heavy burden they are too heavy for me. My
wounds stink and are corrupt because of my
foolishness

I am troubled; I am bowed down greatly; I   Psalm 38:6-8
go mourning all the day long. For my loins
are filled with a loathsome disease: and there
is no soundness in my flesh. I am feeble and
sore broken: I have roared by reason of the
disquietness of my heart

Lord, all my desire is before Thee; and my   Psalm 38:9-12
groaning is not hid from Thee. My heart
panteth, my strength faileth me: as for the light
of mine eyes, it also is gone from me. My lovers
and my friends stand aloof from my sore; and
my kinsmen stand afar off. They also that seek
after my life lay snares for me: and they that
seek my hurt speak mischievous things, and
imagine deceits all the day long

But I, as a deaf man, heard not; and I was as a   Psalm 38:13-17
dumb man that openeth not his mouth. Thus
I was as a man that heareth not, and in whose
mouth are no reproofs. For in Thee, O LORD,
do I hope: Thou wilt hear, O Lord my God.
For I said, Hear me, lest otherwise they should
rejoice over me: when my foot slippeth, they
magnify themselves against me. For I am ready
to halt, and my sorrow is continually before me

For I will declare mine iniquity; I will be sorry   Psalm 38:18
for my sin

But mine enemies are lively, and they are   Psalm 38:19-20
strong: and they that hate me wrongfully are
multiplied. They also that render evil for good
are mine adversaries; because I follow the thing
that good is

Forsake me not, O LORD: O my God, be not   Psalm 38:21-22
far from me. Make haste to help me, O Lord
my salvation

I said, I will take heed to my ways, that I sin   Psalm 39:1-5
not with my tongue: I will keep my mouth
with a bridle, while the wicked is before me. I
was dumb with silence, I held my peace, even
from good; and my sorrow was stirred. My
heart was hot within me, while I was musing
the fire burned: then spake I with my tongue,
LORD, make me to know mine end, and
the measure of my days, what it is: that I may
know how frail I am. Behold, Thou hast made
my days as an handbreadth; and mine age is as
nothing before Thee: verily every man at his
best state is altogether vanity

Surely every man walketh in a vain show: Psalm 39:6
surely they are disquieted in vain: he heapeth
up riches, and knoweth not who shall gather
them

And now, Lord, what wait I for? my hope is in   Psalm 39:7
Thee

Deliver me from all my transgressions: make   Psalm 39:8
me not the reproach of the foolish

I was dumb, I opened not my mouth; because Thou didst it. Remove Thy Stroke away from me: I am consumed by the Blow of Thine Hand. When Thou with rebukes dost correct man for iniquity, Thou makest his beauty to consume away like a moth: surely every man is vanity — Psalm 39:9-11

Hear my prayer, O LORD, and give ear unto my cry; hold not Thy Peace at my tears: for I am a stranger with Thee, and a sojourner, as all my fathers were — Psalm 39:12

O spare me, that I may recover strength, before I go hence, and be no more — Psalm 39:13

Many, O LORD my God, are Thy Wonderful Works which Thou hast done, and Thy Thoughts which are to us-ward: They cannot be reckoned up in order unto Thee: if I would declare and speak of Them, They are more than can be numbered — Psalm 40:5

Sacrifice and offering Thou didst not desire; mine ears hast Thou opened; burnt offering and sin offering hast Thou not required — Psalm 40:6 [Hebrews 10:5b-8a]

Lo, I come: in the volume of the Book it is written of me, I delight to do Thy Will, O my God: yea, Thy Law is within my heart — Psalm 40:7-8 [Hebrews 10:7,9a]

I have preached righteousness in the great assembly: lo, I have not refrained my lips, O LORD, Thou knowest — Psalm 40:9

I have not hid Thy Righteousness within
my heart; I have declared Thy Faithfulness
and Thy Salvation: I have not concealed Thy
Lovingkindness and Thy Truth from the great
congregation

Psalm 40:10

Withhold not Thou Thy Tender Mercies from
me, O LORD: let Thy Lovingkindness and
Thy Truth continually preserve me

Psalm 40:11

For innumerable evils have compassed me
about: mine iniquities have taken hold upon
me, so that I am not able to look up; they are
more than the hairs of mine head: therefore my
heart faileth me

Psalm 40:12

Be pleased, O LORD, to deliver me: O
LORD, make haste to help me

Psalm 40:13

Let them be ashamed and confounded together
that seek after my soul to destroy it; let all be
driven backward and put to shame that wish me
evil

Psalm 40:14

Let them be desolate for a reward of their
shame that say unto me, Aha, aha

Psalm 40:15

Let all that seek Thee rejoice and be glad in
Thee: let such as love Thy Salvation always say,
The LORD be magnified

Psalm 40:16

But I am poor and needy; yet The Lord
thinketh upon me: Thou art my help and my
deliverer; make no delay, O my God

Psalm 40:17

Blessed is he that considereth the poor: The LORD will deliver him in time of trouble. The LORD will preserve him, and keep him alive; and he shall be blessed upon the earth: and Thou wilt not deliver him unto the will of his enemies. The LORD will strengthen him upon the bed of languishing: Thou wilt make all his bed in his sickness
Psalm 41:1-3

LORD, be merciful unto me: heal my soul; for I have sinned against Thee
Psalm 41:4

Mine enemies speak evil of me, When shall he die, and his name perish? And if he come to see me, he speaketh vanity: his heart gathereth iniquity to itself; when he goeth abroad, he telleth it
Psalm 41:5-6

All that hate me whisper together against me: against me do they devise my hurt. An evil disease, say they, cleaveth fast unto him: and now that he lieth he shall rise up no more
Psalm 41:7-8

Yea, mine own familiar friend, in whom I trusted, which did eat of my bread, hath lifted up his heel against me. But Thou, O LORD, be merciful unto me, and raise me up, that I may requite them
Psalm 41:9-10

By this I know that Thou favourest me, because mine enemy doth not triumph over me
Psalm 41:11

And as for me, Thou upholdest me in mine integrity, and settest me before Thy Face for ever
Psalm 41:12

Blessed be The LORD God of Israel from everlasting, and to everlasting. Amen, and amen.
Psalm 41:13

Judge me, O God, and plead my cause, against an ungodly nation: O deliver me from the deceitful and unjust man	Psalm 43:1
For Thou art The God of my strength: why dost Thou cast me off? why go I mourning because of the oppression of the enemy?	Psalm 43:2
O send out Thy Light and Thy Truth: let Them lead me; let Them bring me unto Thy Holy Hill, and to Thy Tabernacles	Psalm 43:3
Then will I go unto the altar of God, unto God my exceeding joy: yea, upon the harp will I praise Thee, O God my God	Psalm 43:4
But Thou hast cast off, and put us to shame; and goest not forth with our armies	Psalm 44:9
Thou makest us to turn back from the enemy: and they which hate us spoil for themselves	Psalm 44:10
Thou hast given us like sheep appointed for meat; and hast scattered us among the heathen	Psalm 44:11
Thou sellest Thy people for nought, and dost not increase Thy Wealth by their price	Psalm 44:12
Thou makest us a reproach to our neighbours, a scorn and a derision to them that are round about us	Psalm 44:13
Thou makest us a byword among the heathen, a shaking of the head among the people	Psalm 44:14
My confusion is continually before me, and the shame of my face hath covered me, For the voice of him that reproacheth and blasphemeth; by reason of the enemy and avenger	Psalm 44:15-16

All this is come upon us; yet have we not forgotten Thee, neither have we dealt falsely in Thy Covenant	Psalm 44:17
Our heart is not turned back, neither have our steps declined from Thy Way; though Thou hast sore broken us in the place of dragons, and covered us with the shadow of death	Psalm 44:18-19
If we have forgotten the Name of our God, or stretched out our hands to a strange god; shall not God search this out? For He knoweth the secrets of the heart	Psalm 44:20-21
Yea, for Thy Sake are we killed all the day long; we are counted as sheep for the slaughter	Psalm 44:22
Awake, why sleepest Thou, O Lord? Arise, cast us not off for ever	Psalm 44:23
Wherefore hidest Thou Thy Face, and forgettest our affliction and our oppression?	Psalm 44:24
For our soul is bowed down to the dust; our belly cleaveth unto the earth	Psalm 44:25
Arise for our help, and redeem us for Thy Mercies' Sake	Psalm 44:26
Save me, O God; by Thy Name, and judge me by Thy Strength	Psalm 54:1
Hear my prayer, O God: give ear to the words of my mouth	Psalm 54:2
Cut them off in Thy Truth	Psalm 54:5b
I will freely sacrifice unto Thee: I will praise Thy Name, O LORD, for it is good	Psalm 54:6

Give ear to my prayer, O God; and hide not
Thyself from my supplication

Psalm 55:1

Attend unto me, and hear me: I mourn in my
complaint, and make a noise; because of the
voice of the enemy, because of the oppression of
the wicked: for they cast iniquity upon me, and
in wrath they hate me

Psalm 55:2-3

My heart is sore pained within me: and the
terrors of death are fallen upon me

Psalm 55:4

Fearfulness and trembling are come upon me,
and horror hath overwhelmed me

Psalm 55:5

And I said, Oh that I had wings like a dove!
for then would I fly away, and be at rest. Lo,
then would I wander far off, and remain in the
wilderness. Selah. I would hasten my escape
from the windy storm and tempest

Psalm 55:6-8

Destroy, O Lord, and divide their tongues:
for I have seen violence and strife in the city.
Day and night they go about it upon the walls
thereof: mischief also and sorrow are in the
midst of it. Wickedness is in the midst thereof:
deceit and guile depart not from her streets

Psalm 55:9-11

But Thou, O God, shalt bring them down into
the pit of destruction: bloody and deceitful men
shall not live out half their days; but I will trust
in Thee

Psalm 55:23

Break their teeth, O God, in their mouth: Psalm 58:6-8
break out the great teeth of the young lions, O
LORD. Let them melt away as waters which
run continually: when he bendeth his bow to
shoot his arrows, let them be as cut in pieces.
As a snail which melteth, let every one of them
pass away: like the untimely birth of a woman,
that they may not see the sun.

Deliver me from mine enemies, O my God: Psalm 59:1
defend me from them that rise up against me

Deliver me from the workers of iniquity, and   Psalm 59:2
save me from bloody men

For, lo, they lie in wait for my soul: the   Psalm 59:3-4
mighty are gathered against me; not for my
transgression, not for my sin, O LORD. They
run and prepare themselves without my fault:
awake to help me, and behold

Thou therefore, O LORD God of hosts, The   Psalm 59:5
God of Israel, awake to visit all the heathen: be
not merciful to any wicked transgressors

They return at evening: they make a noise like   Psalm 59:6-8
a dog, and go round about the city. Behold,
they belch out with their mouth: swords are
in their lips: for who, say they, doth hear? But
Thou, O LORD, shalt laugh at them; Thou
shalt have all the heathen in derision

Because of His Strength will I wait upon Thee: Psalm 59:9-13
for God is my defence. The God of my mercy
shall prevent me: God shall let me see my desire
upon mine enemies. Slay them not, lest my
people forget: scatter them by Thy Power; and
bring them down, O Lord our shield. For the
sin of their mouth and the words of their lips
let them even be taken in their pride: and for
cursing and lying which they speak. Consume
them in wrath, consume them, that they may
not be: and let them know that God ruleth in
Jacob unto the ends of the earth

And at evening let them return; and let them   Psalm 59:14-16
make a noise like a dog, and go round about the
city. Let them wander up and down for meat,
and grudge if they be not satisfied. But I will
sing of Thy Power; yea, I will sing aloud of
Thy Mercy in the morning: for Thou hast been
my defence and refuge in the day of my trouble

Unto Thee, O my strength, will I sing: for God   Psalm 59:17
is my defence, and The God of my mercy

O God, Thou hast cast us off, Thou hast   Psalm 60:1-4
scattered us, Thou hast been displeased; O
turn Thyself to us again. Thou hast made the
earth to tremble; Thou hast broken it: heal
the breaches thereof; for it shaketh. Thou hast
shown Thy People hard things: Thou hast
made us to drink the wine of astonishment.
Thou hast given a banner to them that fear
Thee, that it may be displayed because of the
truth

That Thy Beloved may be delivered; save with   Psalm 60:5;
Thy Right Hand, and hear me   108:6

Who will bring me into the strong city? who will lead me into Edom? Wilt not Thou, O God, which hadst cast us off? and Thou, O God, which didst not go out with our armies? Give us help from trouble: for vain is the help of man. Through our God we shall do valiantly: for He it is that shall tread down our enemies.

Psalm 60:9-12; 108:10-13

Hear my cry, O God; attend unto my prayer

Psalm 61:1

From the end of the earth will I cry unto Thee, when my heart is overwhelmed: lead me to The Rock that is higher than I

Psalm 61:2

For Thou hast been a shelter for me, and a strong tower from the enemy. I will abide in Thy Tabernacle for ever: I will trust in the covert of Thy Wings

Psalm 61:3-4

For Thou, O God, hast heard my vows: Thou hast given me the heritage of those that fear Thy Name

Psalm 61:5

Thou wilt prolong the king's life: and his years as many generations. He shall abide before God for ever: O prepare mercy and truth, which may preserve him. So will I sing praise unto Thy Name for ever, that I may daily perform my vows

Psalm 61:6-8

Hear my voice, O God, in my prayer: preserve my life from fear of the enemy

Psalm 64:1

Hide me from the secret counsel of the wicked;   Psalm 64:2-4
from the insurrection of the workers of
iniquity: Who whet their tongue like a sword,
and bend their bows to shoot their arrows, even
bitter words: That they may shoot in secret at
the perfect: suddenly do they shoot at him, and
fear not

Save me, O God; for the waters are come in   Psalm 69:1-3
unto my soul. I sink in deep mire, where there
is no standing: I am come into deep waters,
where the floods overflow me. I am weary of
my crying: my throat is dried: mine eyes fail
while I wait for my God

They that hate me without cause are more than   Psalm 69:4-5
the hairs of mine head: they that would destroy
me, being mine enemies wrongfully, are
mighty; then I restored that which I took not
away. O God, Thou knowest my foolishness;
and my sins are not hid from Thee

Let not them that wait on Thee, O Lord GOD   Psalm 69:6-7
of Hosts, be ashamed for my sake: let not those
that seek Thee be confounded for my sake,
O God of Israel. Because for Thy Sake I have
borne reproach; shame hath covered my face

I am become a stranger unto my brethren, and   Psalm 69:8-9
an alien unto my mother's children. For the   [John 2:17b]
zeal of Thine House hath eaten me up; and the
reproaches of them that reproached Thee are
fallen upon me

When I wept, and chastened my soul with   Psalm 69:10-12
fasting, that was to my reproach. I made
sackcloth also my garment; and I became a
proverb to them. They that sit in the gate speak
against me; and I was the song of the drunkards

But as for me, my prayer is unto Thee, O
LORD, in an acceptable time: O God, in the
multitude of Thy Mercy hear me, in the truth
of Thy Salvation. Deliver me out of the mire,
and let me not sink: let me be delivered from
them that hate me, and out of the deep waters.
Let not the waterflood overflow me, neither let
the deep swallow me up, and let not the pit shut
her mouth upon me

Psalm 69:13-15

Hear me, O LORD; for Thy Lovingkindness is
good: turn unto me according to the multitude
of Thy Tender Mercies. And hide not Thy Face
from Thy Servant; for I am in trouble: hear me
speedily

Psalm 69:16-17

Draw nigh unto my soul, and redeem it: deliver
me because of mine enemies

Psalm 69:18

Thou hast known my reproach, and my shame,
and my dishonour: mine adversaries are all
before Thee

Psalm 69:19

Reproach hath broken my heart; and I am full
of heaviness: and I looked for some to take pity,
but there was none; and for comforters, but I
found none

Psalm 69:20

They gave Me also gall for My Meat; and in
My Thirst they gave Me vinegar to drink

Psalm 69:21

Let their table become a snare before them: and
that which should have been for their welfare,
let it become a trap

Psalm 69:22

Let their eyes be darkened, that they see not;
and make their loins continually to shake

Psalm 69:23

Pour out Thine Indignation upon them, and let Thy Wrathful Anger take hold of them	Psalm 69:24
Let their habitation be desolate; and let none dwell in their tents. For they persecute Him whom Thou hast smitten; and they talk to the grief of those whom Thou hast wounded	Psalm 69:25-26 [Acts 1:20a]
Add iniquity unto their iniquity: and let them not come into Thy Righteousness. Let them be blotted out of the book of the living, and not be written with the righteous. But I am poor and sorrowful: let Thy Salvation, O God, set me up on high	Psalm 69:27-29
Make haste, O God, to deliver me; make haste to help me, O LORD	Psalm 70:1
Let them be ashamed and confounded that seek after my soul: let them be turned backward, and put to confusion, that desire my hurt. Let them be turned back for a reward of their shame that say, Aha, aha	Psalm 70:2-3
Let all those that seek Thee rejoice and be glad in Thee: and let such as love Thy Salvation say continually, Let God be magnified	Psalm 70:4
But I am poor and needy: make haste unto me, O God: Thou art my help and my deliverer; O LORD, make no tarrying	Psalm 70:5
In Thee, O LORD, do I put my trust: let me never be put to confusion	Psalm 71:1
Deliver me in Thy righteousness, and cause me to escape: incline Thine Ear unto me, and save me	Psalm 71:2

Be Thou my strong habitation, whereunto   Psalm 71:3
I may continually resort: Thou hast given
commandment to save me; for Thou art my
rock and my fortress

Deliver me, O my God, out of the hand of the   Psalm 71:4-5
wicked, out of the hand of the unrighteous
and cruel man. For Thou art my hope, O Lord
GOD: Thou art my trust from my youth

By Thee have I been holden up from the   Psalm 71:6
womb: Thou art He that took me out of my
mother's bowels: my praise shall be continually
of Thee

I am as a wonder unto many; but Thou art my   Psalm 71:7
strong refuge

Let my mouth be filled with Thy Praise and   Psalm 71:8
with Thy Honour all the day

Cast me not off in the time of old age; forsake Psalm 71:9
me not when my strength faileth

For mine enemies speak against me; and they   Psalm 71:10-11
that lay wait for my soul take counsel together,
Saying, God hath forsaken him: persecute and
take him; for there is none to deliver him

O God, be not far from me: O my God, make   Psalm 71:12
haste for my help

Let them be confounded and consumed that   Psalm 71:13-14
are adversaries to my soul; let them be covered
with reproach and dishonour that seek my hurt.
But I will hope continually, and will yet praise
Thee more and more

My mouth shall show forth Thy Righteousness   Psalm 71:15
and Thy Salvation all the day; for I know not
the numbers thereof

I will go in the strength of The Lord GOD: I   Psalm 71:16
will make mention of Thy Righteousness, even
of Thine only

O God, Thou hast taught me from my youth: Psalm 71:17-18
and hitherto have I declared Thy Wondrous
Works. Now also when I am old and
grayheaded, O God, forsake me not; until I
have shown Thy Strength unto this generation,
and Thy Power to every one that is to come

Thy Righteousness also, O God; is very high,   Psalm 71:19
Who hast done great things: O God, who is
like unto Thee!

Thou, which hast shown me great and sore   Psalm 71:20-21
troubles, shalt quicken me again, and shalt
bring me up again from the depths of the earth.
Thou shalt increase my greatness, and comfort
me on every side

I will also praise Thee with the psaltery, even   Psalm 71:22-24
Thy Truth, O my God: unto Thee will I sing
with the harp, O Thou Holy One of Israel. My
lips shall greatly rejoice when I sing unto Thee;
and my soul, which Thou hast redeemed. My
tongue also shall talk of Thy Righteousness all
the day long: for they are confounded, for they
are brought unto shame, that seek my hurt

Give the king Thy Judgments, O God, and   Psalm 72:1-5
Thy Righteousness unto the king's son. He
shall judge Thy People with righteousness, and
Thy Poor with judgment. The mountains shall
bring peace to the people, and the little hills,
by righteousness. He shall judge the poor of the
people, he shall save the children of the needy,
and shall break in pieces the oppressor. They
shall fear Thee as long as the sun and moon
endure, throughout all generations

And he shall live, and to him shall be given of   Psalm 72:15-17
the gold of Sheba: prayer also shall be made for
him continually; and daily shall he be praised.
There shall be an handful of corn in the earth
upon the top of the mountains; the fruit thereof
shall shake like Lebanon: and they of the
city shall flourish like grass of the earth. His
name shall endure for ever: his name shall be
continued as long as the sun: and men shall be
blessed in him: all nations shall call him blessed

O God, why hast Thou cast us off for ever?   Psalm 74:1-2
why doth Thine Anger smoke against the sheep
of Thy Pasture? Remember Thy Congregation,
which Thou hast purchased of old; the rod of
Thine Inheritance, which Thou hast redeemed;
this mount Zion, wherein Thou hast dwelt

Lift up Thy Feet unto the perpetual desolations;   Psalm 74:3
even all that the enemy hath done wickedly in
the sanctuary

Thine Enemies roar in the midst of Thy   Psalm 74:4
Congregations; they set up their ensigns for
signs

A man was famuos according as he had lifted up axes upon the thick trees. But now they break down the carved work thereof at once with axes and hammers. They have cast fire into Thy Sanctuary, they have defiled by casting down the dwellingplace of Thy Name to the ground. They said in their hearts, Let us destroy them together: they have burned up all the synagogues of God in the land

Psalm 74:5-8

We see not our signs: there is no more any prophet: neither is there among us any that knoweth how long

Psalm 74:9

O God, how long shall the adversary reproach? Shall the enemy blaspheme Thy Name for ever? Why withdrawest Thou Thy Hand, even Thy Right Hand? pluck it out of Thy Bosom

Psalm 74:10-11

For God is my King of old, working salvation in the midst of the earth

Psalm 74:12

Thou didst divide the sea by Thy Strength; Thou brakest the heads of the dragons in the waters. Thou brakest the heads of leviathan in pieces, and gavest him to be meat to the people inhabiting the wilderness. Thou didst cleave the fountain and the flood: Thou driedst up mighty rivers

Psalm 74:13-15

The day is Thine, the night also is Thine: Thou hast prepared the light and the sun. Thou hast set all the borders of the earth: Thou hast made summer and winter

Psalm 74:16-17

Remember this, that the enemy hath reproached, O LORD, and that the foolish people have blasphemed Thy Name

Psalm 74:18

O deliver not the soul of Thy Turtledoves unto the multitude of the wicked: forget not the congregation of Thy Poor for ever — Psalm 74:19

Have respect unto the covenant: for the dark places of the earth are full of the habitations of cruelty — Psalm 74:20

O let not the oppressed return ashamed: let the poor and needy praise Thy Name — Psalm 74:21

Arise, O God, plead Thine Own Cause: remember how the foolish man reproacheth Thee daily. Forget not the voice of Thine Enemies: the tumult of those that rise up against Thee increaseth continually — Psalm 74:22-23

I remembered God, and was troubled: I complained, and my spirit was overwhelmed — Psalm 77:3

Thou holdest mine eyes waking: I am so troubled that I cannot speak — Psalm 77:4

I have considered the days of old, the years of ancient times — Psalm 77:5

I call to remembrance my song in the night: I commune with mine own heart: and my spirit made diligent search — Psalm 77:6

Will The Lord cast off for ever? and will He be favourable no more? Is His Mercy clean gone for ever? doth His Promise fail for evermore? Hath God forgotten to be gracious? hath He in anger shut up His Tender Mercies? — Psalm 77:7-9

And I said, This is my infirmity; but I will
remember the years of The Right Hand of The
Most High. I will remember the Works of The
LORD: surely I will remember Thy Wonders
of Old

Psalm 77:10-11

O God, the heathen are come into Thine
Inheritance; Thy Holy Temple have they
defiled; they have laid Jerusalem on heaps

Psalm 79:1

The dead bodies of Thy Servants have they
given to be meat unto the fowls of the heaven,
the flesh of Thy Saints unto the beasts of the
earth

Psalm 79:2

Their blood have they shed like water round
about Jerusalem; and there was none to bury
them

Psalm 79:3

We are become a reproach to our neighbors, a
scorn and derision to them that are round about
us

Psalm 79:4

How long, LORD? wilt Thou be angry for
ever? shall Thy Jealousy burn like fire?

Psalm 79:5

Pour out Thy Wrath upon the heathen that
have not known Thee, and upon the kingdoms
that have not called upon Thy Name. For
they have devoured Jacob, and laid waste his
dwellingplace

Psalm 79:6-7

O remember not against us former iniquities:
let Thy Tender Mercies speedily prevent us: for
we are brought very low

Psalm 79:8

Help us, O God of our salvation, for the glory
of Thy Name: and deliver us, and purge away
our sins, for Thy Name's sake

Psalm 79:9

Wherefore should the heathen say, Where
is their God? let Him be known among the
heathen in our sight by the revenging of the
blood of Thy Servants which is shed

Psalm 79:10

Let the sighing of the prisoner come before
Thee; according to the greatness of Thy Power
preserve Thou those that are appointed to die

Psalm 79:11

And render unto our neighbors sevenfold into
their bosom their reproach, wherewith they
have reproached Thee, O Lord

Psalm 79:12

So we Thy People and sheep of Thy Pasture
will give Thee thanks for ever: we will show
forth Thy Praise to all generations

Psalm 79:13

Give ear, O Shepherd of Israel, Thou that
leadest Joseph like a flock; Thou that dwellest
between the cherubims, shine forth

Psalm 80:1

Before Ephraim and Benjamin and Manasseh
stir up Thy Strength, and come and save us.
Turn us again, O God, and cause Thy Face to
shine; and we shall be saved

Psalm 80:2-
3,7,19

O LORD God of Hosts, how long wilt Thou
be angry against the prayer of Thy People?
Thou feedest them with the bread of tears; and
givest them tears to drink in great measure.
Thou makest us a strife unto our neighbours:
and our enemies laugh among themselves

Psalm 80:4-6

Turn us again, O God of Hosts, and cause Thy
Face to shine; and we shall be saved

Psalm 80:7,3,19

Thou hast brought a vine out of Egypt: Thou   Psalm 80:8-11
hast cast out the heathen, and planted it. Thou
preparedst room before it, and didst cause it to
take deep root, and it filled the land. The hills
were covered with the shadow of it, and the
boughs thereof were like the goodly cedars.
She sent out her boughs unto the sea, and her
branches unto the river

Why hast Thou then broken down her hedges,   Psalm 80:12-15
so that all they which pass by the way do pluck
her? The boar out of the wood doth waste it,
and the wild beast of the field doth devour it.
Return, we beseech Thee, O God of Hosts:
look down from heaven, and behold, and visit
this vine; And the vineyard which Thy Right
Hand hath planted, and the branch that Thou
madest strong for Thyself

It is burned with fire, it is cut down: they   Psalm 80:16
perish at the rebuke of Thy Countenance

Let Thy Hand be upon the man of Thy Right   Psalm 80:17
Hand, upon the son of man whom Thou
madest strong for Thyself

So will not we go back from Thee: quicken us,   Psalm 80:18
and we will call upon Thy Name

Turn us again, O LORD God of Hosts, cause   Psalm 80:19,3,7
Thy Face to shine; and we shall be saved

Arise, O God, judge the earth: for Thou shalt   Psalm 82:8
inherit all nations

Keep not Thou silence, O God: hold not Thy   Psalm 83:1
peace, and be not still, O God

For, lo, Thine Enemies make a tumult: and   Psalm 83:2-4
they that hate Thee have lifted up the head.
They have taken crafty counsel against Thy
People, and consulted against Thy Hidden
Ones. They have said, Come, and let us cut
them off from being a nation; that the name of
Israel may be no more in remembrance

For they have consulted together with one   Psalm 83:5-8
consent: they are confederate against Thee:
the tabernacles of Edom, and the Ishmaelites;
of Moab, and the Hagarenes; Gebal, and
Ammon, and Amalek; the Philistines with the
inhabitants of Tyre; Assure also is joined with
them: they have helped the children of Lot

Do unto them as unto the Midianites; as to   Psalm 83:9-10
Sisera, as to Jabin, at the brook of Kison: Which
perished at En-dor: they became as dung for
the earth

Make their nobles like Oreb, and like   Psalm 83:11-12
Zeeb: yea, all their princes as Zebah, and as
Zalmunna: Who said, Let us take to ourselves
the houses of God in possession

O my God, make them like a wheel; as the   Psalm 83:13-15
stubble before the wind. As the fire burneth a
wood, and as the flame setteth the mountains
on fire; So persecute them with Thy Tempest,
and make them afraid with Thy Storm

Fill their faces with shame; that they may   Psalm 83:16-18
seek Thy Name, O LORD. Let them be
confounded and troubled for ever; yea, let
them be put to shame, and perish: That men
may know that Thou, whose Name alone is
JEHOVAH, art the Most High over all the
earth

LORD, Thou hast been favourable unto Thy Land: Thou hast brought back the captivity of Jacob. Thou hast forgiven the iniquity of Thy People, Thou hast covered all their sin. Selah. Thou hast taken away all Thy Wrath: Thou hast turned Thyself from the fierceness of Thine Anger

Psalm 85:1-3

Turn us, O God of our salvation, and cause Thine Anger toward us to cease. Wilt Thou be angry with us for ever? Wilt Thou draw out Thine Anger to all generations?

Psalm 85:4-5

Wilt Thou not revive us again: that Thy People may rejoice in Thee?

Psalm 85:6

Show us Thy Mercy, O LORD, and grant us Thy Salvation

Psalm 85:7

I will hear what God The LORD will speak: for He will speak peace unto His People, and to His Saints: but let them not turn again to folly

Psalm 85:8

Surely His Salvation is nigh them that fear Him; that glory may dwell in our land

Psalm 85:9

Mercy and truth are met together; righteousness and peace have kissed each other. Truth shall spring out of the earth; and righteousness shall look down from heaven

Psalm 85:10-11

Yea, The Lord shall give that which is good; and our land shall yield her increase. Righteousness shall go before him; and shall set us in the way of His Steps

Psalm 85:12-13

Bow down Thine Ear, O LORD, hear me: for I am poor and needy

Psalm 86:1

Preserve my soul; for I am holy: O Thou my   Psalm 86:2
God, save Thy Servant that trusteth in Thee

Be merciful unto me, O Lord, for I cry unto   Psalm 86:3
Thee daily

Rejoice the soul of Thy Servant: for unto Thee,   Psalm 86:4
O Lord, do I lift up my soul

For Thou, Lord, art good, and ready to forgive;   Psalm 86:5
and plenteous in mercy unto all them that call
upon Thee

Give ear, O LORD, unto my prayer; and attend   Psalm 86:6
to the voice of my supplications

In the day of my trouble I will call upon Thee: Psalm 86:7
for Thou wilt answer me

Among the gods there is none like unto Thee,   Psalm 86:8
O Lord; neither are there any works like unto
Thy Works

All nations whom Thou hast made shall come   Psalm 86:9-10
and worship before Thee, O Lord, and shall
glorify Thy Name. For Thou art great, and
doest wondrous things: Thou art God alone

Teach me Thy Way, O LORD; I will walk in   Psalm 86:11
Thy Truth: unite my heart to fear Thy Name

I will praise Thee, O Lord my God, with all   Psalm 86:12-13
my heart: and I will glorify Thy Name for
evermore. For great is Thy Mercy toward me:
and Thou hast delivered my soul from the
lowest hell

O God, the proud are risen against me, and the assemblies of violent men have sought after my soul; and have not set Thee before them	Psalm 86:14
But Thou, O Lord, art a God full of compassion, and gracious, longsuffering, and plenteous in mercy and truth	Psalm 86:15
O turn unto me, and have mercy upon me; give Thy Strength unto Thy Servant, and save the son of Thine Handmaid	Psalm 86:16
Show me a token for good; that they which hate me may see it, and be ashamed: because Thou, LORD, hast helped me, and comforted me	Psalm 86:17
O LORD God of my salvation, I have cried day and night before Thee	Psalm 88:1 [some of Jonah 2 throughout this Psalm]
Let my prayer come before Thee: incline Thine Ear unto my cry; For my soul is full of troubles: and my life draweth nigh unto the grave	Psalm 88:2-3
I am counted with them that go down into the pit: I am as a man that hath no strength: Free among the dead, like the slain that lie in the grave, whom Thou rememberest no more: and they are cut off from Thy Hand	Psalm 88:4-5
Thou hast laid me in the lowest pit, in darkness, in the deeps. Thy Wrath lieth hard upon me, and Thou hast afflicted me with all Thy Waves	Psalm 88:6-7

Thou hast put away mine acquaintenance far from me; Thou hast made me an abomination unto them: I am shut up, and I cannot come forth	Psalm 88:8
Mine eye mourneth by reason of affliction: LORD, I have called daily upon Thee, I have stretched out my hands unto Thee	Psalm 88:9
Wilt Thou show wonders to the dead? shall the dead arise and praise Thee?	Psalm 88:10
Shall Thy Lovingkindness be declared in the grave? or Thy Faithfulness in destruction? Shall Thy Wonders be known in the dark? and Thy Righteousness in the land of forgetfulness?	Psalm 88:11-12
But unto Thee have I cried, O LORD; and in the morning shall my prayer prevent Thee	Psalm 88:13
LORD, why castest Thou off my soul? why hidest Thou Thy Face from me?	Psalm 88:14
I am afflicted and ready to die from my youth up: while I suffer Thy Terrors I am distracted	Psalm 88:15
Thy Fierce Wrath goeth over me; Thy Terrors have cut me off. They came round about me daily like water; they compassed me about together	Psalm 88:16-17
Lover and friend hast Thou put far from me, and mine acquaintance into darkness	Psalm 88:18
LORD, Thou hast been our Dwellingplace in all generations	Psalm 90:1

Before the mountains were brought forth,   Psalm 90:2
or ever Thou hadst formed the earth and the
world, even from everlasting to everlasting,
Thou art God

Thou turnest man to destruction; and sayest,   Psalm 90:3
Return, ye children of men

For a thousand years in Thy Sight are but as   Psalm 90:4
yesterday when it is past, and as a watch in the
night

Thou carriest them away as with a flood; they   Psalm 90:5-6
are as a sleep: in the morning they are like
grass which groweth up. In the morning it
flourisheth, and groweth up; in the evening it is
cut down, and withereth

For we are consumed by Thine Anger, and by   Psalm 90:7-9
Thy Wrath are we troubled. Thou hast set our
iniquities before Thee, our secret sins in the
light of Thy Countenance. For all our days are
passed away in Thy Wrath: we spend our years
as a tale that is told

The days of our years are threescore years   Psalm 90:10
and ten; and if by reason of strength they be
fourscore years, yet is their strength labour and
sorrow; for it is soon cut off, and we fly away

Who knoweth the power of Thine Anger? even Psalm 90:11
according to Thy Fear, so is Thy Wrath

So teach us to number our days, that we may   Psalm 90:12
apply our hearts unto wisdom

Return, O LORD, how long? And let it repent   Psalm 90:13-14
Thee concerning Thy Servants. O satisfy us
early with Thy Mercy; that we may rejoice and
be glad all our days

Make us glad according to the days wherein   Psalm 90:15
Thou hast afflicted us, and the years wherein
we have seen evil

Let Thy Work appear unto Thy Servants, and   Psalm 90:16
Thy Glory unto their children

And let the Beauty of the LORD our God be   Psalm 90:17
upon us: and establish Thou the work of our
hands upon us; yea, the work of our hands
establish Thou it

O LORD God, to Whom vengeance   Psalm 94:1-2
belongeth; O God, to Whom vengeance
belongeth, show Thyself. Lift up Thyself, Thou
Judge of the Earth: render a reward to the
proud

LORD, how long shall the wicked, how long   Psalm 94:3-4
shall the wicked triumph? How long shall they
utter and speak hard things? and all the workers
of iniquity boast themselves?

They break in pieces Thy People, O LORD,   Psalm 94:5-7
and afflict Thine Heritage. They slay the
widow and the stranger, and murder the
fatherless. Yet they say, The LORD shall not
see, neither shall The God of Jacob regard it

Blessed is the man whom Thou chastenest, O   Psalm 94:12-13
LORD, and teachest him out of Thy Law; That
Thou mayest give him rest from the days of
adversity, until the pit be digged for the wicked

For the LORD will not cast off His People,   Psalm 94:14-16
neither will He forsake His Inheritance. But
judgment shall return unto righteousness: and
all the upright in heart shall follow it. Who
will rise up for me against the evildoers? or
who will stand up for me against the workers of
iniquity?

Unless The LORD had been my help, my soul   Psalm 94:17-18
had almost dwelt in silence. When I said, My
foot slippeth; Thy Mercy, O LORD, held me
up

In the multitude of my thoughts within me   Psalm 94:19-20
Thy Comforts delight my soul. Shall the throne
of iniquity have fellowship with Thee, which
frameth mischief by a law?

Hear my prayer, O LORD, and let my cry   Psalm 102:1
come unto Thee

Hide not Thy Face from me in the day when I   Psalm 102:2-3
am in trouble; incline Thine Ear unto me: in
the day when I call answer me speedily. For my
days are consumed like smoke, and my bones
are burned as an hearth

My heart is smitten, and withered like grass; so   Psalm 102:4-5
that I forget to eat my bread. By reason of the
voice of my groaning my bones cleave to my
skin

I am like a pelican of the wilderness: I am   Psalm 102:6-7
like an owl of the desert. I watch, and am as a
sparrow alone upon the house top

Mine enemies reproach me all the day; and they   Psalm 102:8
that are mad against me are sworn against me

For I have eaten ashes like bread, and mingled   Psalm 102:9-10
my drink with weeping, Because of Thine
Indignation and Thy Wrath: for Thou hast
lifted me up, and cast me down

My days are like a shadow that declineth; and   Psalm 102:11-12
I am withered like grass. But Thou, O LORD,
shalt endure for ever; and Thy Remembrance
unto all generations

Thou shalt arise, and have mercy upon Zion: Psalm 102:13-14
for the time to favour her, yea, the set time, is
come. For Thy Servants take pleasure in her
stones, and favour the dust thereof

So the heathen shall fear the Name of The   Psalm 102:15
LORD, and all the kings of the earth Thy
Glory

When The LORD shall build up Zion, He   Psalm 102:16-17
shall appear in His Glory. He will regard the
prayer of the destitute, and not despise their
prayer

This shall be written for the generation to   Psalm 102:18
come: and the people which shall be created
shall praise The LORD

For He hath looked down from the height of   Psalm 102:19-20
His Sanctuary; from heaven did The LORD
behold the earth; To hear the groaning of the
prisoner; to loose those that are appointed to
death

To declare the Name of The LORD in Zion,   Psalm 102:21-22
and His Praise in Jerusalem; When the people
are gathered together, and the kingdoms, to
serve The LORD

He weakened my strength in the way; He shortened my days. I said, O my God, take me not away in the midst of my days: Thy Years are throughout all generations	Psalm 102:23-24
Of old [And, Thou, LORD, in the beginning] hast Thou laid the foundation of the earth: and the heavens are the Work[s] of Thy [Thine] Hands. They shall perish, but Thou shalt endure [remainest]: yea,all of them [they all] shall wax old like [as doth] a garment; [and] as a vesture shalt Thou change [fold] them [up,] and they shall be changed: but Thou art the same, and Thy Years have no end [shall not fail]	Psalm 102:25-27 [Hebrews 1:10-12]
The children of Thy Servants shall continue, and their seed shall be established before Thee	Psalm 102:28
Remember me, O LORD, with the favour that Thou bearest unto Thy People: O visit me with Thy Salvation; That I may see the good of Thy Chosen, that I may rejoice in the gladness of Thy Nation, that I may glory with Thine Inheritance	Psalm 106:4-5
We have sinned with our fathers, we have committed iniquity, we have done wickedly	Psalm 106:6
Our fathers understood not Thy Wonders in Egypt; they remembered not the multitude of Thy Mercies; but provoked Him at the sea, even at the Red Sea	Psalm 106:7
Save us, O LORD our God, and gather us from among the heathen, to give thanks unto Thy Holy Name, and to triumph in Thy Praise	Psalm 106:47 [1 Chronicles 16:35]

Blessed be The LORD God of Israel from everlasting to everlasting: and let all the people say, Amen. Praise ye The LORD	Psalm 106:48 [1 Chronicles 16:36]

That Thy Beloved may be delivered: save with Thy Right Hand, and answer me	Psalm 108:6; 60:5

Who will bring me into the strong city? who will lead me into Edom? Wilt not Thou, O God, who hast cast us off? and wilt not Thou, O God, go forth with our hosts?	Psalm 108:10-11; 60:9-10

Give us help from trouble: for vain is the help of man. Through God we shall do valiantly: for He it is that shall tread down our enemies	Psalm 108:12-13; 60:11-12

Hold not Thy Peace, O God of my praise; For the mouth of the wicked and the mouth of the deceitful are opened against me: they have spoken against me with a lying tongue	Psalm 109:1-2

They compassed me about also with words of hatred; and fought against me without a cause	Psalm 109:3

For my love they are my adversaries: but I give myself unto prayer	Psalm 109:4

And they have rewarded me evil for good, and hatred for my love	Psalm 109:5

But do Thou for me, O GOD The LORD, for Thy Name's Sake: because Thy Mercy is good, deliver Thou me	Psalm 109:21

For I am poor and needy, and my heart is wounded within me	Psalm 109:22

I am gone like the shadow when it declineth: I am tossed up and down as the locust	Psalm 109:23
My knees are weak through fasting; and my flesh faileth of fatness	Psalm 109:24
I became also a reproach unto them: when they looked upon me they shaked their heads	Psalm 109:25
Help me, O LORD my God: O save me according to Thy Mercy: That they may know that this is Thy Hand; that Thou LORD, hast done it	Psalm 109:26-27
Let them curse, but bless Thou: when they arise, let them be ashamed; but let Thy Servant rejoice	Psalm 109:28
Let mine adversaries be clothed with shame, and let them cover themselves with their own confusion, as with a mantle	Psalm 109:29
I will greatly praise The LORD with my mouth; yea, I will praise Him among the multitude. For He shall stand at the right hand of the poor, to save him from those that condemn his soul	Psalm 109:30-31
O LORD, I beseech Thee, deliver my soul	Psalm 116:4
Deliver my soul, O LORD, from lying lips, and from a deceitful tongue	Psalm 120:2
Unto Thee lift I up mine eyes, O Thou that dwellest in the heavens	Psalm 123:1

Behold, as the eyes of servants look unto the hand of their masters, and as the eyes of a maiden unto the hand of her mistress; so our eyes wait upon The LORD our God, until that He have mercy upon us	Psalm 123:2
Have mercy upon us, O LORD, have mercy upon us: for we are exceedingly filled with contempt. Our soul is exceedingly filled with the scorning of those that are at ease, and with the contempt of the proud	Psalm 123:3-4
Do good, O LORD, unto those that be good, and to them that are upright in their hearts	Psalm 125:4
Turn again our captivity, O LORD, as the streams in the south	Psalm 126:4
Let them all be confounded and turned back that hate Zion. Let them be as the grass upon the housetops, which withereth afore it groweth up	Psalm 129:5-6
Out of the depths have I cried unto Thee, O LORD	Psalm 130:1
LORD, hear my voice: let Thine Ears be attentive to the voice of my supplications	Psalm 130:2
If Thou, LORD, shouldest mark iniquities, O Lord, who shall stand? But there is forgiveness with Thee, that Thou mayest be feared	Psalm 130:3-4
LORD, remember David, and all his afflictions	Psalm 132:1 (2-7)
Arise, O LORD, into Thy Rest; Thou, and the ark of Thy Strength	Psalm 132:8

Let Thy Priests be clothed with righteousness; and let Thy Saints shout for joy	Psalm 132:9
For Thy Servant David's sake turn not away the face of Thine Anointed	Psalm 132:10
Remember, O LORD, the children of Edom in the day of Jerusalem; who said, Rase it, rase it, even to the foundation thereof	Psalm 137:7
Deliver me, O LORD, from the evil man: preserve me from the violent man; Which imagine mischiefs in their heart; continually are they gathered together for war. They have sharpened their tongues like a serpent; adders' poison is under their lips	Psalm 140:1-3
Keep me, O LORD, from the hands of the wicked; preserve me from the violent man; who have purposed to overthrow my goings	Psalm 140:4
The proud have hid a snare for me, and cords; they have spread a net by the wayside; they have set gins for me	Psalm 140:5
I said unto The LORD, Thou art my God: hear the voice of my supplications, O LORD	Psalm 140:6
O GOD The Lord, the strength of my salvation, Thou hast covered my head in the day of battle. Grant not, O LORD, the desires of the wicked: further not his wicked device; lest they exalt themselves	Psalm 140:7-8
As for the head of those that compass me about, let the mischief of their own lips cover them	Psalm 140:9

Let burning coals fall upon them: let them be cast into the fire; into deep pits, that they rise not up again	Psalm 140:10
Let not an evil speaker be established in the earth: evil shall hunt the violent man to overthrow him	Psalm 140:11
I know that The LORD will maintain the cause of the afflicted, and the right of the poor	Psalm 140:12
Surely the righteous shall give thanks unto Thy Name: the upright shall dwell in Thy Presence	Psalm 140:13

LORD, I cry unto Thee: make haste unto me; give ear unto my voice, when I cry unto Thee	Psalm 141:1
Let my prayer be set forth before Thee as incense; and the lifting up of my hands as the evening sacrifice	Psalm 141:2
Set a watch, O LORD, before my mouth; keep the door of my lips	Psalm 141:3
Incline not my heart to any evil thing, to practise wicked works with men that work iniquity: and let me not eat of their dainties	Psalm 141:4
Let the righteous smite me; it shall be a kindness: and let him reprove me; it shall be an excellent oil, which shall not break my head	Psalm 141:5a
for yet my prayer also shall be in their calamities. When their judges are overthrown in stony places, they shall hear my words; for they are sweet.	Psalm 141:5b-6

Our bones are scattered at the grave's mouth, as when one cutteth and cleaveth wood upon the earth	Psalm 141:7
But mine eyes are unto Thee, O GOD The LORD: in Thee is my trust; leave not my soul destitute	Psalm 141:8
Keep me from the snares which they have laid for me, and the gins of the workers of iniquity	Psalm 141:9
Let the wicked fall into their own nets, whilst that I withal escape	Psalm 141:10
I cried unto The LORD with my voice; with my voice unto The LORD did I make my supplication. I poured out my complaint before Him; I showed before Him my trouble	Psalm 142:1-2
When my spirit was overwhelmed within me, then Thou knewest my path. In the way wherein I walked have they privily laid a snare for me	Psalm 142:3
I looked on my right hand, and beheld, but there was no man that would know me: refuge failed me; no man cared for my soul	Psalm 142:4
I cried unto Thee, O LORD: I said, Thou art my refuge and my portion in the land of the living	Psalm 142:5
Attend unto my cry; for I am brought very low: deliver me from my persecutors; for they are stronger than I	Psalm 142:6
Bring my soul out of prison, that I may praise Thy Name: the righteous shall compass me about; for Thou shalt deal bountifully with me	Psalm 142:7

Hear my prayer, O LORD, give ear to my
supplications: in Thy Faithfulness answer me,
and in Thy Righteousness

Psalm 143:1

And enter not into judgment with Thy Servant:
for in Thy Sight shall no man living be justified

Psalm 143:2

For the enemy hath persecuted my soul; he
hath smitten my life down to the ground; he
hath made me to dwell in darkness, as those
that have been long dead. Therefore is my spirit
overwhelmed within me; my heart within me
is desolate

Psalm 143:3-4

I remember the days of old; I meditate on all
Thy Works; I muse on the Work of Thy Hands

Psalm 143:5

I stretch forth my hands unto Thee: my soul
thirsteth after Thee, as a thirsty land

Psalm 143:6

Hear me speedily, O LORD: my spirit faileth:
hide not Thy Face from me, lest I be like unto
them that go down into the pit

Psalm 143:7

Cause me to hear Thy Lovingkindness in the
morning; for in Thee do I trust: cause me to
know the way wherein I should walk; for I lift
up my soul unto Thee

Psalm 143:8

Deliver me, O LORD, from mine enemies: I
flee unto Thee to hide me

Psalm 143:9

Teach me to do Thy Will; for Thou art my
God: Thy Spirit is good; lead me into the land
of uprightness

Psalm 143:10

Quicken me, O LORD, for Thy Name's Sake:
for Thy Righteousness' Sake bring my soul out
of trouble

Psalm 143:11

And of Thy Mercy cut off mine enemies, and destroy all them that afflict my soul: for I am Thy Servant	Psalm 143:12
LORD, what is man, that Thou takest knowledge of him! or the son of man, that Thou makest account of him!	Psalm 144:3
Man is like to vanity: his days are as a shadow that passeth away	Psalm 144:4
Bow Thy Heavens, O LORD, and come down: touch the mountains, and they shall smoke	Psalm 144:5
Cast forth lightning, and scatter them: shoot out Thine Arrows, and destroy them	Psalm 144:6
Send Thine Hand from above; rid me, and deliver me out of great waters, from the hand of strange children; Whose mouth speaketh vanity, and their right hand is a right hand of falsehood	Psalm 144:7-8
I will sing a new song unto Thee, O God: upon a psaltery and an instrument of ten strings will I sing praises unto Thee	Psalm 144:9
It is He that giveth salvation unto kings: who delivereth David His Servant from the hurtful sword	Psalm 144:10
Rid me, and deliver me from the hand of strange children, whose mouth speaketh vanity, and their right hand is a right hand of falsehood	Psalm 144:11
That our sons may be as plants grown up in their youth; that our daughters may be as corner stones, polished after the similitude of a palace	Psalm 144:12

That our garners may be full, affording all manner of store: that our sheep may bring forth thousands and ten thousands in our streets	Psalm 144:13
That our oxen may be strong to labour; that there be no breaking in, nor going out; that there be no complaining in our streets	Psalm 144:14
Happy is that people, that is in such a case: yea, happy is that people, whose God is The LORD	Psalm 144:15
Two things have I required of Thee; deny me them not before I die: Remove far from me vanity and lies: give me neither poverty nor riches; feed me with food convenient for me: Lest I be full, and deny Thee, and say, Who is The LORD? or lest I be poor, and steal, and take the Name of my God in vain	Proverbs 30:7-9
O LORD, be gracious unto us; we have waited for Thee: be Thou their arm every morning, our salvation also in the time of trouble	Isaiah 33:2
At the noise of the tumult the people fled; at the lifting up of Thyself the nations were scattered	Isaiah 33:3
O LORD of Hosts, God of Israel, that dwellest between the cherubims, Thou art The God, even Thou Alone, of all the kingdoms of the earth: Thou hast made heaven and earth	Isaiah 37:16 [2 Kings 19:15]
Incline Thine Ear, O LORD, and hear; open Thine Eyes, O LORD, and see: and hear all the words of Sennacherib, which hath sent to reproach The Living God	Isaiah 37:17 [2 Kings 19:16]

Of a truth, LORD, the kings of Assyria have laid waste all the nations, and their countries, And have cast their gods into the fire: for they were no gods, but the work of men's hands, wood and stone: therefore they have destroyed them. Now therefore, O LORD our God, save us from his hand, that all the kingdoms of the earth may know that Thou art The LORD, even Thou Only

Isaiah 37:18-20 [2 Kings 19:17-19]

Remember now, O LORD, I beseech Thee, how I have walked before Thee in truth and with a perfect heart, and have done that which is good in Thy Sight

Isaiah 38:3a [2 Kings 20:3a]

I said in the cutting off of my days, I shall go to the gates of the grave: I am deprived of the residue of my years. I said, I shall not see The LORD, even The LORD, in the land of the living: I shall behold man no more with the inhabitants of the world. Mine age is departed, and is removed from me as a shepherd's tent: I have cut off like a weaver my life: He will cut me off with pining sickness: from day even to night wilt Thou make an end of me. I reckoned till morning, that, as a lion, so will He break all my bones: from day even to night wilt Thou make an end of me. Like a crane or a swallow, so did I chatter: I did mourn as a dove: mine eyes fail with looking upward: O LORD, I am oppressed; undertake for me

Isaiah 38:10-14

What shall I say? He hath both spoken unto me, and Himself hath done it: I shall go softly all my years in the bitterness of my soul. O LORD, by these things men live, and in all these things is the life of my spirit: so wilt Thou recover me, and make me to live

Isaiah 38:15-16

Behold, for peace I had great bitterness: but   Isaiah 38:17-20
Thou hast in love to my soul delivered it from
the pit of corruption: for Thou hast cast all my
sins behind Thy Back. For the grave cannot
praise Thee, death can not celebrate Thee: they
that go down into the pit cannot hope for Thy
Truth. The living, the living, he shall praise
Thee, as I do this day: the father to the children
shall make known Thy Truth. The LORD was
ready to save me: therefore we will sing my
songs to the stringed instruments all the days of
our life in the House of The LORD

...So didst Thou lead Thy People, to make   Isaiah 63:7-14
Thyself a Glorious Name

Look down from heaven, and behold from the   Isaiah 63:15
habitation of Thy Holiness and of Thy Glory:
where is Thy Zeal and Thy Strength, the
sounding of Thy Bowels and of Thy Mercies
toward me? are They restrained?

Doubtless Thou art our Father, though   Isaiah 63:16
Abraham be ignorant of us, and Israel
acknowledge us not: Thou, O LORD, art
our Father, our Redeemer; Thy Name is from
everlasting

O LORD, why hast Thou made us to err from   Isaiah 63:17
Thy Ways, and hardened our heart from Thy
Fear? Return for Thy Servants' sake, the tribes
of Thine Inheritance

The people of Thy Holiness have possessed it   Isaiah 63:18
but a little while: our adversaries have trodden
down Thy Sanctuary

We are Thine: Thou never barest rule over   Isaiah 63:19
them; they were not called by Thy Name

Oh that Thou wouldest rend the heavens, that
Thou wouldest come down, that the mountains
might flow down at Thy Presence, As when the
melting fire burneth, the fire causeth the waters
to boil, to make Thy Name known to Thine
Adversaries, that the nations may tremble at
Thy Presence!

Isaiah 64:1-2

When Thou didst terrible things which
we looked not for, Thou camest down, the
mountains flowed down at Thy Presence

Isaiah 64:3

For since the beginning of the world men have
not heard, nor perceived by the ear, neither
hath the eye seen, O God, beside Thee, what
He hath prepared for him that waiteth for Him

Isaiah 64:4

Thou meetest him that rejoiceth and worketh
righteousness, those that remember Thee in
Thy Ways: behold, Thou art wroth; for we
have sinned: in those is continuance, and we
shall be saved

Isaiah 64:5

But we are all as an unclean thing, and all our
righteousnesses are as filthy rags; and we all do
fade as a leaf; and our iniquities, like the wind,
have taken us away

Isaiah 64:6

And there is none that calleth upon Thy Name,
that stirreth up himself to take hold of Thee:
for Thou hast hid Thy Face from us, and hast
consumed us, because of our iniquities

Isaiah 64:7

But now, O LORD, Thou art our Father; we
are the clay, and Thou our Potter; and we all
are the Work of Thy Hand

Isaiah 64:8

Be not wroth very sore, O LORD, neither remember iniquity for ever: behold, see, we beseech Thee, we are all Thy People	Isaiah 64:9
Thy Holy Cities are a wilderness, Zion is a wilderness, Jerusalem a desolation	Isaiah 64:10
Our holy and our beautiful house, where our fathers praised Thee, is burned up with fire: and all our pleasant things are laid waste	Isaiah 64:11
Wilt Thou refrain Thyself for these things, O LORD? wilt Thou hold Thy Peace, and afflict us very sore?	Isaiah 64:12
Arise, and save us	Jeremiah 2:27b
O LORD, I know that the way of man is not in himself: it is not in man that walketh to direct his steps	Jeremiah 10:23
O LORD, correct me, but with judgment; not in Thine Anger, lest Thou bring me to nothing	Jeremiah 10:24
Pour out Thy Fury upon the heathen that know Thee not, and upon the families that call not on Thy Name: for they have eaten up Jacob, and devoured him, and consumed him, and have made his habitation desolate	Jeremiah 10:25
But, O LORD of Hosts, that judgest righteously, that triest the reins and the heart, let me see Thy Vengeance on them: for unto Thee have I revealed my cause	Jeremiah 11:20

Righteous art Thou, O LORD, when I plead
with Thee: yet let me talk with Thee of Thy
Judgments: Wherefore doth the way of the
wicked prosper? wherefore are all they happy
that deal very treacherously? Thou hast planted
them, yea, they have taken root: they grow,
yea, they bring forth fruit: Thou art near in
their mouth, and far from their reins

Jeremiah 12:1-2

But Thou, O LORD, knowest me: Thou hast
seen me, and tried mine heart toward Thee:
pull them out like sheep for the slaughter, and
prepare them for the day of slaughter

Jeremiah 12:3

How long shall the land mourn, and the
herbs of every field wither, for the wickedness
of them that dwell therein? the beasts are
consumed, and the birds; because they said, He
shall not see our last end

Jeremiah 12:4

O LORD, though our iniquities testify against
us, do Thou it for Thy Name's Sake: for our
backslidings are many; we have sinned against
Thee

Jeremiah 14:7

O the Hope of Israel, the Saviour thereof in
time of trouble, why shouldest Thou be as a
stranger in the land, and as a wayfaring man
that turneth aside to tarry for a night?

Jeremiah 14:8

Why shouldest Thou be as a man astonied, as
a mighty man that cannot save? yet Thou, O
LORD, art in the midst of us, and we are called
by Thy Name; leave us not

Jeremiah 14:9

Hast Thou utterly rejected Judah? hath Thy Soul loathed Zion? why hast Thou smitten us, and there is no healing for us? we looked for peace, and there is no good; and for the time of healing, and behold trouble!	Jeremiah 14:19
We acknowledge, O LORD, our wickedness, and the iniquity of our fathers: for we have sinned against Thee	Jeremiah 14:20
Do not abhor us, for Thy Name's Sake, do not disgrace the throne of Thy Glory: remember, break not Thy Covenant with us	Jeremiah 14:21
Are there any among the vanities of the Gentiles that can cause rain? or can the heavens give showers? art not Thou He, O LORD our God? therefore we will wait upon Thee: for Thou hast made all these things	Jeremiah 14:22

O LORD, Thou knowest: remember me, and visit me, and revenge me of my persecutors; take me not away in Thy Longsuffering: know that for Thy Sake I have suffered rebuke	Jeremiah 15:15
Thy Words were found, and I did eat them; and Thy Word was unto me the joy and rejoicing of mine heart: for I am called by Thy Name, O LORD God of Hosts	Jeremiah 15:16
I sat not in the assembly of the mockers, nor rejoiced; I sat alone because of Thy Hand: for Thou hast filled me with indignation	Jeremiah 15:17
Why is my pain perpetual, and my wound incurable, which refuseth to be healed? wilt Thou be altogether unto me as a liar, and as waters that fail?	Jeremiah 15:18

A glorious high throne from the beginning is the place of our sanctuary — Jeremiah 17:12

O LORD, The Hope of Israel, all that forsake Thee shall be ashamed, and they that depart from me shall be written in the earth, because they have forsaken The LORD, the fountain of living waters — Jeremiah 17:13

Heal me, O LORD, and I shall be healed; save me, and I shall be saved: for Thou art my praise — Jeremiah 17:14

Behold, they say unto me, Where is The Word of The LORD? let it come now — Jeremiah 17:15

As for me, I have not hastened from being a pastor to follow Thee: neither have I desired the woeful day; Thou knowest: that which came out of my lips was right before Thee — Jeremiah 17:16

Be not a terror unto me: Thou art my hope in the day of evil — Jeremiah 17:17

Let them be confounded that persecute me, but let not me be confounded: let them be dismayed, but let not me be dismayed: bring upon them the day of evil, and destroy them with double destruction — Jeremiah 17:18

Give heed to me, O LORD, and hearken to the voice of them that contend with me — Jeremiah 18:19

Shall evil be recompensed for good? for they have digged a pit for my soul. Remember that I stood before Thee to speak good for them, and to turn away Thy Wrath from them — Jeremiah 18:20

Therefore deliver up their children to the   Jeremiah 18:21
famine, and pour out their blood by the force
of the sword; and let their wives be bereaved
of their children, and be widows; and let their
men be put to death; let their young men be
slain by the sword in battle

Let a cry be heard from their houses, when   Jeremiah 18:22
Thou shalt bring a troop suddenly upon them:
for they have digged a pit to take me, and hid
snares for my feet

Yet, LORD, Thou knowest all their counsel   Jeremiah 18:23
against me to slay me: forgive not their iniquity,
neither blot out their sin from Thy Sight, but
let them be overthrown before Thee; deal thus
with them in the time of Thine Anger

O LORD, Thou hast deceived me, and I was   Jeremiah 20:7
deceived; Thou art stronger than I, and hast
prevailed: I am in derision daily, every one
mocketh me

For since I spake, I cried out, I cried violence   Jeremiah 20:8
and spoil; because The Word of The LORD
was made a reproach unto me, and a derision,
daily

Then I said, I will not make mention of Him,   Jeremiah 20:9
nor speak any more in His Name. But His
Word was in mine heart as a burning fire
shut up in my bones, and I was weary with
forbearing, and I could not stay

For I heard the defaming of many, fear on every side. Report, say they, and we will report it. All my familiars watched for my halting, saying, Peradventure he will be enticed, and we shall prevail against him, and we shall take our revenge on him	Jeremiah 20:10
But The LORD is with me as a Mighty Terrible One: therefore my persecutors shall stumble, and they shall not prevail: they shall be greatly ashamed; for they shall not prosper: their everlasting confusion shall never be forgotten	Jeremiah 20:11
But, O LORD of Hosts, that triest the righteous, and seest the reins and the heart, let me see Thy Vengeance on them: for unto Thee have I opened my cause	Jeremiah 20:12; 17:10a [Revelation 2:23b]
O LORD, save Thy People, the remnant of Israel	Jeremiah 31:7b
Thou hast chastised me, and I was chastised, as a bullock unaccustomed to the yoke: turn Thou me, and I shall be turned; for Thou art The LORD my God	Jeremiah 31:18b
Surely after that I was turned, I repented; and after that I was instructed, I smote upon my thigh: I was ashamed, yea, even confounded, because I did bear the reproach of my youth	Jeremiah 31:19
O Thou Sword of The LORD, how long will it be ere Thou be quiet? put up Thyself into Thy Scabbard, rest, and be still	Jeremiah 47:6
O LORD, behold my affliction: for the enemy hath magnified himself	Lamentations 1:9b

See, O LORD, and consider; for I am become vile	Lamentations 1:11b
Behold, O LORD; for I am in distress: my bowels are troubled; mine heart is turned within me; for I have grievously rebelled: abroad the sword bereaveth, at home there is as death	Lamentations 1:20
They have heard that I sigh: there is none to comfort me: all mine enemies have heard of my trouble; they are glad that Thou hast done it: Thou wilt bring the day that Thou hast called, and they shall be like unto me	Lamentations 1:21
Let all their wickedness come before Thee; and do unto them, as Thou hast done unto me for all my transgressions: for my sighs are many, and my heart is faint	Lamentations 1:22
Behold, O LORD, and consider to whom Thou hast done this. Shall the women eat their fruit, and children of a span long? shall the priest and the prophet be slain in the sanctuary of The Lord?	Lamentations 2:20
The young and the old lie on the ground in the streets: my virgins and my young men are fallen by the sword; Thou hast slain them in the day of Thine Anger; Thou hast killed, and not pitied	Lamentations 2:21
Thou hast called as in a solemn day my terrors round about, so that in the day of The LORD'S Anger none escaped nor remained: those that I have swaddled and brought up hath mine enemy consumed	Lamentations 2:22

171

We have transgressed and have rebelled: Thou hast not pardoned	Lamentations 3:42
Thou hast covered with anger, and persecuted us: Thou hast slain, Thou hast not pitied	Lamentations 3:43
Thou hast covered Thyself with a cloud, that our prayer should not pass through	Lamentations 3:44
Thou hast made us as the offscouring and refuse in the midst of the people	Lamentations 3:45
All our enemies have opened their mouths against us	Lamentations 3:46
Fear and a snare is come upon us, desolation and destruction	Lamentations 3:47
Mine eye runneth down with rivers of water for the destruction of the daughter of my people	Lamentations 3:48
Mine eye trickleth down, and ceaseth not, without any intermission. Till The LORD look down, and behold from heaven	Lamentations 3:49-50
Mine eye affecteth mine heart because of all the daughters of my city	Lamentations 3:51
Mine enemies chased me sore, like a bird, without cause	Lamentations 3:52
They have cut off my life in the dungeon, and cast a stone upon me. Waters flowed over mine head; then I said, I am cut off	Lamentations 3:53-54
I called upon Thy Name, O LORD, out of the low dungeon	Lamentations 3:55

Thou hast heard my voice: hide not Thine Ear at my breathing, at my cry	Lamentations 3:56
Thou drewest near in the day that I called upon Thee: Thou saidst, Fear not	Lamentations 3:57
O Lord, Thou hast pleaded the causes of my soul; Thou hast redeemed my life	Lamentations 3:58
O LORD, Thou hast seen my wrong: judge Thou my cause	Lamentations 3:59
Thou hast seen all their vengeance and all their imaginations against me	Lamentations 3:60
Thou hast heard their reproach, O LORD, and all their imaginations against me; The lips of those that rose up against me, and their device against me all the day	Lamentations 3:61-62
Behold their sitting down, and their rising up; I am their music	Lamentations 3:63
Render unto them a recompence, O LORD, according to the work of their hands	Lamentations 3:64
Give them sorrow of heart, Thy Curse unto them	Lamentations 3:65
Persecute and destroy them in anger from under the heavens of The LORD	Lamentations 3:66
Remember, O LORD, what is come upon us: consider, and behold our reproach	Lamentations 5:1
Our inheritance is turned to strangers, our houses to aliens	Lamentations 5:2

We are orphans and fatherless, our mothers are as widows	Lamentations 5:3
We have drunken our water for money; our wood is sold unto us	Lamentations 5:4
Our necks are under persecution: we labour, and have no rest	Lamentations 5:5
We have given the hand to the Egyptians, and to the Assyrians, to be satisfied with bread	Lamentations 5:6
Our fathers have sinned, and are not; and we have borne their iniquities	Lamentations 5:7
Servants have ruled over us: there is none that doth deliver us out of their hand	Lamentations 5:8
We gat our bread with the peril of our lives because of the sword of the wilderness	Lamentations 5:9
Our skin was black like an oven because of the terrible famine	Lamentations 5:10
They ravished the women in Zion, and the maids in the cities of Judah	Lamentations 5:11
Princes are hanged up by their hand: the faces of elders were not honoured	Lamentations 5:12
They took the young men to grind, and the children fell under the wood	Lamentations 5:13
The elders have ceased from the gate, the young men from their music	Lamentations 5:14
The joy of our heart is ceased; our dance is turned into mourning	Lamentations 5:15

The crown is fallen from our head: woe unto us, that we have sinned!	Lamentations 5:16
For this our heart is faint; for these things our eyes are dim. Because of the mountain of Zion, which is desolate, the foxes walk upon it	Lamentations 5:17-18
Thou, O LORD, remainest for ever; Thy Throne from generation to generation	Lamentations 5:19
Wherefore dost Thou forget us for ever, and forsake us so long time?	Lamentations 5:20
Turn Thou us unto Thee, O LORD, and we shall be turned; renew our days as of old. But Thou hast utterly rejected us; Thou art very wroth against us	Lamentations 5:21-22
Take away all iniquity, and receive us graciously: so will we render the calves of our lips	Hosea 14:2b
Asshur shall not save us; we will not ride upon horses: neither will we say any more to the work of our hands, Ye are our gods: for in Thee the fatherless findeth mercy	Hosea 14:3
O LORD, to Thee will I cry: for the fire hath devoured the pastures of the wilderness, and the flame hath burned all the trees of the field	Joel 1:19
The beasts of the field cry also unto Thee: for the rivers of waters are dried up, and the fire hath devoured the pastures of the wilderness	Joel 1:20
Spare Thy People, O LORD, and give not Thine Heritage to reproach, that the heathen should rule over them: wherefore should they say among the people, Where is their God?	Joel 2:17b

Thither cause Thy Mighty Ones to come down, O LORD	Joel 3:11b
O Lord GOD, forgive, I beseech Thee: by whom shall Jacob arise? for he is small	Amos 7:2b
O Lord GOD, cease, I beseech Thee: by whom shall Jacob arise? for he is small	Amos 7:5
We beseech Thee, O LORD, we beseech Thee, let us not perish for this man's life, and lay not upon us innocent blood: for Thou, O LORD, hast done as it pleased Thee	Jonah 1:14
I cried by reason of mine affliction unto The LORD, and He heard me; out of the belly of hell cried I, and Thou heardest my voice	Jonah 2:2 [Psalm 18:4-6; 22:23-24; 88 & 89 throughout this prayer]
For Thou hadst cast me into the deep, in the midst of the seas; and the floods compassed me about: all Thy Billows and Thy Waves passed over me	Jonah 2:3 [Psalm 42:7]
Then I said, I am cast out of Thy Sight; yet I will look again toward Thy Holy Temple	Jonah 2:4
The waters compassed me about, even to the soul: the depth closed me round about, the weeds were wrapped about my head. I went down to the bottoms of the mountains; the earth with her bars was about me for ever: yet hast Thou brought up my life from corruption, O LORD my God	Jonah 2:5-6
When my soul fainted within me I remembered The LORD: and my prayer came in unto Thee, into Thine Holy Temple	Jonah 2:7

They that observe lying vanities forsake their own mercy. But I will sacrifice unto Thee with the voice of thanksgiving; I will pay that that I have vowed. Salvation is of The LORD — Jonah 2:8-9

I pray Thee, O LORD, was not this my saying, when I was yet in my country? Therefore I fled before unto Tarshish: for I knew that Thou art A Gracious God, and merciful, slow to anger, and of great kindness, and repentest Thee of the evil — Jonah 4:2

Therefore now, O LORD, take, I beseech Thee, my life from me; for it is better for me to die than to live — Jonah 4:3

O LORD, I have heard Thy Speech, and was afraid: O LORD, revive Thy Work in the midst of the years, in the midst of the years make known; in wrath remember mercy — Habakkuk 3:2

God came from Teman, and the Holy One from mount Paran. Selah. His Glory covered the heavens, and the earth was full of His Praise — Habakkuk 3:3

And His Brightness was as the light; He had horns coming out of His Hand: and there was the hiding of His Power — Habakkuk 3:4

Before Him went the pestilence, and burning coals went forth at His Feet — Habakkuk 3:5

He stood, and measured the earth: He beheld, and drove asunder the nations; and the everlasting mountains were scattered, the perpetual hills did bow: His Ways are everlasting — Habakkuk 3:6

I saw the tents of Cushan in affliction: and the curtains of the land of Midian did tremble	Habakkuk 3:7
Was The LORD displeased against the rivers? was Thine Anger against the rivers? was Thy Wrath against the sea, that Thou didst ride upon Thine Horses and Thy Chariots of Salvation?	Habakkuk 3:8
Thy Bow was made quite naked, according to the oaths of the tribes, even Thy Word. Selah. Thou didst cleave the earth with rivers	Habakkuk 3:9
The mountains saw Thee, and they trembled: the overflowing of the water passed by: the deep uttered his voice, and lifted up his hands on high	Habakkuk 3:10
The sun and moon stood still in their habitation: at the Light of Thine Arrows they went, and at the Shining of Thy Glittering Spear	Habakkuk 3:11
Thou didst march through the land in indignation, Thou didst thresh the heathen in anger	Habakkuk 3:12
Thou wentest forth for the salvation of Thy People, even for salvation with Thine Anointed; Thou woundedst the head out of the house of the wicked, by discovering the foundation unto the neck	Habakkuk 3:13
Thou didst strike through with his staves the head of his villages: they came out as a whirlwind to scatter me: their rejoicing was as to devour the poor secretly	Habakkuk 3:14

Thou didst walk through the sea with Thine Horses, through the heap of great waters. When I heard, my belly trembled; my lips quivered at the voice: rottenness entered into my bones, and I trembled in myself, that I might rest in the day of trouble: when he cometh up unto the people, he will invade them with his troops	Habakkuk 3:15–16
Although the fig tree shall not blossom, neither shall fruit be in the vines; the labour of the olive shall fail, and the fields shall yield no meat; the flock shall be cut off from the fold, and there shall be no herd in the stalls: Yet I will rejoice in The LORD, I will joy in The God of my salvation	Habakkuk 3:17–18
The LORD God is my strength, and He will make my feet like hinds' feet, and He will make me to walk upon mine high places	Habakkuk 3:19
Our Father Which art in heaven, Hallowed by Thy Name. Thy Kingdom come. Thy Will be done in earth, as it is in heaven. Give us this day our daily bread. And forgive us our debts, as we forgive our debtors. And lead us not into temptation, but deliver us from evil: For Thine is the kingdom, and the power, and the glory, for ever. Amen	Matthew 6:9–13; Luke 11:2-4
Lord, if Thou wilt, Thou canst make me clean	Matthew 8:2b; Luke 5:12b
Lord, my servant lieth at home sick of the palsy, grievously tormented	Matthew 8:6
Lord, I am not worthy that Thou shouldest come under my roof: but speak the Word only, and my servant shall be healed	Matthew 8:8; Luke 7:6b-7

Lord, save us: we perish	Matthew 8:25b; Mark 4:38b; Luke 8:24a
If Thou cast us out, suffer us to go away into the herd of swine	Matthew 8:31; Mark 5:12; Luke 8:32
My daughter is even now dead: but come and lay Thy Hand upon her, and she shall live	Matthew 9:18b
Thou Son of David, have mercy on us	Matthew 9:27b
Declare unto us the parable of the tares of the field	Matthew 13:36b
Lord, if it be Thou, bid me come unto Thee on the water	Matthew 14:28
Lord, save me	Matthew 14:30b
Have mercy on me, O Lord, Thou Son of David; my daughter is grievously vexed with a devil	Matthew 15:22b
Lord, help me	Matthew 15:25b
Lord, have mercy on my son: for he is lunatic, and sore vexed: for ofttimes he falleth into the fire, and oft into the water. And I brought him to Thy Disciples, and they could not cure him	Matthew 17:15–16; Mark 9:17b–22; Luke 9:38b–40
Grant that these my two sons may sit, the one on Thy Right Hand, and the other on the left, in Thy Kingdom	Matthew 20:21b; Mark 10:37
Have mercy on us, O Lord, Thou Son of David	Matthew 20:30b,31b

Have mercy on us, O Lord, Thou Son of David	Matthew 20:31b,30b
Lord, that our eyes may be opened	Matthew 20:33
O My Father, if it be possible, let this cup pass from Me: nevertheless not as I will, but as Thou wilt	Matthew 26:39, 44; Mark 14:36; Luke 22:42
Master, carest Thou not that we perish?	Mark 4:38b; Matthew 8:25b; Luke 8:24a
Send us into the swine, that we may enter into them	Mark 5:12; Matthew 8:31; Luke 8:32
My little daughter lieth at the point of death: I pray Thee, come and lay Thy Hands on her, that she may be healed; and she shall live	Mark 5:23
Master, I have brought unto Thee my son, which hath a dumb spirit; And wheresoever he taketh him, he teareth him: and he foameth, and gnasheth with his teeth, and pineth away: and I spake to Thy Disciples that they should cast him out; and they could not	Mark 9:17b-18; Matthew 17:15-16; Luke 9:38b-40
Of a child. And ofttimes it hath cast him into the fire, and into the waters, to destroy him: but if Thou canst do any thing, have compassion on us, and help us	Mark 9:21b-22; Matthew 17:15; Luke 9:38-42
Lord, I believe; help Thou mine unbelief	Mark 9:24b
Master, we would that Thou shouldest do for us whatsoever we shall desire	Mark 10:35b

181

Grant unto us that we may sit, one on Thy Right Hand, and the other on Thy Left Hand, in Thy Glory	Mark 10:37; Matthew 20:21b
[Jesus,] Thou Son of David, have mercy on me	Mark 10:47b,48b; Luke 18:38,39b
Lord, that I might [may] receive my sight	Mark 10:51b; Luke 18:41b
Abba, Father, all things are possible unto Thee; take away this cup from Me: nevertheless not what I will, but what Thou wilt	Mark 14:36; Matthew 26:39, 44; Luke 22:42
Lord, now lettest Thou Thy Servant depart in peace, according to Thy Word: For mine eyes have seen Thy Salvation, Which Thou hast prepared before the face of all people; A light to lighten the Gentiles, and the glory of Thy People Israel	Luke 2:29-32
Lord, if Thou wilt, Thou canst make me clean	Luke 5:12b; Matthew 8:2b
That he was worthy for whom he should do this: For he loveth our nation, and he hath built us a synagogue	Luke 7:4b-5
Lord, trouble not Thyself: for I am not worthy that Thou shouldest enter under my roof: Wherefore neither thought I myself worthy to come unto Thee: but say in a Word, and my servant shall be healed	Luke 7:6b-7; Matthew 8:8
Master, Master, we perish	Luke 8:24a; Matthew 8:25b; Mark 4:38b

I beseech Thee, torment me not	Luke 8:28b; Matthew 8:31; Mark 5:7-12
Master, I beseech Thee, look upon my son: for he is mine only child. And, lo, a spirit taketh him, and he suddenly crieth out; and it teareth him that he foameth again, and bruising him hardly departeth from him. And I besought Thy Disciples to cast him out; and they could not	Luke 9:38b-40; Matthew 17:15-16; Mark 9:17b-22
Lord, teach us to pray, as John also taught his disciples	Luke 11:1b
Our Father Which art in heaven, Hallowed be Thy Name. Thy Kingdom come. Thy Will be done, as in heaven, so in earth. Give us day by day our daily bread. And forgive us our sins; for we also forgive every one that is indebted to us. And lead us not into temptation; but deliver us from evil	Luke 11:2-4; Matthew 6:9-13
Lord, increase our faith	Luke 17:5
Jesus, Master, have mercy on us	Luke 17:13
God be merciful to me a sinner	Luke 18:13b
[Jesus,] Thou Son of David, have mercy on me	Luke 18:38,39b; Mark 10:47b,48b
Lord, that I might [may] receive my sight	Luke 18:41b; Mark 10:51b
Father, if Thou be willing, remove this cup from me: nevertheless not my will, but Thine, be done	Luke 22:42; Matthew 26:39, 44; Mark 14:36

Father, forgive them; for they know not what they do	Luke 23:34a
Lord, remember me when Thou comest into Thy Kingdom	Luke 23:42
Sir, come down ere my child die	John 4:49
Lord, behold, he whom Thou lovest is sick	John 11:3
Lord, if Thou hadst been here, my brother had not died. But I know, that even now, whatsoever Thou wilt ask of God, God will give it Thee	John 11:21-22
Father, glorify Thy Name	John 12:28a
Lord, show us The Father, and it sufficeth us	John 14:8
Father, the hour is come; glorify Thy Son, that Thy Son also may glorify Thee:	John 17:1
Let his habitation be desolate, and let no man dwell therein: and his bishopric let another take	Acts 1:20 [Psalm 69:25a; 109:8b]
Thou, Lord, Which knowest the hearts of all men, show whether of these two Thou hast chosen, that he may take part of this ministry and apostleship, from which Judas by transgression fell, that he might go to his own place	Acts 1:24-25
Lord, Thou art God, which hast made heaven, and earth, and the sea, and all that in them is: Who by the mouth of Thy Servant David hast said, Why did the heathen rage, and the people imagine vain things? The kings of the earth stood up, and the rulers were gathered together against The Lord, and against His Christ	Acts 4:24-26 [Psalm 2:1-2]

For of a truth against Thy Holy Child Jesus, Whom Thou hast anointed, both Herod, and Pontius Pilate, with the Gentiles, and the people of Israel, were gathered together, for to do whatsoever Thy Hand and Thy Counsel determined before to be done	Acts 4:27-28
And now, Lord, behold their threatenings: and grant unto Thy Servants, that with all boldness they may speak Thy Word, by stretching forth Thine Hand to heal; and that signs and wonders may be done by The Name of Thy Holy Child Jesus	Acts 4:29-30
Lord Jesus, receive my spirit	Acts 7:59b
Lord, lay not this sin to their charge	Acts 7:60a
Maranatha	1 Corinthians 16:22b
For this cause I bow my knees unto the Father of our Lord Jesus Christ, Of Whom the whole family in heaven and earth is named, That He would grant you, according to the riches of His Glory, to be strengthened with might by His Spirit in the inner man; That Christ may dwell in your hearts by faith; that ye, being rooted and grounded in love, May be able to comprehend with all saints what is the breadth, and length, and depth, and height; And to know the Love of Christ, which passeth knowledge, that ye might be filled with all the Fulness of God. Now unto Him that is able to do exceeding abundantly above all that we ask or think, according to the power that worketh in us, Unto Him be glory in the church by Christ Jesus throughout all ages, world without end. Amen	Ephesians 3:14-21

Now The God of Peace, that brought again from the dead our Lord Jesus, That Great Shepherd of the sheep, through the blood of the everlasting covenant, Make you perfect in every good work to do His Will, working in you that which is wellpleasing in His Sight, through Jesus Christ; to Whom be glory for ever and ever. Amen	Hebrews 13:20-21
But The God of All Grace, Who hath called us unto His Eternal Glory by Christ Jesus, after that ye have suffered a while, make you perfect, stablish, strengthen, settle you. To Him be glory and dominion for ever and ever. Amen	1 Peter 5:10-11
How long, O Lord, holy and true, dost Thou not judge and avenge our blood on them that dwell on the earth?	Revelation 6:10
Even so, come, Lord Jesus	Revelation 22:20b

Prayer portions that contain Petitions in them

Genesis 15:2-3	Psalm 68:30
Numbers 14:17-19	Psalm 84:8-9
Deuteronomy 33:6-17	Psalm 118:25
Deuteronomy 33:24-25	Psalm 119:8
1 Samuel 24:19b	Psalm 119:10
2 Samuel 7:25 [1 Chronicles 17:23]	Psalm 119:12
2 Samuel 7:26 [1 Chronicles 17:24]	Psalm 119:17-19
2 Samuel 7:29 [1 Chronicles 17:27]	Psalm 119:22
1 Chronicles 17:23 [2 Samuel 7:25]	Psalm 119:25-43
1 Chronicles 17:24 [2 Samuel 7:26]	Psalm 119:49
1 Chronicles 17:27 [2 Samuel 7:29]	Psalm 119:58
1 Chronicles 22:11-12	Psalm 119:64-66
Nehemiah 9:32-33	Psalm 119:68

Job 7:7

Job 10:2-9

Job 10:18-22

Job 14:1-6

Job 14:13-14

Job 30:27-28

Psalm 9:13-14

Psalm 9:19-20

Psalm 22:1 [Matthew 27:46b;
Mark 15:34b]

Psalm 22:11-21

Psalm 30:8-10

Psalm 36:10-11

Psalm 44:4

Psalm 51:1-3

Psalm 51:7-15

Psalm 51:18

Psalm 56:1-2

Psalm 56:4-8

Psalm 57:1-4

Psalm 63:1-2

Psalm 67:1-2

Psalm 68:1-3

Psalm 68:28

Psalm 119:73-88

Psalm 119:94

Psalm 119:107-108

Psalm 119:116-117

Psalm 119:121-126

Psalm 119:132-135

Psalm 119:145-149

Psalm 119:153-154

Psalm 119:156

Psalm 119:159

Psalm 119:169-176

Psalm 138:8

Psalm 139:19-24

Isaiah 26:11

Isaiah 26:16-18

Daniel 9:16-19

Habakkuk 1:2-4

Matthew 15:23b

John 17:9-11

John 17:15-17

John 17:20

John 17:23

Revelation 11:18

Prayers of Praise

And blessed be The Most High God, which   Genesis 14:20
hath delivered thine enemies into thy hand

Thy Right Hand, O LORD, is become   Exodus 15:6
glorious in power: Thy Right Hand, O
LORD, hath dashed in pieces the enemy

And in the greatness of Thine Excellency Thou   Exodus 15:7
hast overthrown them that rose up against
Thee: Thou sentest forth Thy Wrath, which
consumed them as stubble

And with the blast of Thy Nostrils the waters   Exodus 15:8
were gathered together, the floods stood upright
as an heap, and the depths were congealed in
the heart of the sea

The enemy said, I will pursue, I will overtake, Exodus 15:9
I will divide the spoil; my lust shall be satisfied
upon them; I will draw my sword, my hand
shall destroy them

Thou didst blow with Thy Wind, the sea   Exodus 15:10
covered them: they sank as lead in the mighty
waters

Who is like unto Thee, O LORD, among the   Exodus 15:11
gods? Who is like Thee, glorious in holiness,
fearful in praises, doing wonders?

Thou stretchedst out Thy Right Hand, the earth swallowed them	Exodus 15:12
Thou in Thy Mercy hast led forth the people which Thou hast redeemed: Thou hast guided them in Thy Strength unto Thy Holy Habitation	Exodus 15:13
The people shall hear, and be afraid: sorrow shall take hold on the inhabitants of Palestina	Exodus 15:14
Then the dukes of Edom shall be amazed; the mighty men of Moab, trembling shall take hold upon them; all the inhabitants of Canaan shall melt away	Exodus 15:15
Fear and dread shall fall upon them; by the greatness of Thine Arm they shall be as still as a stone; till Thy People pass over, O LORD, till the people pass over, which Thou hast purchased	Exodus 15:16
Thou shalt bring them in, and plant them in the mountain of Thine Inheritance, in the place, O LORD, which Thou hast made for Thee to dwell in, in the Sanctuary, O LORD, which Thy Hands have established	Exodus 15:17
The LORD shall reign for ever and ever	Exodus 15:18

Blessed be The LORD, Who hath delivered you out of the hand of the Egyptians, and out of the hand of Pharaoh, Who hath delivered the people from under the hand of the Egyptians	Exodus 18:10

LORD, when Thou wentest out of Seir, when Thou marchedst out of the field of Edom, the earth trembled, and the heavens dropped, the clouds also dropped water. The mountains melted from before The LORD, even that Sinai from before The LORD God of Israel — Judges 5:4-5

My heart rejoiceth in The LORD, mine horn is exalted in The LORD: my mouth is enlarged over mine enemies; because I rejoice in Thy Salvation — 1 Samuel 2:1

There is none holy as The LORD: for there is none beside Thee: neither is there any rock like our God — 1 Samuel 2:2

Talk no more so exceeding proudly; let not arrogancy come out of your mouth: for The LORD is a God of knowledge, and by Him actions are weighed — 1 Samuel 2:3

The bows of the mighty men are broken, and they that stumbled are girded with strength. — 1 Samuel 2:4

They that were full have hired out themselves for bread; and they that were hungry ceased: so that the barren hath born seven; and she that hath many children is waxed feeble. — 1 Samuel 2:5

The LORD killeth, and maketh alive: He bringeth down to the grave, and bringeth up. — 1 Samuel 2:6

The LORD maketh poor, and maketh rich: He bringeth low, and lifteth up. — 1 Samuel 2:7

He raiseth up the poor out of the dust, and
lifteth up the beggar from the dunghill, to set
them among princes, and to make them inherit
the throne of glory: for the pillars of the earth
are The LORD'S, and he hath set the world
upon them

1 Samuel 2:8

He will keep the feet of His Saints, and the
wicked shall be silent in darkness; for by
strength shall no man prevail

1 Samuel 2:9

The adversaries of The LORD shall be broken
to pieces; out of heaven shall He thunder upon
them: The LORD shall judge the ends of the
earth; and He shall give strength unto His
King, and exalt the horn of His Anointed

1 Samuel 2:10

Blessed be The LORD, that hath pleaded the
cause of my reproach from the hand of Nabal,
and hath kept His Servant from evil: for The
LORD hath returned the wickedness of Nabal
upon his own head

1 Samuel 25:39a

Who am I, O Lord GOD? and what is my
house, that Thou hast brought me hitherto?

2 Samuel 7:18
[1 Chronicles
17:16]

And this was yet a small thing in Thy Sight, O
Lord GOD; but Thou hast spoken also of Thy
Servant's house for a great while to come. And
is this the manner of man, O Lord GOD?

2 Samuel 7:19
[1 Chronicles
17:17]

And what can David say more unto Thee? for
Thou, Lord GOD, knowest Thy Servant

2 Samuel 7:20
[1 Chronicles
17:18]

For Thy Word's Sake, and according to Thine Own Heart, hast Thou done all these great things, to make Thy Servant know them	2 Samuel 7:21 [1 Chronicles 17:19]
Wherefore Thou art Great, O LORD God: for there is none like Thee, neither is there any God beside Thee, according to all that we have heard with our ears	2 Samuel 7:22 [1 Chronicles 17:20]
And what one nation in the earth is like Thy People, even like Israel, whom God went to redeem for a people to Himself, and to make Him a Name, and to do for You great things and terrible, for Thy Land, before Thy People, which Thou redeemedst to Thee from Egypt, from the nations and their gods?	2 Samuel 7:23 [1 Chronicles 17:21]
For Thou hast confirmed to Thyself Thy People Israel to be a people unto Thee for ever: and Thou, LORD, art become their God	2 Samuel 7:24 [1 Chronicles 17:22]
And now, O LORD God, The Word that Thou hast spoken concerning Thy Servant, and concerning his house, establish it for ever, and do as Thou hast said	2 Samuel 7:25 [1 Chronicles 17:23]
And let Thy Name be magnified for ever, saying, The LORD of Hosts is The God over Israel: and let the house of Thy Servant David be established before Thee	2 Samuel 7:26 [1 Chronicles 17:24]
For Thou, O LORD of Hosts, God of Israel, hast revealed to Thy Servant, saying, I will build Thee an house: therefore hath Thy Servant found in his heart to pray this prayer unto Thee	2 Samuel 7:27 [1 Chronicles 17:25]

And now, O Lord GOD, Thou art That God, and Thy Words be True, and Thou hast promised this goodness unto Thy Servant	2 Samuel 7:28 [1 Chronicles 17:26]
Therefore now let it please Thee to bless the house of Thy Servant, that it may continue for ever before Thee: for Thou, O Lord GOD, hast spoken it: and with Thy Blessing let the house of Thy Servant be blessed for ever	2 Samuel 7:29 [1 Chronicles 17:27]
The LORD is my rock, and my fortress, and my deliverer; The God of my rock; in Him will I trust: He is my shield, and the horn of my salvation, my high tower, and my refuge, my Saviour; Thou savest me from violence	2 Samuel 22:2-3 (4-15) [Psalm 18]
And the channels of the sea appeared, the foundations of the world were discovered, at the rebuking of The LORD, at the blast of the Breath of His Nostrils	2 Samuel 22:16 [Psalm 18]
He sent from above, He took me; He drew me out of many waters	2 Samuel 22:17 [Psalm 18]
He delivered me from my strong enemy, and from them that hated me: for they were too strong for me. They prevented me in the day of my calamity: but The LORD was my stay	2 Samuel 22:18-19 [Psalm 18]
He brought me forth also into a large place: He delivered me, because He delighted in me	2 Samuel 22:20 [Psalm 18]

The LORD rewarded me according to my righteousness: according to the cleanness of my hands hath he recompensed me. For I have kept The Ways of The LORD, and have not wickedly departed from my God. For all His Judgments were before me: and as for His Statutes, I did not depart from them. I was also upright before Him, and have kept myself from mine iniquity. Therefore The LORD hath recompensed me according to my righteousness; according to my cleanness in His Eyesight

2 Samuel 22:21-25 [Psalm 18]

With the merciful Thou wilt show Thyself merciful, and with the upright man Thou wilt show Thyself upright. With the pure Thou wilt show Thyself pure; and with the froward Thou wilt show Thyself unsavoury. And the afflicted people Thou wilt save: but Thine Eyes are upon the haughty, that Thou mayest bring them down

2 Samuel 22:26-28 [Psalm 18]

For Thou art my lamp, O LORD: and The LORD will lighten my darkness

2 Samuel 22:29 [Psalm 18]

For by Thee I have run through a troop: by my God have I leaped over a wall

2 Samuel 22:30 [Psalm 18]

As for God, His Way is perfect; The Word of The LORD is tried: He is a buckler to all them that trust in Him. For who is God, save The LORD? and who is a rock, save our God?

2 Samuel 22:31-32 [Psalm 18]

God is my strength and power: and He maketh my way perfect. He maketh my feet like hinds' feet: and setteth me upon my high places. He teacheth my hands to war; so that a bow of steel is broken by mine arms

2 Samuel 22:33-35 [Psalm 18]

Thou hast also given me the shield of Thy Salvation: and Thy Gentleness hath made me great	2 Samuel 22:36 [Psalm 18]
Thou hast enlarged my steps under me; so that my feet did not slip	2 Samuel 22:37 [Psalm 18]
I have pursued mine enemies, and destroyed them; and turned not again until I had consumed them. And I have consumed them, and wounded them, that they could not arise: yea, they are fallen under my feet. For Thou hast girded me with strength to battle: them that rose up against me hast Thou subdued under me. Thou hast also given me the necks of mine enemies, that I might destroy them that hate me	2 Samuel 22:38-41 [Psalm 18]
They looked, but there was none to save; even unto The LORD, but He answered them not	2 Samuel 22:42 [Psalm 18]
Then did I beat them as small as the dust of the earth, I did stamp them as the mire of the street, and did spread them abroad	2 Samuel 22:43 [Psalm 18]
Thou also hast delivered me from the strivings of my people, Thou hast kept me to be head of the heathen: a people which I knew not shall serve me. Strangers shall submit themselves unto me: as soon as they hear, they shall be obedient unto me. Strangers shall fade away, and they shall be afraid out of their close places	2 Samuel 22:44-46 [Psalm 18]
The LORD liveth; and blessed be my rock; and exalted be The God of the rock of my salvation	2 Samuel 22:47 [Psalm 18]

It is God that avengeth me, and that bringeth down the people under me. And that bringeth me forth from mine enemies: Thou also hast lifted me up on high above them that rose up against me: Thou hast delivered me from the violent man. Therefore I will give thanks unto Thee, O LORD, among the heathen, and I will sing praises unto Thy Name	2 Samuel 22:48-50 [Psalm 18]
He is the tower of salvation for his king: and showeth mercy to his anointed, unto David, and to his seed for evermore	2 Samuel 22:51 [Psalm 18]
Blessed be The LORD God of Israel, Which hath given one to sit on my throne this day, mine eyes even seeing it	1 Kings 1:48
Blessed be The LORD this day, which hath given unto David a wise son over this great people	1 Kings 5:7b [2 Chronicles 2:12]
Blessed be The LORD God of Israel, which spake with His mouth unto David my father, and hath with His Hand fulfilled it, saying...	1 Kings 8:15(-21) [2 Chronicles 6:4(-11)]
Blessed be The LORD thy God, which delighted in thee, to set thee on the throne of Israel	1 Kings 10:9a [2 Chronicles 9:8a]
Save us, O God of our salvation, and gather us together, and deliver us from the heathen, that we may give thanks to Thy Holy Name, and glory in Thy Praise	1 Chronicles 16:35-36a [Psalm 106:47-48]
Blessed be The LORD God of Israel for ever and ever	

Who am I, O LORD God, and what is mine house, that Thou hast brought me hitherto?	1 Chronicles 17:16 [2 Samuel 7:18]
And yet this was a small thing in Thine Eyes, O God; for Thou hast also spoken of Thy Servant's house for a great while to come, and hast regarded me according to the estate of a man of high degree, O LORD God	1 Chronicles 17:17 [2 Samuel 7:19]
What can David speak more to Thee for the honour of Thy Servant? for Thou knowest Thy Servant	1 Chronicles 17:18 [2 Samuel 7:20]
O LORD, for Thy Servant's Sake, and according to Thine Own Heart, hast Thou done all this greatness, in making known all these great things	1 Chronicles 17:19 [2 Samuel 7:21]
O LORD, there is none like Thee, neither is there any God beside Thee, according to all that we have heard with our ears	1 Chronicles 17:20 [2 Samuel 7:22]
And what one nation in the earth is like Thy People Israel, whom God went to redeem to be His Own People, to make Thee A Name of Greatness and Terribleness, by driving out nations from before Thy People whom Thou hast redeemed out of Egypt? For Thy People Israel didst Thou make Thine Own People for ever; and Thou, LORD, becamest their God	1 Chronicles 17:21-22 [2 Samuel 7:23-24]
Therefore now, LORD, let the thing that Thou hast spoken concerning Thy Servant and concerning his house be established for ever, and do as Thou hast said	1 Chronicles 17:23 [2 Samuel 7:25]

Let it even be established, that Thy Name may be magnified for ever, saying, The LORD of Hosts is The God of Israel, even a God to Israel: and let the house of David Thy Servant be established before Thee	1 Chronicles 17:24 [2 Samuel 7:26]
For Thou, O my God, hast told Thy Servant that Thou wilt build him an house: therefore Thy Servant hath found in his heart to pray before Thee	1 Chronicles 17:25 [2 Samuel 7:27]
And now, LORD, Thou art God, and hast promised this goodness unto Thy Servant	1 Chronicles 17:26 [2 Samuel 7:28]
Now therefore let it please Thee to bless the house of Thy Servant, that it may be before Thee for ever: for Thou blessest, O LORD, and it shall be blessed for ever	1 Chronicles 17:27 [2 Samuel 7:29]
Blessed be Thou, LORD God of Israel our father, for ever and ever	1 Chronicles 29:10
Thine, O LORD is the greatness, and the power, and the glory, and the victory, and the majesty: for all that is in the heaven and in the earth is Thine; Thine is the Kingdom, O LORD, and Thou art exalted as Head above all. Both riches and honour come of Thee, and Thou reignest over all; and in Thine Hand is power and might; and in Thine Hand it is to make great, and to give strength unto all	1 Chronicles 29:11-12
Now therefore, our God, we thank Thee, and praise Thy Glorious Name	1 Chronicles 29:13

But who am I, and what is my people, that we should be able to offer so willingly after this sort? for all things come of Thee, and of Thine Own have we given Thee. For we are strangers before Thee, and sojourners, as were all our fathers: our days on the earth are as a shadow, and there is none abiding	1 Chronicles 29:14-15
O LORD our God, all this store that we have prepared to build Thee an house for Thine Holy Name cometh of Thine Hand, and is All Thine Own	1 Chronicles 29:16
I know also, my God, that Thou triest the heart, and hast pleasure in uprightness. As for me, in the uprightness of mine heart I have willingly offered all these things: and now have I seen with joy Thy People, which are present here, to offer willingly unto Thee	1 Chronicles 29:17
O LORD God of Abraham, Isaac, and of Israel, our fathers, keep this for ever in the imagination of the thoughts of the heart of Thy People, and prepare their heart unto Thee	1 Chronicles 29:18
And give unto Solomon my son a perfect heart, to keep Thy Commandments, Thy Testimonies, and Thy Statutes, and to do all these things, and to build the palace, for the which I have made provision	1 Chronicles 29:19
Blessed be The LORD God of Israel, that made heaven and earth, Who hath given to David the king a wise son, endued with prudence and understanding, that might build an house for The LORD, and an house for His Kingdom	2 Chronicles 2:12 [1 Kings 5:7b]

Blessed be The LORD God of Israel, Who hath with His Hands fulfilled that Which He spake with His Mouth to my father David, saying	2 Chronicles 6:4(-11) [1 Kings 8:15(-21)]
Blessed be The LORD thy God, which delighted in thee to set thee on his throne, to be king for The LORD thy God: because thy God loved Israel, to establish them for ever, therefore made He thee king over them, to do judgment and justice	2 Chronicles 9:8a [1 Kings 10:9a]
Blessed be The LORD God of our fathers, Which hath put such a thing as this in the king's heart, to beautify the house of The LORD which is in Jerusalem: And hath extended mercy unto me before the king, and his counsellors, and before all the king's mighty princes	Ezra 7:27-28a
Stand up and bless The LORD your God for ever and ever: and blessed be Thy Glorious Name, Which is exalted above all blessing and praise. Thou, even Thou, art LORD Alone; Thou hast made heaven, the heaven of heavens, with all their host, the earth, and all things that are therein, the seas, and all that is therein, and Thou preservest them all; and the host of heaven worshippeth Thee	Nehemiah 9:5b-6
Thou art The LORD The God, Who didst choose Abram, and broughtest him forth out of Ur of the Chaldees, and gavest him the name of Abraham; And foundest his heart faithful before Thee, and madest a covenant with him to give the land of the Canaanites, the Hittites, the Amorites, and the Perizzites, and the Jebusites, and the Girgashites, to give it, I say, to his seed, and hast performed Thy Words; for Thou art righteous	Nehemiah 9:7-8

And didst see the affliction of our fathers in
Egypt, and heardest their cry by the Red sea;
And showedst signs and wonders upon Pharaoh,
and on all his servants, and on all the people
of his land: for Thou knewest that they dealt
proudly against them. So didst Thou get Thee
a Name, as it is this day. And Thou didst divide
the sea before them, so that they went through
the midst of the sea on the dry land; and their
persecutors thou threwest into the deeps, as a
stone into the mighty waters. Moreover Thou
leddest them in the day by a cloudy pillar; and
in the night by a pillar of fire, to give them
light in the way wherein they should go

Nehemiah 9:9–12

Thou camest down also upon mount Sinai,
and spakest with them from heaven, and gavest
them right judgments, and true laws, good
statutes and commandments: And madest
known unto them Thy Holy Sabbath, and
commandedst them precepts, statutes, and laws,
by the hand of Moses Thy Servant: And gavest
them bread from heaven for their hunger, and
broughtest forth water for them out of the rock
for their thirst, and promisedst them that they
should go in to possess the land which Thou
hadst sworn to give them

Nehemiah 9:13–15

But they and our fathers dealt proudly, and
hardened their necks, and hearkened not to Thy
Commandments, And refused to obey, neither
were mindful of Thy Wonders that Thou didst
among them; but hardened their necks, and in
their rebellion appointed a captain to return
to their bondage: but Thou art a God ready to
pardon, gracious and merciful, slow to anger,
and of great kindness, and forsookest them not

Nehemiah 9:16–17

Yea, when they had made them a molten
calf, and said, This is thy God that brought
thee up out of Egypt, and had wrought great
provocations; Yet Thou in Thy Manifold
Mercies forsookest them not in the wilderness:
the pillar of the cloud departed not from them
by day, to lead them in the way; neither the
pillar of fire by night, to show them light, and
the way wherein they should go

Nehemiah 9:18–
19

Thou gavest also Thy Good Spirit to instruct
them, and withheldest not Thy Manna from
their mouth, and gavest them water for their
thirst. Yea, forty years didst Thou sustain them
in the wilderness, so that they lacked nothing;
their clothes waxed not old, and their feet
swelled not

Nehemiah 9:20–
21

Moreover Thou gavest them kingdoms and
nations, and didst divide them into corners: so
they possessed the land of Sihon, and the land
of the king of Heshbon, and the land of Og
king of Bashan

Nehemiah 9:22

Their children also multipliedst Thou as the
stars of heaven, and broughtest them into the
land, concerning which Thou hadst promised
to their fathers, that they should go in to possess
it. So the children went in and possessed the
land, and Thou subduedst before them the
inhabitants of the land, the Canaanites, and
gavest them into their hands, with their kings,
and the people of the land, that they might do
with them as they would. And they took strong
cities, and a fat land, and possessed houses
full of all goods, wells digged, vineyards, and
oliveyards, and fruit trees in abundance: so they
did eat, and were filled, and became fat, and
delighted themselves in Thy Great Goodness

Nehemiah 9:23–
25

Nevertheless they were disobedient, and rebelled against Thee, and cast Thy Law behind their backs, and slew Thy prophets which testified against them to turn them to Thee, and they wrought great provocations. Therefore Thou deliveredst them into the hand of their enemies, who vexed them: and in the time of their trouble, when they cried unto Thee, Thou heardest them from heaven; and according to Thy Manifold Mercies Thou gavest them saviours, who saved them out of the hand of their enemies

Nehemiah 9:26–27

But after they had rest, they did evil again before Thee: therefore leftest Thou them in the land of their enemies, so that they had the dominion over them: yet when they returned, and cried unto Thee, Thou heardest them from heaven; and many times didst Thou deliver them according to Thy Mercies; And testifiedst against them, that Thou mightest bring them again unto Thy Law: yet they dealt proudly, and hearkened not unto Thy Commandments, but sinned against Thy Judgments, (which if a man do, he shall live in them;) and withdrew the shoulder, and hardened their neck, and would not hear

Nehemiah 9:28–29

Yet many years didst Thou forbear them, and testifiedst against them by Thy Spirit in Thy Prophets: yet would they not give ear: therefore gavest Thou them into the hand of the people of the lands. Nevertheless for Thy Great Mercies' Sake Thou didst not utterly consume them, nor forsake them; for Thou art a gracious and merciful God

Nehemiah 9:30–31

Now therefore, our God, The Great, The Mighty, and The Terrible God, Who keepest covenant and mercy, let not all the trouble seem little before Thee, that hath come upon us, on our kings, on our princes, and on our priests, and on our prophets, and on our fathers, and on all Thy People, since the time of the kings of Assyria unto this day. Howbeit Thou art just in all that is brought upon us; for Thou hast done right, but we have done wickedly

Nehemiah 9:32-33

Neither have our kings, our princes, our priests, nor our fathers, kept Thy Law, nor hearkened unto Thy Commandments and Thy Testimonies, wherewith Thou didst testify against them. For they have not served Thee in their kingdom, and in Thy Great Goodness that Thou gavest them, and in the large and fat land which Thou gavest before them, neither turned they from their wicked works

Nehemiah 9:34-35

Behold, we are servants this day, and for the land that Thou gavest unto our fathers to eat the fruit thereof and the good thereof, behold, we are servants in it: And it yieldeth much increase unto the kings whom Thou hast set over us because of our sins: also they have dominion over our bodies, and over our cattle, at their pleasure, and we are in great distress

Nehemiah 9:36-37

And because of all this we make a sure covenant, and write it; and our princes, Levites, and priests, seal unto it

Nehemiah 9:38

Naked came I out of my mother's womb, and naked shall I return thither: The LORD gave, and The LORD hath taken away; blessed be the Name of The LORD

Job 1:21

But Thou, O LORD, art a shield for me; my glory, and the lifter up of mine head. I cried unto The LORD with my voice, and He heard me out of His Holy Hill	Psalm 3:3-4
I laid me down and slept; I awaked; for The LORD sustained me	Psalm 3:5
I will not be afraid of ten thousands of people, that have set themselves against me round about	Psalm 3:6
Arise, O LORD; save me, O my God: for Thou hast smitten all mine enemies upon the cheek bone; Thou hast broken the teeth of the ungodly	Psalm 3:7
Salvation belongeth unto The LORD: Thy Blessing is upon Thy People	Psalm 3:8
O LORD our Lord, how excellent is Thy Name in all the earth! who hast set Thy Glory above the heavens	Psalm 8:1,9a
Out of the mouth of babes and sucklings hast Thou ordained strength because of Thine Enemies, that Thou mightest still the enemy and the avenger	Psalm 8:2
When I consider Thy Heavens, the Work of Thy Fingers, the moon and the stars, which Thou hast ordained; What is man, that Thou art mindful of him? and [or] the son of man, that Thou visitest him? [For] Thou hast made [madest] him a little lower than the angels, [and] [Thou] hast crowned [crownedest] him with glory and honour	Psalm 8:3-5 [Hebrews 2:6b-7a]

Thou madest him to have dominion over the Works of Thy Hands; Thou hast put all things under his feet: All sheep and oxen, yea, and the beasts of the field; The fowl of the air, and the fish of the sea, and whatsoever passeth through the paths of the seas	Psalm 8:6-8 [Hebrews 2:7b-8a]
O LORD our Lord, how excellent is Thy Name in all the earth! who hast set Thy Glory above the heavens	Psalm 8:9a,1
I will praise Thee, O LORD, with my whole heart; I will show forth all Thy Marvellous Works	Psalm 9:1
I will be glad and rejoice in Thee: I will sing praise to Thy Name, O Thou Most High	Psalm 9:2
When mine enemies are turned back, they shall fall and perish at Thy Presence. For Thou hast maintained my right and my cause; Thou satest in the throne judging right	Psalm 9:3-4
Thou hast rebuked the heathen, Thou hast destroyed the wicked, Thou hast put out their name for ever and ever. O thou enemy, destructions are come to a perpetual end: and Thou hast destroyed cities; their memorial is perished with them	Psalm 9:5-6
But The LORD shall endure for ever: He hath prepared His Throne for judgment. And He shall judge the world in righteousness, He shall minister judgment to the people in uprightness	Psalm 9:7-8
The LORD also will be a refuge for the oppressed, a refuge in times of trouble	Psalm 9:9

And they that know Thy Name will put their   Psalm 9:10
trust in Thee: for Thou, LORD, hast not
forsaken them that seek Thee

Sing praises to The LORD, Which dwelleth   Psalm 9:11-12
in Zion: declare among the people His Doings.
When He maketh inquisition for blood, He
remembereth them: He forgetteth not the cry
of the humble

Have mercy upon me, O LORD; consider my   Psalm 9:13-14
trouble which I suffer of them that hate me,
Thou that liftest me up from the gates of death:
That I may show forth all Thy Praise in the
gates of the daughter of Zion: I will rejoice in
Thy Salvation

The heathen are sunk down in the pit that they   Psalm 9:15
made: in the net which they hid is their own
foot taken

The LORD is known by the judgment which   Psalm 9:16
He executeth: the wicked is snared in the work
of his own hands. Higgaion

The wicked shall be turned into hell, and all   Psalm 9:17
the nations that forget God

For the needy shall not always be forgotten: the   Psalm 9:18
expectation of the poor shall not perish for ever

Arise, O LORD; let not man prevail: let the   Psalm 9:19-20
heathen be judged in Thy Sight. Put them in
fear, O LORD: that the nations may know
themselves to be but men

Preserve me, O God: for in Thee do I put my   Psalm 16:1
trust

O my soul, thou hast said unto The LORD,   Psalm 16:2-3
Thou art my Lord: my goodness extendeth not
to Thee; But to the saints that are in the earth,
and to the excellent, in whom is all my delight

Their sorrows shall be multiplied that hasten   Psalm 16:4-6
after another god: their drink offerings of blood
will I not offer, nor take up their names into
my lips. The LORD is the portion of mine
inheritance and of my cup: Thou maintainest
my lot. The lines are fallen unto me in pleasant
places; yea, I have a goodly heritage

I will bless The LORD, Who hath given me   Psalm 16:7-8
counsel: my reins also instruct me in the night
seasons. I have set The LORD always before
me: because He is at my right hand, I shall not
be moved

Therefore my heart is glad, and my glory   Psalm 16:9-10
rejoiceth: my flesh also shall rest in hope. For
Thou wilt not leave my soul in hell; neither
wilt Thou suffer Thine Holy One to see
corruption

Thou wilt show me the path of life: in Thy   Psalm 16:11
Presence is fulness of joy; at Thy Right Hand
there are pleasures for evermore

I will love Thee, O LORD, my strength. The   Psalm 18:1-2
LORD is my rock, and my fortress, and my   (3-14) [2 Samuel
deliverer; my God, my strength, in Whom   22]
I will trust; my buckler, and the horn of my
salvation, and my high tower

Then the channels of waters were seen, and   Psalm 18:15 [2
the foundations of the world were discovered   Samuel 22]
at Thy Rebuke, O LORD, at the blast of the
Breath of Thy Nostrils

He sent from above, He took me, He drew me out of many waters	Psalm 18:16 [2 Samuel 22]
He delivered me from my strong enemy, and from them which hated me: for they were too strong for me. They prevented me in the day of my calamity: but The LORD was my stay	Psalm 18:17-18 [2 Samuel 22]
He brought me forth also into a large place; He delivered me, because He delighted in me	Psalm 18:19 [2 Samuel 22]
The LORD rewarded me according to my righteousness; according to the cleanness of my hands hath He recompensed me. For I have kept The Ways of The LORD, and have not wickedly departed from my God. For all His Judgments were before me, and I did not put away His Statutes from me. I was also upright before Him, and I kept myself from mine iniquity. Therefore hath The LORD recompensed me according to my righteousness, according to the cleanness of my hands in His Eyesight	Psalm 18:20-24 [2 Samuel 22]
With the merciful Thou wilt show Thyself Merciful; with an upright man Thou wilt show Thyself Upright; With the pure Thou wilt show Thyself Pure; and with the froward Thou wilt show Thyself Froward. For Thou wilt save the afflicted people; but wilt bring down high looks	Psalm 18:25-27 [2 Samuel 22]
For Thou wilt light my candle: The LORD my God will enlighten my darkness	Psalm 18:28 [2 Samuel 22]
For by Thee I have run through a troop; and by my God have I leaped over a wall.	Psalm 18:29 [2 Samuel 22]

As for God, His Way is perfect: The Word of The LORD is tried: He is a buckler to all those that trust in him. For who is God save The LORD? or who is a rock save our God?	Psalm 18:30-31 [2 Samuel 22]
It is God that girdeth me with strength, and maketh my way perfect. He maketh my feet like hinds' feet, and setteth me upon my high places. He teacheth my hands to war, so that a bow of steel is broken by mine arms	Psalm 18:32-34 [2 Samuel 22]
Thou hast also given me the shield of Thy Salvation: and Thy Right Hand hath holden me up, and Thy Gentleness hath made me great	Psalm 18:35 [2 Samuel 22]
Thou hast enlarged my steps under me, that my feet did not slip	Psalm 18:36 [2 Samuel 22]
I have pursued mine enemies, and overtaken them: neither did I turn again till they were consumed. I have wounded them that they were not able to rise: they are fallen under my feet. For Thou hast girded me with strength unto the battle: Thou hast subdued under me those that rose up against me. Thou hast also given me the necks of mine enemies; that I might destroy them that hate me	Psalm 18:37-40 [2 Samuel 22]
They cried, but there was none to save them: even unto The LORD, but He answered them not	Psalm 18:41 [2 Samuel 22]
Then did I beat them small as the dust before the wind: I did cast them out as the dirt in the streets	Psalm 18:42 [2 Samuel 22]

Thou hast delivered me from the strivings of the people; and Thou hast made me the head of the heathen: a people whom I have not known shall serve me. As soon as they hear of me, they shall obey me: the strangers shall submit themselves unto me. The strangers shall fade away, and be afraid out of their close places

Psalm 18:43–45 [2 Samuel 22]

The LORD liveth; and blessed be my rock; and let The God of my salvation be exalted

Psalm 18:46 [2 Samuel 22]

It is God that avengeth me, and subdueth the people under me. He delivereth me from mine enemies: yea, Thou liftest me up above those that rise up against me: Thou hast delivered me from the violent man. Therefore will I give thanks unto Thee, O LORD, among the heathen, and sing praises unto Thy Name

Psalm 18:47–49 [2 Samuel 22]

Great deliverance giveth He to His King; and showeth mercy to His Anointed, to David, and to his seed for evermore

Psalm 18:50 [2 Samuel 22]

The LORD is my shepherd; I shall not want. He maketh me to lie down in green pastures: He leadeth me beside the still waters. He restoreth my soul: He leadeth me in the paths of righteousness for His Name's Sake. Yea, though I walk through the valley of the shadow of death, I will fear no evil: for Thou art with me; Thy Rod and Thy Staff They comfort me. Thou preparest a table before me in the presence of mine enemies: Thou anointest my head with oil; my cup runneth over. Surely goodness and mercy shall follow me all the days of my life: and I will dwell in the house of The LORD for ever

Psalm 23:1–6

Thy Mercy, O LORD, is in the heavens; and Thy Faithfulness reacheth unto the clouds. Thy Righteousness is like the great mountains; Thy Judgments are a great deep: O LORD, Thou preservest man and beast. How excellent is Thy Lovingkindness, O God! therefore the children of men put their trust under the Shadow of Thy Wings. They shall be abundantly satisfied with the Fatness of Thy House; and Thou shalt make them drink of the river of Thy Pleasures. For with Thee is the fountain of life: in Thy Light shall we see light | Psalm 36:5-9

O continue Thy Lovingkindness unto them that know Thee; and Thy Righteousness to the upright in heart | Psalm 36:10

Let not the foot of pride come against me, and let not the hand of the wicked remove me | Psalm 36:11

There are the workers of iniquity fallen: they are cast down, and shall not be able to rise | Psalm 36:12

We have heard with our ears, O God, our fathers have told us, what work Thou didst in their days, in the times of old. How Thou didst drive out the heathen with Thy Hand, and plantedst them; how Thou didst afflict the people, and cast them out | Psalm 44:1-2

For they got not the land in possession by their own sword, neither did their own arm save them: but Thy Right Hand, and Thine Arm, and the light of Thy Countenance, because Thou hadst a favour unto them | Psalm 44:3

Thou art my King, O God: command deliverances for Jacob | Psalm 44:4

Through Thee will we push down our
enemies: through Thy Name will we tread
them under that rise up against us

Psalm 44:5

For I will not trust in my bow, neither shall my
sword save me

Psalm 44:6

But Thou hast saved us from our enemies, and
hast put them to shame that hated us

Psalm 44:7

In God we boast all the day long, and praise
Thy Name for ever

Psalm 44:8

For, lo, the kings were assembled, they
passed by together. They saw it, and so they
marvelled; they were troubled, and hasted away.
Fear took hold upon them there, and pain, as of
a woman in travail. Thou breakest the ships of
Tarshish with an east wind

Psalm 48:4-7

As we have heard, so have we seen in the city
of The LORD of Hosts, in the city of our God:
God will establish it for ever

Psalm 48:8

We have thought of Thy Lovingkindness, O
God, in the midst of Thy Temple

Psalm 48:9

According to Thy Name, O God, so is Thy
praise unto the ends of the earth: Thy Right
Hand is full of righteousness

Psalm 48:10

Let mount Zion rejoice, let the daughters of
Judah be glad, because of Thy Judgments

Psalm 48:11

I will praise Thee for ever, because Thou hast
done it: and I will wait on Thy Name; for it is
good before Thy Saints

Psalm 52:9

Be merciful unto me, O God: for man would swallow me up: he fighting daily oppresseth me

Psalm 56:1

Mine enemies would daily swallow me up: for they be many that fight against me, O Thou Most High

Psalm 56:2

What time I am afraid, I will trust in Thee

Psalm 56:3

In God I will praise His Word, in God I have put my trust; I will not fear what flesh can do unto me. Every day they wrest my words: all their thoughts are against me for evil. They gather themselves together, they hide themselves, they mark my steps, when they wait for my soul. Shall they escape by iniquity? in Thine Anger cast down the people, O God

Psalm 56:4-7

Thou tellest my wanderings: put Thou my tears into Thy Bottle: are they not in Thy Book?

Psalm 56:8

When I cry unto Thee, then shall mine enemies turn back: this I know, for God is for me

Psalm 56:9

In God will I praise His Word: in The LORD will I praise His Word

Psalm 56:10

In God have I put my trust: I will not be afraid what man can do unto me

Psalm 56:11

Thy Vows are upon me, O God: I will render praises unto Thee. For Thou hast delivered my soul from death: will not Thou deliver my feet from falling, that I may walk before God in the light of the living?

Psalm 56:12-13

God hath spoken once; twice have I heard this;   Psalm 62:11-12
that power belongeth unto God. Also unto
Thee, O Lord, belongeth mercy: for Thou
renderst to every man according to his work

Praise waiteth for Thee, O God, in Sion: and   Psalm 65:1
unto Thee shall the vow be performed

O Thou that hearest prayer, unto Thee shall all   Psalm 65:2
flesh come

Iniquities prevail against me: as for our   Psalm 65:3
transgressions, Thou shalt purge them away

Blessed is the man whom Thou choosest, and   Psalm 65:4
causest to approach unto Thee, that he may dwell
in Thy Courts: we shall be satisfied with the
goodness of Thy House, even of Thy Holy Temple

By terrible things in righteousness wilt Thou   Psalm 65:5-7
answer us, O God of our salvation; Who art the
confidence of all the ends of the earth, and of
them that are afar off upon the sea: Which by
His Strength setteth fast the mountains; being
girded with power: Which stilleth the noise
of the seas, the noise of their waves, and the
tumult of the people

They also that dwell in the uttermost parts   Psalm 65:8
are afraid at Thy Tokens: Thou makest the
outgoings of the morning and evening to rejoice

Thou visitest the earth, and waterest it: Thou   Psalm 65:9-10
greatly enrichest it with the river of God, which
is full of water: Thou preparest them corn, when
Thou hast so provided for it. Thou waterest
the ridges thereof abundantly: Thou settlest
the furrows thereof: Thou makest it soft with
showers: Thou blessest the springing thereof

Thou crownest the year with Thy Goodness; and Thy Paths drop fatness. They drop upon the pastures of the wilderness: and the little hills rejoice on every side. The pastures are clothed with flocks; the valleys also are covered over with corn; they shout for joy, they also sing

Psalm 65:11-13

How terrible art Thou in Thy Works! through the greatness of Thy Power shall Thine Enemies submit themselves unto Thee. All the earth shall worship Thee, and shall sing unto Thee; they shall sing to Thy Name

Psalm 66:3-4

God be merciful unto us, and bless us; and cause His Face to shine upon us; Selah. That Thy Way may be known upon earth, Thy Saving Health among all nations

Psalm 67:1-2

Let the people praise Thee, O God; let all the people praise Thee. Then shall the earth yield her increase; and God, even our own God, shall bless us. God shall bless us; and all the ends of the earth shall fear him

Psalm 67:3, 5-7

O let the nations be glad and sing for joy: for Thou shalt judge the people righteously, and govern the nations upon earth

Psalm 67:4

Let God arise, let His enemies be scattered: let them also that hate Him flee before Him. As smoke is driven away, so drive them away: as wax melteth before the fire, so let the wicked perish at the presence of God. But let the righteous be glad; let them rejoice before God: yea, let them exceedingly rejoice

Psalm 68:1-3

O God, when Thou wentest forth before Thy   Psalm 68:7-8
People, when Thou didst march through the
wilderness. Selah: The earth shook, the heavens
also dropped at the presence of God: even Sinai
itself was moved at the Presence of God , The
God of Israel

Thou, O God, didst send a plentiful   Psalm 68:9-10
rain, whereby Thou didst confirm Thine
Inheritance, when it was weary. Thy
Congregation hath dwelt therein: Thou, O
God, hast prepared of Thy Goodness for the
poor

Thou hast ascended on high, Thou hast led   Psalm 68:18-19
captivity captive: Thou hast received gifts
for men; yea, for the rebellious also, that The
LORD God might dwell among them. Blessed
be The Lord, who daily loadeth us with
benefits, even The God of our salvation

They have seen Thy Goings, O God; even the   Psalm 68:24-27
goings of my God, my King, in the sanctuary.
The singers went before, the players on
instruments followed after; among them were
the damsels playing with timbrels. Bless ye
God in the congregations, even the Lord, from
the fountain of Israel. There is little Benjamin
with their ruler, the princes of Judah and their
council, the princes of Zebulun, and the princes
of Naphtali

Thy God hath commanded Thy Strength: Psalm 68:28
strengthen, O God, that which Thou hast
wrought for us

Because of Thy Temple at Jerusalem shall kings   Psalm 68:29
bring presents unto Thee

217

Rebuke the company of spearmen, the
multitude of the bulls, with the calves of the
people, till every one submit himself with
pieces of silver: scatter Thou the people that
delight in war

Psalm 68:30

O God, Thou art terrible out of Thy Holy
Places: The God of Israel is He that giveth
strength and power unto His People. Blessed be
God

Psalm 68:35

I will sing of the Mercies of The LORD for
ever: with my mouth will I make known Thy
Faithfulness to all generations. For I have
said, Mercy shall be built up for ever: Thy
Faithfulness shalt Thou establish in the very
heavens

Psalm 89:1-2
[some of Jonah
2 throughout
this Psalm]

And the heavens shall praise Thy Wonders,
O LORD: Thy Faithfulness also in the
congregation of the saints

Psalm 89:5

For who in the heaven can be compared unto
The LORD? who among the sons of the
mighty can be likened unto The LORD? God
is greatly to be feared in the assembly of the
saints, and to be had in reverence of all them
that are about Him

Psalm 89:6-7

O LORD God of Hosts, who is a Strong
LORD like unto Thee? or to Thy Faithfulness
round about Thee? Thou rulest the raging of
the sea: when the waves thereof arise, Thou
stillest them

Psalm 89:8-9

Thou hast broken Rahab in pieces, as one that
is slain: Thou hast scattered Thine Enemies
with Thy Strong Arm

Psalm 89:10

The heavens are Thine, the earth also is Thine: Psalm 89:11-12
as for the world and the fulness thereof, Thou
hast founded them. The north and the south
Thou hast created them: Tabor and Hermon
shall rejoice in Thy Name

Thou hast a Mighty Arm: strong is Thy Hand,   Psalm 89:13-14
and high is Thy Right Hand. Justice and
judgment are the habitation of Thy Throne:
mercy and truth shall go before Thy Face

Blessed is the people that know the joyful   Psalm 89:15-17
sound: they shall walk, O LORD, in the light
of Thy Countenance. In Thy Name shall they
rejoice all the day: and in Thy Righteousness
shall they be exalted. For Thou art the Glory
of their strength: and in Thy Favour our horn
shall be exalted

For The LORD is our Defence; and the Holy   Psalm 89:18-19
One of Israel is our King. Then Thou spakest in   (20-45)
vision to Thy Holy One, and saidst, I have laid
help upon one that is mighty; I have exalted
one chosen out of the people....

It is a good thing to give thanks unto The   Psalm 92:1-3
LORD, and to sing praises unto Thy Name, O
Most High: To show forth Thy Lovingkindness
in the morning, and Thy Faithfulness every
night, Upon an instrument of ten strings, and
upon the psaltery; upon the harp with a solemn
sound

For Thou, LORD, hast made me glad through   Psalm 92:4
Thy Work: I will triumph in the works of Thy
Hands

O LORD, how great are Thy Works! and Thy   Psalm 92:5
Thoughts are very deep

A brutish man knoweth not; neither doth a fool
understand this. When the wicked spring as
the grass, and when all the workers of iniquity
do flourish; it is that they shall be destroyed
for ever: But Thou, LORD, art Most High for
evermore

Psalm 92:6-8

For, lo, Thine Enemies, O LORD, for, lo,
Thine Enemies shall perish; all the workers of
iniquity shall be scattered. But my horn shalt
Thou exalt like the horn of an unicorn: I shall
be anointed with fresh oil

Psalm 92:9-10

Mine eye also shall see my desire on mine
enemies, and mine ears shall hear my desire of
the wicked that rise up against me

Psalm 92:11

The righteous shall flourish like the palm tree:
he shall grow like a cedar in Lebanon. Those
that be planted in the House of The LORD
shall flourish in the courts of our God. They
shall still bring forth fruit in old age; they
shall be fat and flourishing; To show that The
LORD is upright: He is my rock, and there is
no unrighteousness in Him

Psalm 92:12-15

Bless The LORD, O my soul, O LORD my
God, Thou art Very Great, Thou art Clothed
with Honour and Majesty

Psalm 104:1

Who coverest Thyself with light as with a
garment: Who stretchest out the heavens
like a curtain: Who layeth the beams of His
Chambers in the waters: Who maketh the
clouds His Chariot: Who walketh upon the
wings of the wind

Psalm 104:2-3

Who maketh His Angels spirits; His Ministers a
flaming fire

Psalm 104:4

Who laid the foundations of the earth, that it should not be removed for ever. Thou coveredst it with the deep as with a garment: the waters stood above the mountains	Psalm 104:5-6

At Thy Rebuke they fled; at the voice of Thy Thunder they hasted away. They go up by the mountains; they go down by the valleys unto the place which Thou hast founded for them. Thou hast set a bound that they may not pass over; that they turn not again to cover the earth	Psalm 104:7-9

He sendeth the springs into the valleys, which run among the hills. They give drink to every beast of the field: the wild asses quench their thirst. By them shall the fowls of the heaven have their habitation, which sing among the branches	Psalm 104:10-12

He watereth the hills from His Chambers: the earth is satisfied with the fruit of Thy Works	Psalm 104:13

He causeth the grass to grow for the cattle, and herb for the service of man: that he may bring forth food out of the earth; And wine that maketh glad the heart of man, and oil to make his face to shine, and bread which strengtheneth man's heart	Psalm 104:14-15

The trees of The LORD are full of sap; the cedars of Lebanon, which He hath planted; Where the birds make their nests: as for the stork, the fir trees are her house	Psalm 104:16-17

The high hills are a refuge for the wild goats; and the rocks for the conies. He appointed the moon for seasons: the sun knoweth his going down	Psalm 104:18-19

Thou makest darkness, and it is night: wherein all the beasts of the forest do creep forth	Psalm 104:20
The young lions roar after their prey, and seek their meat from God. The sun ariseth, they gather themselves together, and lay them down in their dens. Man goeth forth unto his work and to his labour until the evening	Psalm 104:21-23
O LORD, how manifold are Thy Works! In wisdom hast Thou made them all: the earth is full of Thy Riches. So is this great and wide sea, wherein are things creeping innumerable, both small and great beasts	Psalm 104:24-25
There go the ships: there is that leviathan, whom Thou hast made to play therein	Psalm 104:26
These wait all upon Thee; that Thou mayest give them their meat in due season. That Thou givest them they gather: Thou openest Thine Hand, they are filled with good	Psalm 104:27-28
Thou hidest Thy Face, they are troubled: Thou takest away their breath, they die, and return to their dust	Psalm 104:29
Thou sendest forth Thy Spirit, they are created: and Thou renewest the face of the earth	Psalm 104:30
O GOD, my heart is fixed; I will sing and give praise, even with my glory. Awake, psaltery and harp: I myself will awake early	Psalm 108:1-2
I will praise Thee, O LORD, among the people: and I will sing praises unto Thee among the nations. For Thy Mercy is great above the heavens: and Thy Truth reacheth unto the clouds	Psalm 108:3-4

Be Thou exalted, O God, above the heavens: and Thy Glory above the earth	Psalm 108:5

For Thou hast delivered my soul from death, mine eyes from tears, and my feet from falling. I will walk before The LORD in the land of the living — Psalm 116:8-9

O LORD, truly I am Thy Servant; I am Thy Servant, and the son of Thine Handmaid: Thou hast loosed my bonds — Psalm 116:16

I will offer to Thee the sacrifice of thanksgiving, and will call upon the Name of The LORD — Psalm 116:17

I will praise Thee with my whole heart: before the gods will I sing praise unto Thee — Psalm 138:1

I will worship toward Thy Holy Temple, and praise Thy Name for Thy Lovingkindness and for Thy Truth: for Thou hast magnified Thy Word above all Thy Name — Psalm 138:2

In the day when I cried Thou answeredst me, and strengthenedst me with strength in my soul — Psalm 138:3

All the kings of the earth shall praise Thee, O LORD, when they hear The Words of Thy Mouth. Yea, they shall sing in The Ways of The LORD: for great is The Glory of The LORD — Psalm 138:4-5

Though the LORD be high, yet hath He respect unto the lowly: but the proud He knoweth afar off — Psalm 138:6

Though I walk in the midst of trouble, Thou wilt revive me: Thou shalt stretch forth Thine Hand against the wrath of mine enemies, and Thy Right Hand shall save me

Psalm 138:7

The LORD will perfect that which concerneth me: Thy Mercy, O LORD, endureth for ever: forsake not The Works of Thine Own Hands

Psalm 138:8

O LORD, Thou hast searched me, and known me

Psalm 139:1

Thou knowest my downsitting and mine uprising, Thou understandest my thought afar off

Psalm 139:2

Thou compassest my path and my lying down, and art acquainted with all my ways

Psalm 139:3

For there is not a word in my tongue, but, lo, O LORD, Thou knowest it altogether

Psalm 139:4

Thou hast beset me behind and before, and laid Thine Hand upon me. Such knowledge is too wonderful for me; it is high, I cannot attain unto it

Psalm 139:5-6

Whither shall I go from Thy Spirit? or whither shall I flee from Thy Presence? If I ascend up into heaven, Thou art there: if I make my bed in hell, behold, Thou art there

Psalm 139:7-8

If I take the wings of the morning, and dwell in the uttermost parts of the sea; Even there shall Thy Hand lead me, and Thy Right Hand shall hold me

Psalm 139:9-10

If I say, Surely the darkness shall cover me; even the night shall be light about me. Yea, the darkness hideth not from Thee; but the night shineth as the day: the darkness and the light are both alike to Thee	Psalm 139:11-12
For Thou hast possessed my reins: Thou hast covered me in my mother's womb	Psalm 139:13
I will praise Thee; for I am fearfully and wonderfully made: marvellous are Thy Works; and that my soul knoweth right well	Psalm 139:14
My substance was not hid from Thee, when I was made in secret, and curiously wrought in the lowest parts of the earth. Thine Eyes did see my substance, yet being unperfect; and in Thy Book all my members were written, which in continuance were fashioned, when as yet there was none of them	Psalm 139:15-16
How precious also are Thy Thoughts unto me, O God! how great is the sum of Them! If I should count Them, they are more in number than the sand: when I awake, I am still with Thee	Psalm 139:17-18
Surely Thou wilt slay the wicked, O God: depart from me therefore, ye bloody men	Psalm 139:19
For they speak against Thee wickedly, and Thine Enemies take Thy Name in vain	Psalm 139:20
Do not I hate them, O LORD, that hate Thee? and am not I grieved with those that rise up against Thee? I hate them with perfect hatred: I count them mine enemies	Psalm 139:21-22

Search me, O God, and know my heart: try me, and know my thoughts: And see if there be any wicked way in me, and lead me in the way everlasting	Psalm 139:23–24
I will sing a new song unto Thee, O God: upon a psaltery and an instrument of ten strings will I sing praises unto Thee	Psalm 144:9
It is He that giveth salvation unto kings: who delivereth David His Servant from the hurtful sword	Psalm 144:10
I will extol Thee, my God, O King; and I will bless Thy Name for ever and ever	Psalm 145:1
Every day will I bless Thee; and I will praise Thy Name for ever and ever	Psalm 145:2
Great is The LORD, and greatly to be praised; and His Greatness is unsearchable	Psalm 145:3
One generation shall praise Thy Works to another, and shall declare Thy Mighty Acts	Psalm 145:4
I will speak of the glorious honour of Thy Majesty, and of Thy Wondrous Works	Psalm 145:5
And men shall speak of the might of Thy Terrible Acts: and I will declare Thy Greatness	Psalm 145:6
They shall abundantly utter the memory of Thy Great Goodness, and shall sing of Thy Righteousness	Psalm 145:7
The LORD is gracious, and full of compassion; slow to anger, and of great mercy	Psalm 145:8

The LORD is good to all: and His Tender Mercies are over all His Works	Psalm 145:9
All Thy Works shall praise Thee, O LORD; and Thy Saints shall bless Thee. They shall speak of the glory of Thy Kingdom, and talk of Thy Power; To make known to the sons of men His Mighty Acts, and the glorious majesty of His Kingdom	Psalm 145:10-12
Thy Kingdom is an Everlasting Kingdom, and Thy Dominion endureth throughout all generations	Psalm 145:13
The LORD upholdeth all that fall, and raiseth up all those that be bowed down	Psalm 145:14
The eyes of all wait upon Thee; and Thou givest them their meat in due season	Psalm 145:15
Thou openest Thine Hand, and satisfiest the desire of every living thing	Psalm 145:16
The LORD is righteous in all His Ways, and holy in all His Works	Psalm 145:17
The LORD is nigh unto all them that call upon Him, to all that call upon Him in truth	Psalm 145:18
He will fulfil the desire of them that fear Him: He also will hear their cry, and will save them	Psalm 145:19
The LORD preserveth all them that love Him: but all the wicked will He destroy	Psalm 145:20
My mouth shall speak the praise of The LORD: and let all flesh bless His Holy Name for ever and ever	Psalm 145:21

O LORD, I will praise Thee: though Thou   Isaiah 12:1b
wast angry with me, Thine Anger is turned
away, and Thou comfortedst me

O LORD, Thou art my God; I will exalt Thee,   Isaiah 25:1
I will praise Thy Name; for Thou hast done
wonderful things; Thy Counsels of old are
faithfulness and truth

For Thou hast made of a city an heap; of a   Isaiah 25:2
defenced city a ruin: a palace of strangers to be
no city; it shall never be built

Therefore shall the strong people glorify Thee,   Isaiah 25:3
the city of the terrible nations shall fear Thee

For Thou hast been a strength to the poor, a   Isaiah 25:4
strength to the needy in his distress, a refuge
from the storm, a shadow from the heat, when
the blast of the terrible ones is as a storm against
the wall

Thou shalt bring down the noise of strangers, as Isaiah 25:5
the heat in a dry place; even the heat with the
shadow of a cloud: the branch of the terrible
ones shall be brought low

We have a strong city; salvation will God   Isaiah 26:1b-2
appoint for walls and bulwarks. Open ye the
gates, that the righteous nation which keepeth
the truth may enter in

Thou wilt keep him in perfect peace, whose   Isaiah 26:3
mind is stayed on Thee: because he trusteth in
Thee

Trust ye in The LORD for ever: for in The   Isaiah 26:4
LORD JEHOVAH is Everlasting Strength

For He bringeth down them that dwell on high; the lofty city, He layeth it low; He layeth it low, even to the ground; He bringeth it even to the dust. The foot shall tread it down, even the feet of the poor, and the steps of the needy

Isaiah 26:5-6

The way of the just is uprightness: Thou, most upright, dost weigh the path of the just

Isaiah 26:7

Yea, in the way of Thy Judgments, O LORD, have we waited for Thee; the desire of our soul is to Thy Name, and to the remembrance of Thee

Isaiah 26:8

With my soul have I desired Thee in the night; yea, with my spirit within me will I seek Thee early: for when Thy Judgments are in the earth, the inhabitants of the world will learn righteousness

Isaiah 26:9

Let favour be shown to the wicked, yet will he not learn righteousness: in the land of uprightness will he deal unjustly, and will not behold The Majesty of The LORD

Isaiah 26:10

LORD, when Thy Hand is lifted up, they will not see: but they shall see, and be ashamed for their envy at the people; yea, the fire of Thine Enemies shall devour them

Isaiah 26:11

LORD, Thou wilt ordain peace for us: for Thou also hast wrought all our works in us

Isaiah 26:12

O LORD our God, other lords beside Thee have had dominion over us: but by Thee only will we make mention of Thy Name. They are dead, they shall not live; they are deceased, they shall not rise: therefore hast Thou visited and destroyed them, and made all their memory to perish

Isaiah 26:13-14

Thou hast increased the nation, O LORD,   Isaiah 26:15
Thou hast increased the nation: Thou art
Glorified: Thou hadst removed it far unto all
the ends of the earth

Lord, in trouble have they visited Thee, they   Isaiah 26:16
poured out a prayer when Thy Chastening was
upon them

Like as a woman with child, that draweth near   Isaiah 26:17
the time of her delivery, is in pain, and crieth
out in her pangs; so have we been in Thy Sight,
O LORD

We have been with child, we have been in   Isaiah 26:18
pain, we have as it were brought forth wind; we
have not wrought any deliverance in the earth;
neither have the inhabitants of the world fallen

O LORD, my strength, and my fortress, and my   Jeremiah 16:19
refuge in the day of affliction, the Gentiles shall
come unto Thee from the ends of the earth, and
shall say, Surely our fathers have inherited lies,
vanity, and things wherein there is no profit

Shall a man make gods unto himself, and they   Jeremiah 16:20
are no gods?

Ah Lord GOD! behold, Thou hast made the   Jeremiah 32:17
heaven and the earth by Thy Great Power and
Stretched Out Arm, and there is nothing too
hard for Thee:

Thou showest lovingkindness unto thousands,   Jeremiah 32:18
and recompensest the iniquity of the fathers
into the bosom of their children after them:
The Great, The Mighty God, The LORD of
Hosts, is His Name,

Great in counsel, and mighty in work: for   Jeremiah
Thine Eyes are open upon all the ways of the   32:19; 17:10b
sons of men: to give every one according to his   [Revelation
ways, and according to the fruit of his doings: 2:23b]

Which hast set signs and wonders in the land   Jeremiah 32:20
of Egypt, even unto this day, and in Israel,
and among other men; and hast made Thee a
Name, as at this day;

And hast brought forth Thy People Israel out of   Jeremiah 32:21
the land of Egypt with signs, and with wonders,
and with a strong hand, and with a stretched
out arm, and with great terror;

And hast given them this land, which Thou   Jeremiah 32:22
didst swear to their fathers to give them, a land
flowing with milk and honey;

And they came in, and possessed it; but they   Jeremiah 32:23
obeyed not Thy Voice, neither walked in Thy
Law; they have done nothing of all that Thou
commandedst them to do: therefore Thou hast
caused all this evil to come upon them:

Behold the mounts, they are come unto the city   Jeremiah 32:24
to take it; and the city is given into the hand
of the Chaldeans, that fight against it, because
of the sword, and of the famine, and of the
pestilence: and what Thou hast spoken is come
to pass; and, behold, Thou seest it

And Thou hast said unto me, O Lord GOD,   Jeremiah 32:25
Buy thee the field for money, and take
witnesses; for the city is given into the hand of
the Chaldeans

I thank Thee, and praise Thee, O Thou God   Daniel 2:23
of my fathers, Who hast given me wisdom and
might, and hast made known unto me now
what we desired of Thee: for Thou hast now
made known unto us the king's matter

Who is a God like unto Thee, that pardoneth   Micah 7:18-20
iniquity, and passeth by the transgression of the
remnant of His Heritage? He retaineth not His
Anger for ever, because He delighteth in mercy.
He will turn again, He will have compassion
upon us; He will subdue our iniquities; and
Thou wilt cast all their sins into the depths of
the sea. Thou wilt perform the truth to Jacob,
and the mercy to Abraham, which Thou hast
sworn unto our fathers from the days of old

Thy Throne, O God, is for ever and ever: [the]   Hebrews 1:8-9
a sceptre of [Thy Kingdom] righteousness is the   [Psalm 45:6-7]
[a right] sceptre of Thy Kingdom. Thou hast
loved [lovest] righteousness, and hated iniquity
[hatest wickedness]; therefore God, [even]
Thy God, hath anointed Thee with the oil of
gladness above Thy Fellows

And, Thou, Lord, in the beginning [of old] hast   Hebrews 1:10-
[Thou] laid the foundation of the earth: and the   12 [Psalm
heavens are the Work[s] of Thine [Thy] Hands.   102:25-27]
They shall perish, but Thou remainest [shalt
endure: yea], they all [all of them] shall wax old
as doth [like] a garment; and as a vesture shalt
Thou fold [change] them up, and they shall be
changed: but Thou art the same, and Thy Years
shall not fail [have no end]

What is man, that Thou art mindful of him? or [and] the son of man, that Thou visitest him? [For] Thou madest [hast made] him a little lower than the angels, [and] Thou crownedest [hast crowned] him with glory and honour, and didst set him over the Works of Thy Hands	Hebrews 2:6b-7 [Psalm 8:4-6a]
Thou hast put all things in subjection under his feet	Hebrews 2:8a [Psalm 8:6b]
I will declare Thy Name unto my brethren, in the midst of the church [congregation] will I [sing] praise [unto] Thee	Hebrews 2:12 [Psalm 22:22]
Thou art worthy, O Lord, to receive glory and honour and power: for Thou hast created all things, and for Thy Pleasure they are and were created	Revelation 4:11
Thou art worthy to take the book, and to open the seals thereof: for Thou wast slain, and hast redeemed us to God by Thy Blood out of every kindred, and tongue, and people, and nation; And hast made us unto our God kings and priests: and we shall reign on the earth	Revelation 5:9-10
Alleluia; Salvation, and glory, and honour, and power, unto The Lord our God: For true and righteous are His Judgments: for He hath judged the great whore, which did corrupt the earth with her fornication, and hath avenged the blood of His Servants at her hand	Revelation 19:1b-2

Alleluia: for The Lord God Omnipotent
reigneth. Let us be glad and rejoice, and give
honour to Him: for the marriage of The Lamb
is come, and His Wife hath made herself ready.
And to her was granted that she should be
arrayed in fine linen, clean and white: for the
fine linen is the righteousness of saints

Revelation
19:6-8

Prayer portions that contain Praises in them

Deuteronomy 33:3-4	Psalm 31:19-24
1 Kings 8:23-25 [2 Chronicles 6:14-42]	Psalm 32:7
1 Kings 8:56	Psalm 35:10
2 Kings 19:15 [Isaiah 37:16]	Psalm 35:18
2 Chronicles 6:14-16 [1 Kings 8:23-53]	Psalm 40:5
2 Chronicles 14:11	Psalm 43:4
2 Chronicles 20:6-9	Psalm 45:6-7 [Hebrews 1:8-9]
Psalm 4:7-8	Psalm 45:17
Psalm 10:17-18	Psalm 51:15
Psalm 12:5-8	Psalm 54:6
Psalm 13:3-6	Psalm 57:7-10
Psalm 21:13	Psalm 59:9-17
Psalm 22:3-5	Psalm 61:2-8
Psalm 22:22 [Hebrews 2:12]	Psalm 69:16-17
Psalm 22:23-25	Psalm 71:3
Psalm 25:6-7	Psalm 71:6-8
Psalm 27:9-10	Psalm 71:13-24
Psalm 28:6	Psalm 72:18-19
Psalm 30:1	Psalm 73:24-28
Psalm 30:11-12	Psalm 74:12-17
Psalm 31:7-8	Psalm 74:21

Psalm 75:1-5

Psalm 76:6-10

Psalm 77:12-20

Psalm 79:13

Psalm 80:1

Psalm 85:1-3

Psalm 86:5

Psalm 86:8-10

Psalm 86:12-15

Psalm 94:17-20

Psalm 97:8

Psalm 101:1

Psalm 102:18-24

Psalm 102:25-27 [Hebrews 1:10-12]

Psalm 102:28

Psalm 106:47 [1 Chronicles 16:35]

Psalm 106:48 [1 Chronicles 16:36]

Psalm 109:30-31

Psalm 115:1

Psalm 118:28

Psalm 119:7

Psalm 119:27

Psalm 119:46

Psalm 119:50

Psalm 119:64

Psalm 119:68

Psalm 119:73

Psalm 119:90-93

Psalm 119:119

Psalm 119:151-152

Psalm 119:164

Psalm 119:171

Psalm 119:175

Psalm 142:7

Isaiah 37:16 [2 Kings 19:15]

Isaiah 38:15-20

Isaiah 63:7-15

Isaiah 64:1-4

Isaiah 64:8

Jeremiah 14:22

Jeremiah 15:16

Jeremiah 20:12; 17:10a

[Revelation 2:23b]

Daniel 9:4b

Jonah 2:2 [Psalm 18:4-6;

    22:23-24; 88 & 89 throughout

    this prayer]

Jonah 2:5-6

Jonah 2:8-9

Habakkuk 3:2-19

Acts 4:24-26 [Psalm 2:1-2]

Ephesians 3:14-21

Revelation 11:17

Response Prayers

I heard Thy Voice in the garden, and I was afraid, because I was naked; and I hid myself	Genesis 3:10
The woman whom Thou gavest to be with me, she gave me of the tree, and I did eat	Genesis 3:12
The serpent beguiled me, and I did eat	Genesis 3:13b
Behold, here I am	Genesis 22:1b
Here am I	Genesis 22:11b
Here am I	Genesis 31:11b
Jacob	Genesis 32:27b
Here am I	Genesis 46:2b
Here am I	Exodus 3:4b
Who am I, that I should go unto Pharaoh, and that I should bring forth the children of Israel out of Egypt?	Exodus 3:11
Behold, when I come unto the children of Israel, and shall say unto them, The God of your fathers hath sent me unto you; and they shall say to me, What is His Name? what shall I say unto them?	Exodus 3:13

But, behold, they will not believe me, nor hearken unto my voice: for they will say, The LORD hath not appeared unto thee — Exodus 4:1

A rod — Exodus 4:2b

O my Lord, I am not eloquent, neither heretofore, nor since Thou hast spoken unto Thy Servant: but I am slow of speech, and of a slow tongue — Exodus 4:10

Behold, the children of Israel have not hearkened unto me; how then shall Pharaoh hear me, who am of uncircumcised lips? — Exodus 6:12

Behold, I am of uncircumcised lips, and how shall Pharaoh hearken unto me? — Exodus 6:30

Then the Egyptians shall hear it, (for Thou broughtest up this people in Thy Might from among them;) And they will tell it to the inhabitants of this land: for they have heard that Thou LORD art among this people, that Thou LORD art seen face to face, and that Thy Cloud standeth over them, and that Thou goest before them, by day time in a pillar of a cloud, and in a pillar of fire by night — Numbers 14:13–14

Now if Thou shalt kill all this people as one man, then the nations which have heard the fame of Thee will speak, saying, Because The LORD was not able to bring this people into the land which He sware unto them, therefore He hath slain them in the wilderness — Numbers 14:15–16

And now, I beseech Thee, let The Power of my LORD be great, according as Thou hast spoken, saying, The LORD is longsuffering, and of great mercy, forgiving iniquity and transgression, and by no means clearing the guilty, visiting the iniquity of the fathers upon the children unto the third and fourth generation	Numbers 14:17-18
Pardon, I beseech Thee, the iniquity of this people according unto the Greatness of Thy Mercy, and as Thou hast forgiven this people, from Egypt even until now	Numbers 14:19
O God, The God of the spirits of all flesh, shall one man sin, and wilt Thou be wroth with all the congregation?	Numbers 16:22
Here am I	1 Samuel 3:4b
How can I go? if Saul hear it, he will kill me	1 Samuel 16:2a
I have been very jealous for The LORD God of hosts: for [because] the children of Israel have forsaken Thy Covenant, thrown down Thine Altars, and slain Thy Prophets with the sword; and I, even I only, am left; and they seek my life, to take it away	1 Kings 19:10,14 [Romans 11:3]
Here am I; send me	Isaiah 6:8
Ah, Lord GOD! Behold, I cannot speak: for I am a child	Jeremiah 1:6
I see a rod of an almond tree	Jeremiah 1:11b
I see a seething pot; and the face thereof is toward the north	Jeremiah 1:13b

So be it, O LORD	Jeremiah 11:5b
Ah, Lord GOD! behold, the prophets say unto them, Ye shall not see the sword, neither shall ye have famine; but I will give you assured peace in this place	Jeremiah 14:13
Figs; the good figs, very good; and the evil, very evil, that cannot be eaten, they are so evil	Jeremiah 24:3b
Ah Lord GOD! behold, my soul hath not been polluted: for from my youth up even till now have I not eaten of that which dieth of itself, or is torn in pieces; neither came there abominable flesh into my mouth	Ezekiel 4:14
Ah Lord GOD! they say of me, Doth he not speak parables?	Ezekiel 20:49
O Lord GOD, Thou knowest	Ezekiel 37:3b
Let my Lord speak; for Thou hast strengthened me	Daniel 10:19b
A plumbline	Amos 7:8b
A basket of summer fruit	Amos 8:2b
I do well to be angry, even unto death	Jonah 4:9b
Yea, Lord	Matthew 13:51b
Thou art the Christ, the Son of the Living God	Matthew 16:16; Luke 9:20b
Which?	Matthew 19:18a
Lord, that our eyes may be opened	Matthew 20:33

My name is Legion: for we are many	Mark 5:9b; Matthew 8:28–32; Luke 8:30b
Thou art the Christ	Mark 8:29b
Of a child. And ofttimes it hath cast him into the fire, and into the waters, to destroy him: but if Thou canst do any thing, have compassion on us, and help us	Mark 9:21b–22; Matthew 17:15; Luke 9:38–42
Lord, I believe; help Thou mine unbelief	Mark 9:24b
Lord, that I might [may] receive my sight	Mark 10:51b; Luke 18:41b
Legion	Luke 8:30b; Matthew 8:28–32; Mark 5:9b
The Christ of God	Luke 9:20b; Matthew 16:16
Lord, that I might [may] receive my sight	Luke 18:41b; Mark 10:51b
Rabbi, Thou art the Son of God; Thou art the King of Israel	John 1:49
How can a man be born when he is old? can he enter the second time into his mother's womb, and be born?	John 3:4
How can these things be?	John 3:9
Sir, Thou hast nothing to draw with, and the well is deep: from whence then hast Thou that Living Water?	John 4:11

Art Thou greater than our father Jacob, which gave us the well, and drank thereof himself, and his children, and his cattle?	John 4:12
Sir, give me this Water, that I thirst not, neither come hither to draw	John 4:15
What shall we do, that we might work the Works of God?	John 6:28
Lord, evermore give us This Bread	John 6:34
Lord, to whom shall we go? Thou hast the Words of eternal life. And we believe and are sure that Thou art That Christ, the Son of the Living God	John 6:68-69
We be Abraham's seed, and were never in bondage to any man: how sayest Thou, Ye shall be made free?	John 8:33
Who is He, Lord, that I might believe on Him?	John 9:36
Yea, Lord: I believe that Thou art The Christ, The Son of God, which should come into the world	John 11:27
Lord, not my feet only, but also my hands and my head	John 13:9
What is truth?	John 18:38a
Rabonni	John 20:16b
My Lord and my God	John 20:28
Yea, Lord; Thou knowest that I love Thee	John 21:15b,16b

Lord, Thou knowest all things; Thou knowest that I love Thee	John 21:17b
Who art Thou, Lord?	Acts 9:5a; 22:8a; 26:15a
Lord, what wilt Thou have me to do?	Acts 9:6a; 22:10a
Behold, I am here, Lord	Acts 9:10b
Lord, I have heard by many of this man, how much evil he hath done to Thy Saints at Jerusalem: and here he hath authority from the chief priests to bind all that call on Thy Name	Acts 9:13-14
Who art Thou, Lord?	Acts 22:8a; 9:5a; 26:15a
What shall I do, Lord?	Acts 22:10a; 9:6a
Lord, they know that I imprisoned and beat in every synagogue them that believed on Thee: And when the blood of Thy Martyr Stephen was shed, I also was standing by, and consenting unto his death, and kept the raiment of them that slew him	Acts 22:19-20
Who art Thou, Lord?	Acts 26:15a; 9:5a; 22:8a
Lord, they have killed Thy Prophets, and digged down Thine Altars; and I am left alone, and they seek my life	Romans 11:3 [1 Kings 19:10,14]

Prayer portions that contain a Response to God in them

Exodus 4:13	Numbers 27:16-17
Exodus 33:15	Psalm 27:8
Exodus 33:18	

Statement Prayers

I heard Thy Voice in the garden, and I was afraid, because I was naked; and I hid myself	Genesis 3:10
The woman whom Thou gavest to be with me, she gave me of the tree, and I did eat	Genesis 3:12
Blessed be The LORD God of Shem; and Canaan shall be his servant. God shall enlarge Japheth, and he shall dwell in the tents of Shem; and Canaan shall be his servant	Genesis 3:13b
I have waited for Thy Salvation, O LORD	Genesis 49:18
If Thou wilt indeed deliver this people into my hand, then I will utterly destroy their cities	Numbers 21:2
Our hands have not shed this blood, neither have our eyes seen it. Be merciful, O LORD, unto Thy People Israel, whom Thou hast redeemed, and lay not innocent blood unto Thy People of Israel's charge	Deuteronomy 21:7-8a
And now, behold, I have brought the firstfruits of the land, which Thou, O LORD, hast given me	Deuteronomy 26:10a
Be it far from me, O LORD, that I should do this: is not this the blood of the men that went in jeopardy of their lives?	2 Samuel 23:17a

Lo, I have sinned, and I have done wickedly: but these sheep, what have they done? let Thine Hand, I pray Thee, be against me, and against my father's house	2 Samuel 24:17 [1 Chronicles 21:17]

Thou hast shown unto Thy Servant David my father great mercy, according as he walked before Thee in truth, and in righteousness, and in uprightness of heart with Thee; and Thou hast kept for him this great kindness, that Thou hast given him a son to sit on his throne, as it is this day. And now, O LORD my God, Thou hast made Thy Servant king instead of David my father: and I am but a little child: I know not how to go out or come in. And Thy Servant is in the midst of Thy People which Thou hast chosen, a great people, that cannot be numbered nor counted for multitude. Give therefore Thy Servant an understanding heart to judge Thy People, that I may discern between good and bad: for who is able to judge this Thy So Great a People?

1 Kings 3:6-9 [2 Chronicles 1:8-10]

The LORD said that He would dwell in the thick darkness. I have surely built Thee an house to dwell in, a settled place for Thee to abide in for ever

1 Kings 8:12-13 [2 Chronicles 6:1-2]

I have been very jealous for The LORD God of hosts: for [because] the children of Israel have forsaken Thy Covenant, thrown down Thine Altars, and slain Thy Prophets with the sword; and I, even I only, am left; and they seek my life, to take it away

1 Kings 19:10,14 [Romans 11:3]

Is it not I that commanded the people to be numbered? even I it is that have sinned and done evil indeed; but as for these sheep, what have they done? let Thine Hand, I pray Thee, O LORD my God, be on me, and on my father's house; but not on Thy People, that they should be plagued

1 Chronicles 21:17 [2 Samuel 24:17]

Thou hast shown great mercy unto David my father, and hast made me to reign in his stead. Now, O LORD God, let Thy Promise unto David my father be established: for Thou hast made me king over a people like the dust of the earth in multitude. Give me now wisdom and knowledge, that I may go out and come in before this people: for who can judge this Thy People, that is so great?

2 Chronicles 1:8-10 [1 Kings 3:6-9]

The LORD hath said that He would dwell in the thick darkness. But I have built an house of habitation for Thee, and a place for Thy Dwelling for ever

2 Chronicles 6:1-2 [1 Kings 8:12-13]

O my God, I am ashamed and blush to lift up my face to Thee, my God: for our iniquities are increased over our head, and our trespass is grown up unto the heavens. Since the days of our fathers have we been in a great trespass unto this day; and for our iniquities have we, our kings, and our priests, been delivered into the hand of the kings of the lands, to the sword, to captivity, and to a spoil, and to confusion of face, as it is this day. And now for a little space grace hath been shown from The LORD our God, to leave us a remnant to escape, and to give us a nail in His Holy Place, that our God may lighten our eyes, and give us a little reviving in our bondage. For we were bondmen; yet our God hath not forsaken us in our bondage, but hath extended mercy unto us in the sight of the kings of Persia, to give us a reviving, to set up the house of our God, and to repair the desolations thereof, and to give us a wall in Judah and in Jerusalem

Ezra 9:6-9

And now, O our God, what shall we
say after this? for we have forsaken Thy
Commandments, Which Thou hast
commanded by Thy Servants the prophets,
saying, The land, unto which ye go to possess
it, is an unclean land with the filthiness of the
people of the lands, with their abominations,
which have filled it from one end to another
with their uncleanness. Now therefore give not
your daughters unto their sons, neither take
their daughters unto your sons, nor seek their
peace or their wealth for ever: that ye may be
strong, and eat the good of the land, and leave it
for an inheritance to your children for ever

Ezra 9:10-12

And after all that is come upon us for our
evil deeds, and for our great trespass, seeing
that Thou our God hast punished us less than
our iniquities deserve, and hast given us such
deliverance as this; Should we again break Thy
Commandments, and join in affinity with
the people of these abominations? wouldest
not Thou be angry with us till Thou hadst
consumed us, so that there should be no
remnant nor escaping? O LORD God of Israel,
Thou art righteous: for we remain yet escaped,
as it is this day: behold, we are before Thee in
our trespasses: for we cannot stand before Thee
because of this

Ezra 9:13-15

O remember that my life is wind: mine eye
shall no more see good

Job 7:7

Therefore I will not refrain my mouth; I
will speak in the anguish of my spirit; I will
complain in the bitterness of my soul

Job 7:11

Am I a sea, or a whale, that Thou settest a
watch over me? When I say, My bed shall
comfort me, my couch shall ease my complaint;
Then Thou scarest me with dreams, and
terrifiest me through visions: So that my soul
chooseth strangling, and death rather than my
life. I loathe it; I would not live always: let me
alone; for my days are vanity

Job 7:12-16

What is man, that Thou shouldest magnify
him? and that Thou shouldest set Thine Heart
upon him? And that Thou shouldest visit him
every morning, and try him every moment?

Job 7:17-18

How long wilt Thou not depart from me, nor
let me alone till I swallow down my spittle?
I have sinned; what shall I do unto Thee, O
Thou Preserver of men? why hast Thou set me
as a mark against Thee, so that I am a burden
to myself? And why dost Thou not pardon my
transgression, and take away mine iniquity? for
now shall I sleep in the dust; and Thou shalt
seek me in the morning, but I shall not be

Job 7:19-21

Do not condemn me; show me wherefore Thou
contendest with me. Is it good unto Thee that
Thou shouldest oppress, that Thou shouldest
despise the Work of Thine Hands, and shine
upon the counsel of the wicked? Hast Thou
eyes of flesh? or seest Thou as man seeth?

Job 10:2-4

Are Thy Days as the days of man? are Thy   Job 10:5-9
Years as man's days, That Thou inquirest after
mine iniquity, and searchest after my sin?
Thou knowest that I am not wicked; and there
is none that can deliver out of Thine Hand.
Thine Hands have made me and fashioned me
together round about; yet Thou dost destroy
me. Remember, I beseech Thee, that Thou hast
made me as the clay; and wilt Thou bring me
into dust again?

Hast Thou not poured me out as milk, and   Job 10:10-11
curdled me like cheese? Thou hast clothed me
with skin and flesh, and hast fenced me with
bones and sinews

Thou hast granted me life and favour, and Thy   Job 10:12-13
Visitation hath preserved my spirit. And these
things hast Thou hid in Thine Heart: I know
that this is with Thee

If I sin, then Thou markest me, and Thou   Job 10:14-17
wilt not acquit me from mine iniquity. If I be
wicked, woe unto me; and if I be righteous,
yet will I not lift up my head. I am full of
confusion; therefore see Thou mine affliction;
For it increaseth. Thou huntest me as a
fierce lion: and again Thou showest Thyself
marvellous upon me. Thou renewest Thy
Witnesses against me, and increasest Thine
Indignation upon me; changes and war are
against me

Wherefore then hast Thou brought me forth out of the womb? Oh that I had given up the ghost, and no eye had seen me! I should have been as though I had not been; I should have been carried from the womb to the grave. Are not my days few? cease then, and let me alone, that I may take comfort a little, Before I go whence I shall not return, even to the land of darkness and the shadow of death; A land of darkness, as darkness itself; and of the shadow of death, without any order, and where the light is as darkness

Job 10:18-22

Wherefore hidest Thou Thy Face, and holdest me for Thine Enemy? Wilt Thou break a leaf driven to and fro? and wilt Thou pursue the dry stubble? For Thou writest bitter things against me, and makest me to possess the iniquities of my youth. Thou puttest my feet also in the stocks, and lookest narrowly unto all my paths; Thou settest a print upon the heels of my feet. And he, as a rotten thing, consumeth, as a garment that is motheaten

Job 13:24-28

Man that is born of a woman is of few days and full of trouble. He cometh forth like a flower, and is cut down: he fleeth also as a shadow, and continueth not. And dost Thou open Thine Eyes upon such an one, and bringest me into judgment with Thee? Who can bring a clean thing out of an unclean? not one. Seeing his days are determined, the number of his months are with Thee, Thou hast appointed his bounds that he cannot pass; Turn from him, that he may rest, till he shall accomplish, as an hireling, his day

Job 14:1-6

For there is hope of a tree, if it be cut down,   Job 14:7-10
that it will sprout again, and that the tender
branch thereof will not cease. Though the root
thereof wax old in the earth, and the stock
thereof die in the ground; Yet through the scent
of water it will bud, and bring forth boughs like
a plant. But man dieth, and wasteth away: yea,
man giveth up the ghost, and where is he?

As the waters fail from the sea, and the flood   Job 14:11-12
decayeth and drieth up: So man lieth down,
and riseth not: till the heavens be no more, they
shall not awake, nor be raised out of their sleep

O that Thou wouldest hide me in the grave,   Job 14:13-14
that Thou wouldest keep me secret, until Thy
Wrath be past, that Thou wouldest appoint me
a set time, and remember me! If a man die, shall
he live again? all the days of my appointed time
will I wait, till my change come

Thou shalt call, and I will answer Thee: Thou   Job 14:15-17
wilt have a desire to the Work of Thine Hands.
For now Thou numberest my steps: dost Thou
not watch over my sin? My transgression is sealed
up in a bag, and Thou sewest up mine iniquity

And surely the mountain falling cometh to   Job 14:18-22
nought, and the rock is removed out of his
place. The waters wear the stones: Thou
washest away the things which grow out of the
dust of the earth; and Thou destroyest the hope
of man. Thou prevailest for ever against him,
and he passeth: Thou changest his countenance,
and sendest him away. His sons come to
honour, and he knoweth it not; and they are
brought low, but he perceiveth it not of them.
But his flesh upon him shall have pain, and his
soul within him shall mourn

But now He hath made me weary: Thou hast made desolate all my company. And Thou hast filled me with wrinkles, which is a witness against me: and my leanness rising up in me beareth witness to my face

Job 16:7-8

Lay down now, put me in a surety with Thee; who is he that will strike hands with me? For Thou hast hid their heart from understanding: therefore shalt Thou not exalt them. He that speaketh flattery to his friends, even the eyes of his children shall fail

Job 17:3-5

I cry unto Thee, and Thou dost not hear me: I stand up, and Thou regardest me not. Thou art become cruel to me: with Thy Strong Hand Thou opposest Thyself against me. Thou liftest me up to the wind; Thou causest me to ride upon it, and dissolvest my substance. For I know that Thou wilt bring me to death, and to the house appointed for all living

Job 30:20-23

Howbeit he will not stretch out his hand to the grave, though they cry in his destruction. Did not I weep for him that was in trouble? was not my soul grieved for the poor? When I looked for good, then evil came unto me: and when I waited for light, there came darkness

Job 30:24-26

My bowels boiled, and rested not: the days of affliction prevented me. I went mourning without the sun: I stood up, and I cried in the congregation

Job 30:27-28

Behold, I am vile; what shall I answer Thee? I will lay mine hand upon my mouth. Once have I spoken; but I will not answer: yea, twice; but I will proceed no further

Job 40:4-5

I know that Thou canst do every thing, and that   Job 42:2-6
no thought can be withholden from Thee. Who
is he that hideth counsel without knowledge?
therefore have I uttered that I understood not;
things too wonderful for me, which I knew
not. Hear, I beseech Thee, and I will speak: I
will demand of Thee, and declare Thou unto
me. I have heard of Thee by the hearing of the
ear: but now mine eye seeth Thee. Wherefore I
abhor myself, and repent in dust and ashes

Hear me when I call, O God of my   Psalm 4:1
righteousness: Thou hast enlarged me when I
was in distress; have mercy upon me, and hear
my prayer

There be many that say, Who will show us any   Psalm 4:6
good? LORD, lift Thou up the Light of Thy
Countenance upon us

Thou hast put gladness in my heart, more than in   Psalm 4:7
the time that their corn and their wine increased

I will both lay me down in peace, and sleep: for   Psalm 4:8
Thou, LORD, only makest me dwell in safety

Give ear to my words, O LORD, consider my   Psalm 5:1-3
meditation. Hearken unto the voice of my cry,
my King, and my God: for unto Thee will I
pray. My voice shalt Thou hear in the morning,
O LORD; in the morning will I direct my
prayer unto Thee, and will look up

For Thou art not a God that hath pleasure   Psalm 5:4-6
in wickedness: neither shall evil dwell with
Thee. The foolish shall not stand in Thy Sight:
Thou hatest all workers of iniquity. Thou shalt
destroy them that speak leasing: The LORD
will abhor the bloody and deceitful man

But as for me, I will come into Thy House in   Psalm 5:7
the multitude of Thy Mercy: and in Thy Fear
will I worship toward Thy Holy Temple

Lead me, O LORD, in Thy Righteousness   Psalm 5:8-10
because of mine enemies; make Thy Way straight
before my face. For there is no faithfulness in
their mouth; their inward part is very wickedness;
their throat is an open sepulchre; they flatter with
their tongue. Destroy Thou them, O God; let
them fall by their own counsels; cast them out
in the multitude of their transgressions; for they
have rebelled against Thee

But let all those that put their trust in Thee   Psalm 5:11-12
rejoice: let them ever shout for joy, because
Thou defendest them: let them also that love
Thy Name be joyful in Thee. For Thou,
LORD, wilt bless the righteous; with favour
wilt Thou compass him as with a shield

O LORD my God, in Thee do I put my trust: Psalm 7:1-2
save me from all them that persecute me, and
deliver me: Lest he tear my soul like a lion,
rending it in pieces, while there is none to
deliver

O LORD my God, If I have done this; if there   Psalm 7:3-5
be iniquity in my hands; If I have rewarded
evil unto him that was at peace with me; (yea,
I have delivered him that without cause is mine
enemy:) Let the enemy persecute my soul, and
take it; yea, let him tread down my life upon
the earth, and lay mine honour in the dust

Arise, O LORD, in Thine Anger, lift up   Psalm 7:6
Thyself because of the rage of mine enemies:
and awake for me to the judgment that Thou
hast commanded

So shall the congregation of the people compass   Psalm 7:7-8
Thee about: for their sakes therefore return
Thou on high. The LORD shall judge the
people: judge me, O LORD, according to my
righteousness, and according to mine integrity
that is in me

Oh let the wickedness of the wicked come to   Psalm 7:9
an end; but establish the just: for the righteous
God trieth the hearts and reins

LORD, who shall abide in Thy Tabernacle?   Psalm 15:1-5
who shall dwell in Thy Holy Hill? He that
walketh uprightly, and worketh righteousness,
and speaketh the truth in his heart. He that
backbiteth not with his tongue, nor doeth evil
to his neighbour, nor taketh up a reproach
against his neighbour. In whose eyes a vile
person is contemned; but he honoureth them
that fear The LORD. He that sweareth to his
own hurt, and changeth not. He that putteth
not out his money to usury, nor taketh reward
against the innocent. He that doeth these things
shall never be moved

Hear the right, O LORD, attend unto my cry,   Psalm 17:1-3
give ear unto my prayer, that goeth not out of
feigned lips. Let my sentence come forth from
Thy Presence; let Thine Eyes behold the things
that are equal. Thou hast proved mine heart;
Thou hast visited me in the night; Thou hast
tried me, and shalt find nothing; I am purposed
that my mouth shall not transgress

Concerning the works of men, by the Word of   Psalm 17:4-5
Thy Lips I have kept me from the paths of the
destroyer. Hold up my goings in Thy Paths,
that my footsteps slip not

I have called upon Thee, for Thou wilt hear   Psalm 17:6
me, O God: incline Thine Ear unto me, and
hear my speech

Show Thy Marvellous Lovingkindness, O   Psalm 17:7
Thou that savest by Thy Right Hand them
which put their trust in Thee from those that
rise up against them

Keep me as the apple of the eye, hide me under   Psalm 17:8-12
the Shadow of Thy Wings, From the wicked
that oppress me, from my deadly enemies, who
compass me about. They are inclosed in their
own fat: with their mouth they speak proudly.
They have now compass sed us in our steps:
they have set their eyes bowing down to the
earth; Like as a lion that is greedy of his prey,
and as it were a young lion lurking in secret
places

Arise, O LORD, disappoint him, cast him   Psalm 17:13-15
down: deliver my soul from the wicked, which
is Thy Sword: From men which are Thy Hand,
O LORD, from men of the world, which have
their portion in this life, and whose belly Thou
fillest with Thy Hid Treasure: they are full of
children, and leave the rest of their substance to
their babes. As for me, I will behold Thy Face
in righteousness: I shall be satisfied, when I
awake, with Thy Likeness

The Law of the LORD is perfect, converting   Psalm 19:7-13
the soul: the Testimony of The LORD is
sure, making wise the simple. The Statutes
of The LORD are right, rejoicing the heart:
the Commandment of The LORD is pure,
enlightening the eyes. The fear of The LORD
is clean, enduring for ever: the Judgments of
The LORD are true and righteous altogether.
More to be desired are They than gold, yea,
than much fine gold: sweeter also than honey
and the honeycomb. Moreover by Them is Thy
Servant warned: and in keeping of Them there
is great reward. Who can understand his errors?
cleanse Thou me from secret faults. Keep back
Thy Servant also from presumptuous sins; let
them not have dominion over me: then shall
I be upright, and I shall be innocent from the
great transgression

Let the words of my mouth, and the meditation   Psalm 19:14
of my heart, be acceptable in Thy Sight, O
LORD, my strength, and my redeemer

The LORD is my shepherd; I shall not want.   Psalm 23:1-6
He maketh me to lie down in green pastures:
He leadeth me beside the still waters. He
restoreth my soul: He leadeth me in the paths
of righteousness for His Name's Sake. Yea,
though I walk through the valley of the shadow
of death, I will fear no evil: for Thou art with
me; Thy Rod and Thy Staff They comfort
me. Thou preparest a table before me in the
presence of mine enemies: Thou anointest my
head with oil; my cup runneth over. Surely
goodness and mercy shall follow me all the days
of my life: and I will dwell in the house of The
LORD for ever

Judge me, O LORD; for I have walked in mine integrity: I have trusted also in The LORD; therefore I shall not slide. Examine me, O LORD, and prove me; try my reins and my heart. For Thy Lovingkindness is before mine eyes: and I have walked in Thy Truth. I have not sat with vain persons, neither will I go in with dissemblers. I have hated the congregation of evil doers; and will not sit with the wicked. I will wash mine hands in innocency: so will I compass Thine Altar, O LORD: That I may publish with the voice of thanksgiving, and tell of all Thy Wondrous Works	Psalm 26:1-7
LORD, I have loved the Habitation of Thy House, and the place where Thine Honour dwelleth	Psalm 26:8
Gather not my soul with sinners, nor my life with bloody men: In whose hands is mischief, and their right hand is full of bribes. But as for me, I will walk in mine integrity: redeem me, and be merciful unto me. My foot standeth in an even place: in the congregations will I bless The LORD	Psalm 26:9-12
When Thou saidst, Seek ye My Face; my heart said unto Thee, Thy Face, LORD, will I seek	Psalm 27:8
Hide not Thy Face far from me; put not Thy Servant away in anger: Thou hast been my help; leave me not, neither forsake me, O God of my salvation	Psalm 27:9
When my father and my mother forsake me, then The LORD will take me up	Psalm 27:10
Teach me Thy Way, O LORD, and lead me in a plain path, because of mine enemies	Psalm 27:11

Deliver me not over unto the will of mine enemies: for false witnesses are risen up against me, and such as breathe out cruelty. I had fainted, unless I had believed to see the Goodness of The LORD in the land of the living. Wait on The LORD: be of good courage, and He shall strengthen thine heart: wait, I say, on The LORD

Psalm 27:12-14

In Thee, O LORD, do I put my trust; let me never be ashamed: deliver me in Thy Righteousness

Psalm 31:1

Bow down Thine Ear to me; deliver me speedily: be Thou my strong rock, for an house of defence to save me. For Thou art my rock and my fortress; therefore for Thy Name's Sake lead me, and guide me

Psalm 31:2-3

Pull me out of the net that they have laid privily for me: for Thou art my strength. Into Thine Hand I commit my spirit: Thou hast redeemed me, O LORD God of truth

Psalm 31:4-5
[Luke 23:46]

I have hated them that regard lying vanities: but I trust in The LORD

Psalm 31:6

I will be glad and rejoice in Thy Mercy: for Thou hast considered my trouble; Thou hast known my soul in adversities; And hast not shut me up into the hand of the enemy: Thou hast set my feet in a large room

Psalm 31:7-8

Have mercy upon me, O LORD, for I am in
trouble: mine eye is consumed with grief, yea,
my soul and my belly. For my life is spent with
grief, and my years with sighing: my strength
faileth because of mine iniquity, and my bones
are consumed. I was a reproach among all mine
enemies, but especially among my neighbours,
and a fear to mine acquaintance: they that did see
me without fled from me. I am forgotten as a dead
man out of mind: I am like a broken vessel. For I
have heard the slander of many: fear was on every
side: while they took counsel together against me,
they devised to take away my life. But I trusted in
Thee, O LORD: I said, Thou art my God

Psalm 31:9-14

My times are in Thy Hand: deliver me from
the hand of mine enemies, and from them that
persecute me

Psalm 31:15

Make Thy Face to shine upon Thy Servant:
save me for Thy Mercies' Sake

Psalm 31:16

Let me not be ashamed, O LORD; for I have
called upon Thee: let the wicked be ashamed,
and let them be silent in the grave

Psalm 31:17

Let the lying lips be put to silence; which speak
grievous things proudly and contemptuously
against the righteous

Psalm 31:18

Oh how great is Thy Goodness, which Thou
hast laid up for them that fear Thee; which
Thou hast wrought for them that trust in Thee
before the sons of men!

Psalm 31:19

Thou shalt hide them in the secret of Thy
Presence from the pride of man: Thou shalt
keep them secretly in a pavilion from the strife
of tongues

Psalm 31:20

Blessed be The LORD: for He hath shown   Psalm 31:21-22
me His Marvellous Kindness in a strong city.
For I said in my haste, I am cut off from before
Thine Eyes: nevertheless Thou heardest the
voice of my supplications when I cried unto
Thee

O love the LORD, all ye His Saints: for The   Psalm 31:23-24
LORD preserveth the faithful, and plentifully
rewardeth the proud doer. Be of good courage,
and He shall strengthen your heart, all ye that
hope in The LORD

O LORD, rebuke me not in Thy Wrath: neither   Psalm 38:1-5
chasten me in Thy Hot Displeasure. For Thine
Arrows stick fast in me, and Thy Hand presseth
me sore. There is no soundness in my flesh
because of Thine Anger; neither is there any
rest in my bones because of my sin. For mine
iniquities are gone over mine head: as an heavy
burden they are too heavy for me. My wounds
stink and are corrupt because of my foolishness

I am troubled; I am bowed down greatly; I   Psalm 38:6-8
go mourning all the day long. For my loins
are filled with a loathsome disease: and there
is no soundness in my flesh. I am feeble and
sore broken: I have roared by reason of the
disquietness of my heart

Lord, all my desire is before Thee; and my   Psalm 38:9-12
groaning is not hid from Thee. My heart
panteth, my strength faileth me: as for the light
of mine eyes, it also is gone from me. My lovers
and my friends stand aloof from my sore; and
my kinsmen stand afar off. They also that seek
after my life lay snares for me: and they that
seek my hurt speak mischievous things, and
imagine deceits all the day long

But I, as a deaf man, heard not; and I was as a dumb man that openeth not his mouth. Thus I was as a man that heareth not, and in whose mouth are no reproofs. For in Thee, O LORD, do I hope: Thou wilt hear, O Lord my God. For I said, Hear me, lest otherwise they should rejoice over me: when my foot slippeth, they magnify themselves against me. For I am ready to halt, and my sorrow is continually before me	Psalm 38:13-17
For I will declare mine iniquity; I will be sorry for my sin	Psalm 38:18
But mine enemies are lively, and they are strong: and they that hate me wrongfully are multiplied. They also that render evil for good are mine adversaries; because I follow the thing that good is	Psalm 38:19-20
Forsake me not, O LORD: O my God, be not far from me. Make haste to help me, O Lord my salvation	Psalm 38:21-22
I said, I will take heed to my ways, that I sin not with my tongue: I will keep my mouth with a bridle, while the wicked is before me. I was dumb with silence, I held my peace, even from good; and my sorrow was stirred. My heart was hot within me, while I was musing the fire burned: then spake I with my tongue, LORD, make me to know mine end, and the measure of my days, what it is: that I may know how frail I am. Behold, Thou hast made my days as an handbreadth; and mine age is as nothing before Thee: verily every man at his best state is altogether vanity	Psalm 39:1-5
Surely every man walketh in a vain show: surely they are disquieted in vain: he heapeth up riches, and knoweth not who shall gather them	Psalm 39:6

And now, Lord, what wait I for? my hope is in Thee | Psalm 39:7

Deliver me from all my transgressions: make me not the reproach of the foolish | Psalm 39:8

I was dumb, I opened not my mouth; because Thou didst it. Remove Thy Stroke away from me: I am consumed by the Blow of Thine Hand. When Thou with rebukes dost correct man for iniquity, Thou makest his beauty to consume away like a moth: surely every man is vanity | Psalm 39:9-11

Hear my prayer, O LORD, and give ear unto my cry; hold not Thy Peace at my tears: for I am a stranger with Thee, and a sojourner, as all my fathers were | Psalm 39:12

O spare me, that I may recover strength, before I go hence, and be no more | Psalm 39:13

As the hart panteth after the water brooks, so panteth my soul after Thee, O God | Psalm 42:1

O my God, my soul is cast down within me: therefore will I remember Thee from the land of Jordan, and of the Hermonites, from the hill Mizar | Psalm 42:6

Deep calleth unto deep at the noise of Thy Waterspouts: all Thy Waves and Thy Billows are gone over me | Psalm 42:7 [Jonah 2:3]

But Thou hast cast off, and put us to shame; and goest not forth with our armies | Psalm 44:9

Thou makest us to turn back from the enemy: and they which hate us spoil for themselves | Psalm 44:10

Thou hast given us like sheep appointed for
meat; and hast scattered us among the heathen

Psalm 44:11

Thou sellest Thy people for nought, and dost
not increase Thy Wealth by their price

Psalm 44:12

Thou makest us a reproach to our neighbours,
a scorn and a derision to them that are round
about us

Psalm 44:13

Thou makest us a byword among the heathen, a
shaking of the head among the people

Psalm 44:14

My confusion is continually before me, and
the shame of my face hath covered me, For the
voice of him that reproacheth and blasphemeth;
by reason of the enemy and avenger

Psalm 44:15-16

All this is come upon us; yet have we not
forgotten Thee, neither have we dealt falsely in
Thy Covenant

Psalm 44:17

Our heart is not turned back, neither have our
steps declined from Thy Way; though Thou
hast sore broken us in the place of dragons, and
covered us with the shadow of death

Psalm 44:18-19

If we have forgotten the Name of our God, or
stretched out our hands to a strange god; shall
not God search this out? For He knoweth the
secrets of the heart

Psalm 44:20-21

Yea, for Thy Sake are we killed all the day
long; we are counted as sheep for the slaughter

Psalm 44:22

Awake, why sleepest Thou, O Lord? Arise, cast
us not off for ever

Psalm 44:23

Wherefore hidest Thou Thy Face, and   Psalm 44:24
forgettest our affliction and our oppression?

For our soul is bowed down to the dust; our   Psalm 44:25
belly cleaveth unto the earth

Arise for our help, and redeem us for Thy   Psalm 44:26
Mercies' Sake

I will praise Thee for ever, because Thou hast Psalm 52:9
done it: and I will wait on Thy Name; for it is
good before Thy Saints

Give ear to my prayer, O God; and hide not   Psalm 55:1
Thyself from my supplication

Attend unto me, and hear me: I mourn in my   Psalm 55:2-3
complaint, and make a noise; because of the
voice of the enemy, because of the oppression of
the wicked: for they cast iniquity upon me, and
in wrath they hate me

My heart is sore pained within me: and the   Psalm 55:4
terrors of death are fallen upon me

Fearfulness and trembling are come upon me,   Psalm 55:5
and horror hath overwhelmed me

And I said, Oh that I had wings like a dove!   Psalm 55:6-8
for then would I fly away, and be at rest. Lo,
then would I wander far off, and remain in the
wilderness. Selah. I would hasten my escape
from the windy storm and tempest

Destroy, O Lord, and divide their tongues: Psalm 55:9-11
for I have seen violence and strife in the city.
Day and night they go about it upon the walls
thereof: mischief also and sorrow are in the
midst of it. Wickedness is in the midst thereof:
deceit and guile depart not from her streets

But Thou, O God, shalt bring them down into   Psalm 55:23
the pit of destruction: bloody and deceitful men
shall not live out half their days; but I will trust
in Thee

Be merciful unto me, O God: for man would   Psalm 56:1
swallow me up: he fighting daily oppresseth me

Mine enemies would daily swallow me up: for   Psalm 56:2
they be many that fight against me, O Thou
Most High

What time I am afraid, I will trust in Thee   Psalm 56:3

In God I will praise His Word, in God I have   Psalm 56:4-7
put my trust; I will not fear what flesh can
do unto me. Every day they wrest my words:
all their thoughts are against me for evil.
They gather themselves together, they hide
themselves, they mark my steps, when they wait
for my soul. Shall they escape by iniquity? in
Thine Anger cast down the people, O God

Thou tellest my wanderings: put Thou my tears   Psalm 56:8
into Thy Bottle: are they not in Thy Book?

When I cry unto Thee, then shall mine enemies   Psalm 56:9
turn back: this I know, for God is for me

In God will I praise His Word: in The LORD   Psalm 56:10
will I praise His Word

In God have I put my trust: I will not be afraid   Psalm 56:11
what man can do unto me

Thy Vows are upon me, O God: I will render   Psalm 56:12-13
praises unto Thee. For Thou hast delivered my
soul from death: will not Thou deliver my feet
from falling, that I may walk before God in the
light of the living?

O God, Thou hast cast us off, Thou hast   Psalm 60:1-4
scattered us, Thou hast been displeased; O
turn Thyself to us again. Thou hast made the
earth to tremble; Thou hast broken it: heal
the breaches thereof; for it shaketh. Thou hast
shown Thy People hard things: Thou hast
made us to drink the wine of astonishment.
Thou hast given a banner to them that fear
Thee, that it may be displayed because of the
truth

That Thy Beloved may be delivered; save with   Psalm 60:5
Thy Right Hand, and hear me

Who will bring me into the strong city? who   Psalm 60:9-12
will lead me into Edom? Wilt not Thou, O
God, which hadst cast us off? and Thou, O
God, which didst not go out with our armies?
Give us help from trouble: for vain is the
help of man. Through our God we shall do
valiantly: for He it is that shall tread down our
enemies.

God hath spoken once; twice have I heard this;   Psalm 62:11-12
that power belongeth unto God. Also unto
Thee, O Lord, belongeth mercy: for Thou
renderst to every man according to his work

O God, Thou art my God, early will I seek   Psalm 63:1-2
Thee: my soul thirsteth for Thee, my flesh
longeth for Thee in a dry and thirsty land,
where no water is; To see Thy Power and Thy
Glory, so as I have seen Thee in the sanctuary

Because Thy Lovingkindness is better than life,   Psalm 63:3-4
my lips shall praise Thee. Thus will I bless Thee
while I live: I will lift up my hands in Thy
Name

My soul shall be satisfied as with marrow and   Psalm 63:5-6
fatness; and my mouth shall praise Thee with
joyful lips: When I remember Thee upon my
bed, and meditate on Thee in the night watches

Because Thou hast been my help, therefore in   Psalm 63:7
the shadow of Thy Wings will I rejoice

My soul followeth hard after Thee: Thy Right   Psalm 63:8
Hand upholdeth me

Hear my voice, O God, in my prayer: preserve   Psalm 64:1
my life from fear of the enemy

Hide me from the secret counsel of the wicked;   Psalm 64:2-4
from the insurrection of the workers of
iniquity: Who whet their tongue like a sword,
and bend their bows to shoot their arrows, even
bitter words: That they may shoot in secret at
the perfect: suddenly do they shoot at him, and
fear not

Save me, O God; for the waters are come in   Psalm 69:1-3
unto my soul. I sink in deep mire, where there
is no standing: I am come into deep waters,
where the floods overflow me. I am weary of
my crying: my throat is dried: mine eyes fail
while I wait for my God

They that hate me without cause are more than   Psalm 69:4-5
the hairs of mine head: they that would destroy
me, being mine enemies wrongfully, are
mighty; then I restored that which I took not
away. O God, Thou knowest my foolishness;
and my sins are not hid from Thee

Let not them that wait on Thee, O Lord GOD   Psalm 69:6-7
of Hosts, be ashamed for my sake: let not those
that seek Thee be confounded for my sake,
O God of Israel. Because for Thy Sake I have
borne reproach; shame hath covered my face

I am become a stranger unto my brethren, and   Psalm 69:8-9
an alien unto my mother's children. For the   [John 2:17b]
zeal of Thine House hath eaten me up; and the
reproaches of them that reproached Thee are
fallen upon me

When I wept, and chastened my soul with   Psalm 69:10-12
fasting, that was to my reproach. I made
sackcloth also my garment; and I became a
proverb to them. They that sit in the gate speak
against me; and I was the song of the drunkards

But as for me, my prayer is unto Thee, O   Psalm 69:13-15
LORD, in an acceptable time: O God, in the
multitude of Thy Mercy hear me, in the truth
of Thy Salvation. Deliver me out of the mire,
and let me not sink: let me be delivered from
them that hate me, and out of the deep waters.
Let not the waterflood overflow me, neither let
the deep swallow me up, and let not the pit shut
her mouth upon me

Hear me, O LORD; for Thy Lovingkindness is good: turn unto me according to the multitude of Thy Tender Mercies. And hide not Thy Face from Thy Servant; for I am in trouble: hear me speedily   Psalm 69:16-17

Draw nigh unto my soul, and redeem it: deliver me because of mine enemies   Psalm 69:18

Thou hast known my reproach, and my shame, and my dishonour: mine adversaries are all before Thee   Psalm 69:19

Reproach hath broken my heart; and I am full of heaviness: and I looked for some to take pity, but there was none; and for comforters, but I found none   Psalm 69:20

They gave Me also gall for My Meat; and in My Thirst they gave Me vinegar to drink   Psalm 69:21

Let their table become a snare before them: and that which should have been for their welfare, let it become a trap   Psalm 69:22

Let their eyes be darkened, that they see not; and make their loins continually to shake   Psalm 69:23

Pour out Thine Indignation upon them, and let Thy Wrathful Anger take hold of them   Psalm 69:24

Let their habitation be desolate; and let none dwell in their tents. For they persecute Him whom Thou hast smitten; and they talk to the grief of those whom Thou hast wounded   Psalm 69:25-26 [Acts 1:20a]

Add iniquity unto their iniquity: and let them
not come into Thy Righteousness. Let them be
blotted out of the book of the living, and not be
written with the righteous. But I am poor and
sorrowful: let Thy Salvation, O God, set me up
on high

Psalm 69:27–29

Give the king Thy Judgments, O God, and
Thy Righteousness unto the king's son. He
shall judge Thy People with righteousness, and
Thy Poor with judgment. The mountains shall
bring peace to the people, and the little hills,
by righteousness. He shall judge the poor of the
people, he shall save the children of the needy,
and shall break in pieces the oppressor. They
shall fear Thee as long as the sun and moon
endure, throughout all generations

Psalm 72:1–5

And he shall live, and to him shall be given of
the gold of Sheba: prayer also shall be made for
him continually; and daily shall he be praised.
There shall be an handful of corn in the earth
upon the top of the mountains; the fruit thereof
shall shake like Lebanon: and they of the
city shall flourish like grass of the earth. His
name shall endure for ever: his name shall be
continued as long as the sun: and men shall be
blessed in him: all nations shall call him blessed

Psalm 72:15–17

If I say, I will speak thus; behold, I should
offend against the generation of Thy Children.
When I thought to know this, it was too
painful for me; Until I went into the sanctuary
of God; then understood I their end. Surely
Thou didst set them in slippery places: Thou
castedst them down into destruction. How are
they brought into desolation, as in a moment!
they are utterly consumed with terrors

Psalm 73:15–19

As a dream when one awaketh; so, O Lord, when Thou awakest, Thou shalt despise their image — Psalm 73:20

Thus my heart was grieved, and I was pricked in my reins. So foolish was I, and ignorant: I was as a beast before Thee. Nevertheless I am continually with Thee: Thou hast holden me by my right hand — Psalm 73:21-23

Thou shalt guide me with Thy Counsel, and afterward receive me to glory. Whom have I in heaven but Thee? and there is none upon earth that I desire beside Thee — Psalm 73:24-25

My flesh and my heart faileth: but God is the strength of my heart, and my portion for ever — Psalm 73:26

For, lo, they that are far from Thee shall perish: Thou hast destroyed all them that go a-whoring from Thee. But it is good for me to draw near to God: I have put my trust in The Lord GOD, that I may declare all Thy Works — Psalm 73:27-28

O God, why hast Thou cast us off for ever? why doth Thine Anger smoke against the sheep of Thy Pasture? Remember Thy Congregation, which Thou hast purchased of old; the rod of Thine Inheritance, which Thou hast redeemed; this mount Zion, wherein Thou hast dwelt — Psalm 74:1-2

Lift up Thy Feet unto the perpetual desolations; even all that the enemy hath done wickedly in the sanctuary — Psalm 74:3

Thine Enemies roar in the midst of Thy Congregations; they set up their ensigns for signs — Psalm 74:4

A man was famuos according as he had lifted
up axes upon the thick trees. But now they
break down the carved work thereof at once
with axes and hammers. They have cast fire
into Thy Sanctuary, they have defiled by
casting down the dwellingplace of Thy Name
to the ground. They said in their hearts, Let us
destroy them together: they have burned up all
the synagogues of God in the land

Psalm 74:5-8

We see not our signs: there is no more any
prophet: neither is there among us any that
knoweth how long

Psalm 74:9

O God, how long shall the adversary reproach?
Shall the enemy blaspheme Thy Name for ever?
Why withdrawest Thou Thy Hand, even Thy
Right Hand? pluck it out of Thy Bosom

Psalm 74:10-11

For God is my King of old, working salvation
in the midst of the earth

Psalm 74:12

Thou didst divide the sea by Thy Strength;
Thou brakest the heads of the dragons in the
waters. Thou brakest the heads of leviathan in
pieces, and gavest him to be meat to the people
inhabiting the wilderness. Thou didst cleave the
fountain and the flood: Thou driedst up mighty
rivers

Psalm 74:13-15

The day is Thine, the night also is Thine: Thou
hast prepared the light and the sun. Thou hast
set all the borders of the earth: Thou hast made
summer and winter

Psalm 74:16-17

Remember this, that the enemy hath
reproached, O LORD, and that the foolish
people have blasphemed Thy Name

Psalm 74:18

O deliver not the soul of Thy Turtledoves unto the multitude of the wicked: forget not the congregation of Thy Poor for ever	Psalm 74:19
Have respect unto the covenant: for the dark places of the earth are full of the habitations of cruelty	Psalm 74:20
O let not the oppressed return ashamed: let the poor and needy praise Thy Name	Psalm 74:21
Arise, O God, plead Thine Own Cause: remember how the foolish man reproacheth Thee daily. Forget not the voice of Thine Enemies: the tumult of those that rise up against Thee increaseth continually	Psalm 74:22-23
Give ear, O Shepherd of Israel, Thou that leadest Joseph like a flock; Thou that dwellest between the cherubims, shine forth	Psalm 80:1
Before Ephraim and Benjamin and Manasseh stir up Thy Strength, and come and save us. Turn us again, O God, and cause Thy Face to shine; and we shall be saved	Psalm 80:2-3,7,19
O LORD God of Hosts, how long wilt Thou be angry against the prayer of Thy People? Thou feedest them with the bread of tears; and givest them tears to drink in great measure. Thou makest us a strife unto our neighbours: and our enemies laugh among themselves	Psalm 80:4-6
Turn us again, O God of Hosts, and cause Thy Face to shine; and we shall be saved	Psalm 80:7,3,19

Thou hast brought a vine out of Egypt: Thou hast cast out the heathen, and planted it. Thou preparedst room before it, and didst cause it to take deep root, and it filled the land. The hills were covered with the shadow of it, and the boughs thereof were like the goodly cedars. She sent out her boughs unto the sea, and her branches unto the river	Psalm 80:8-11
Why hast Thou then broken down her hedges, so that all they which pass by the way do pluck her? The boar out of the wood doth waste it, and the wild beast of the field doth devour it. Return, we beseech Thee, O God of Hosts: look down from heaven, and behold, and visit this vine; And the vineyard which Thy Right Hand hath planted, and the branch that Thou madest strong for Thyself	Psalm 80:12-15
It is burned with fire, it is cut down: they perish at the rebuke of Thy Countenance	Psalm 80:16
Let Thy Hand be upon the man of Thy Right Hand, upon the son of man whom Thou madest strong for Thyself	Psalm 80:17
So will not we go back from Thee: quicken us, and we will call upon Thy Name	Psalm 80:18
Turn us again, O LORD God of Hosts, cause Thy Face to shine; and we shall be saved	Psalm 80:19,3,7
Arise, O God, judge the earth: for Thou shalt inherit all nations	Psalm 82:8
O LORD God of my salvation, I have cried day and night before Thee	Psalm 88:1 [some of Jonah 2 throughout this Psalm]

Let my prayer come before Thee: incline Thine   Psalm 88:2-3
Ear unto my cry; For my soul is full of troubles:
and my life draweth nigh unto the grave

I am counted with them that go down into the   Psalm 88:4-5
pit: I am as a man that hath no strength: Free
among the dead, like the slain that lie in the
grave, whom Thou rememberest no more: and
they are cut off from Thy Hand

Thou hast laid me in the lowest pit, in darkness,   Psalm 88:6-7
in the deeps. Thy Wrath lieth hard upon me,
and Thou hast afflicted me with all Thy Waves

Thou hast put away mine acquaintenance far   Psalm 88:8
from me; Thou hast made me an abomination
unto them: I am shut up, and I cannot come
forth

Mine eye mourneth by reason of affliction: Psalm 88:9
LORD, I have called daily upon Thee, I have
stretched out my hands unto Thee

Wilt Thou show wonders to the dead? shall the   Psalm 88:10
dead arise and praise Thee?

Shall Thy Lovingkindness be declared in the   Psalm 88:11-12
grave? or Thy Faithfulness in destruction? Shall
Thy Wonders be known in the dark? and Thy
Righteousness in the land of forgetfulness?

But unto Thee have I cried, O LORD; and in   Psalm 88:13
the morning shall my prayer prevent Thee

LORD, why castest Thou off my soul? why   Psalm 88:14
hidest Thou Thy Face from me?

I am afflicted and ready to die from my youth   Psalm 88:15
up: while I suffer Thy Terrors I am distracted

Thy Fierce Wrath goeth over me; Thy Terrors   Psalm 88:16-17
have cut me off. They came round about me
daily like water; they compassed me about
together

Lover and friend hast Thou put far from me,   Psalm 88:18
and mine acquaintance into darkness

It is a good thing to give thanks unto The   Psalm 92:1-3
LORD, and to sing praises unto Thy Name, O
Most High: To show forth Thy Lovingkindness
in the morning, and Thy Faithfulness every
night, Upon an instrument of ten strings, and
upon the psaltery; upon the harp with a solemn
sound

For Thou, LORD, hast made me glad through   Psalm 92:4
Thy Work: I will triumph in the works of Thy
Hands

O LORD, how great are Thy Works! and Thy   Psalm 92:5
Thoughts are very deep

A brutish man knoweth not; neither doth a fool   Psalm 92:6-8
understand this. When the wicked spring as
the grass, and when all the workers of iniquity
do flourish; it is that they shall be destroyed
for ever: But Thou, LORD, art Most High for
evermore

For, lo, Thine Enemies, O LORD, for, lo,   Psalm 92:9-10
Thine Enemies shall perish; all the workers of
iniquity shall be scattered. But my horn shalt
Thou exalt like the horn of an unicorn: I shall
be anointed with fresh oil

Mine eye also shall see my desire on mine   Psalm 92:11
enemies, and mine ears shall hear my desire of
the wicked that rise up against me

The righteous shall flourish like the palm tree: Psalm 92:12-15
he shall grow like a cedar in Lebanon. Those
that be planted in the House of The LORD
shall flourish in the courts of our God. They
shall still bring forth fruit in old age; they
shall be fat and flourishing; To show that The
LORD is upright: He is my rock, and there is
no unrighteousness in Him

O LORD God, to Whom vengeance   Psalm 94:1-2
belongeth; O God, to Whom vengeance
belongeth, show Thyself. Lift up Thyself, Thou
Judge of the Earth: render a reward to the
proud

LORD, how long shall the wicked, how long   Psalm 94:3-4
shall the wicked triumph? How long shall they
utter and speak hard things? and all the workers
of iniquity boast themselves?

They break in pieces Thy People, O LORD,   Psalm 94:5-7
and afflict Thine Heritage. They slay the
widow and the stranger, and murder the
fatherless. Yet they say, The LORD shall not
see, neither shall The God of Jacob regard it

Blessed is the man whom Thou chastenest, O   Psalm 94:12-13
LORD, and teachest him out of Thy Law; That
Thou mayest give him rest from the days of
adversity, until the pit be digged for the wicked

For the LORD will not cast off His People,   Psalm 94:14-16
neither will He forsake His Inheritance. But
judgment shall return unto righteousness: and
all the upright in heart shall follow it. Who
will rise up for me against the evildoers? or
who will stand up for me against the workers of
iniquity?

Unless The LORD had been my help, my soul had almost dwelt in silence. When I said, My foot slippeth; Thy Mercy, O LORD, held me up

Psalm 94:17-18

In the multitude of my thoughts within me Thy Comforts delight my soul. Shall the throne of iniquity have fellowship with Thee, which frameth mischief by a law?

Psalm 94:19-20

I will sing of mercy and judgment: unto Thee, O LORD, will I sing

Psalm 101:1

I will behave myself wisely in a perfect way. O when wilt Thou come unto me? I will walk within my house with a perfect heart

Psalm 101:2

I will set no wicked thing before mine eyes: I hate the work of them that turn aside; it shall not cleave to me

Psalm 101:3

A froward heart shall depart from me: I will not know a wicked person

Psalm 101:4

Whoso privily slandereth his neighbour, him will I cut off: him that hath an high look and a proud heart will not I suffer

Psalm 101:5

Mine eyes shall be upon the faithful of the land, that they may dwell with me: he that walketh in a perfect way, he shall serve me

Psalm 101:6

He that worketh deceit shall not dwell within my house: he that telleth lies shall not tarry in my sight

Psalm 101:7

I will early destroy all the wicked of the land; that I may cut off all wicked doers from the city of The LORD

Psalm 101:8

Hear my prayer, O LORD, and let my cry
come unto Thee

Psalm 102:1

Hide not Thy Face from me in the day when I
am in trouble; incline Thine Ear unto me: in
the day when I call answer me speedily. For my
days are consumed like smoke, and my bones
are burned as an hearth

Psalm 102:2-3

My heart is smitten, and withered like grass; so
that I forget to eat my bread. By reason of the
voice of my groaning my bones cleave to my
skin

Psalm 102:4-5

I am like a pelican of the wilderness: I am
like an owl of the desert. I watch, and am as a
sparrow alone upon the house top

Psalm 102:6-7

Mine enemies reproach me all the day; and they
that are mad against me are sworn against me

Psalm 102:8

For I have eaten ashes like bread, and mingled
my drink with weeping, Because of Thine
Indignation and Thy Wrath: for Thou hast
lifted me up, and cast me down

Psalm 102:9-10

My days are like a shadow that declineth; and
I am withered like grass. But Thou, O LORD,
shalt endure for ever; and Thy Remembrance
unto all generations

Psalm 102:11-12

Thou shalt arise, and have mercy upon Zion:
for the time to favour her, yea, the set time, is
come. For Thy Servants take pleasure in her
stones, and favour the dust thereof

Psalm 102:13-14

So the heathen shall fear the Name of The
LORD, and all the kings of the earth Thy
Glory

Psalm 102:15

When The LORD shall build up Zion, He   Psalm 102:16-17
shall appear in His Glory. He will regard the
prayer of the destitute, and not despise their
prayer

This shall be written for the generation to   Psalm 102:18
come: and the people which shall be created
shall praise The LORD

For He hath looked down from the height of   Psalm 102:19-20
His Sanctuary; from heaven did The LORD
behold the earth; To hear the groaning of the
prisoner; to loose those that are appointed to
death

To declare the Name of The LORD in Zion,   Psalm 102:21-22
and His Praise in Jerusalem; When the people
are gathered together, and the kingdoms, to
serve The LORD

He weakened my strength in the way; He   Psalm 102:23-
shortened my days. I said, O my God, take me   24
not away in the midst of my days: Thy Years
are throughout all generations

Of old [And, Thou, LORD, in the beginning]   Psalm 102:25-
hast Thou laid the foundation of the earth: and   27 [Hebrews
the heavens are the Work[s] of Thy [Thine]   1:10-12]
Hands. They shall perish, but Thou shalt
endure [remainest]: yea,all of them [they all]
shall wax old like [as doth] a garment; [and] as
a vesture shalt Thou change [fold] them [up,]
and they shall be changed: but Thou art the
same, and Thy Years have no end [shall not fail]

The children of Thy Servants shall continue,   Psalm 102:28
and their seed shall be established before Thee

Hold not Thy Peace, O God of my praise; For the mouth of the wicked and the mouth of the deceitful are opened against me: they have spoken against me with a lying tongue	Psalm 109:1-2
They compassed me about also with words of hatred; and fought against me without a cause	Psalm 109:3
For my love they are my adversaries: but I give myself unto prayer	Psalm 109:4
And they have rewarded me evil for good, and hatred for my love	Psalm 109:5
But do Thou for me, O GOD The LORD, for Thy Name's Sake: because Thy Mercy is good, deliver Thou me	Psalm 109:21
For I am poor and needy, and my heart is wounded within me	Psalm 109:22
I am gone like the shadow when it declineth: I am tossed up and down as the locust	Psalm 109:23
My knees are weak through fasting; and my flesh faileth of fatness	Psalm 109:24
I became also a reproach unto them: when they looked upon me they shaked their heads	Psalm 109:25
Help me, O LORD my God: O save me according to Thy Mercy: That they may know that this is Thy Hand; that Thou LORD, hast done it	Psalm 109:26-27
Let them curse, but bless Thou: when they arise, let them be ashamed; but let Thy Servant rejoice	Psalm 109:28

Let mine adversaries be clothed with shame, and let them cover themselves with their own confusion, as with a mantle	Psalm 109:29
I will greatly praise The LORD with my mouth; yea, I will praise Him among the multitude. For He shall stand at the right hand of the poor, to save him from those that condemn his soul	Psalm 109:30-31

Blessed are the undefiled in the way, who walk in the Law of the LORD. Blessed are they that keep His Testimonies, and that seek Him with the whole heart. They also do no iniquity: they walk in His Ways	Psalm 119:1-3
Thou hast commanded us to keep Thy Precepts diligently	Psalm 119:4
O that my ways were directed to keep Thy Statutes! Then shall I not be ashamed, when I have respect unto all Thy Commandments	Psalm 119:5-6
I will praise Thee with uprightness of heart, when I shall have learned Thy Righteous Judgments	Psalm 119:7
I will keep Thy Statutes: O forsake me not utterly	Psalm 119:8
Wherewithal shall a young man cleanse His way? By taking heed thereto according to Thy Word	Psalm 119:9
With my whole heart have I sought Thee: O let me not wander from Thy Commandments	Psalm 119:10
Thy Word have I hid in mine heart, that I might not sin against Thee	Psalm 119:11

Blessed art Thou, O LORD: teach me Thy Statutes	Psalm 119:12
With my lips have I declared all the Judgments of Thy Mouth	Psalm 119:13
I have rejoiced in the way of Thy Testimonies, as much as in all riches	Psalm 119:14
I will meditate in Thy Precepts, and have respect unto Thy Ways	Psalm 119:15
I will delight myself in Thy Statutes: I will not forget Thy Word	Psalm 119:16
Deal bountifully with Thy Servant, that I may live, and keep Thy Word	Psalm 119:17
Open Thou mine eyes, that I may behold wondrous things out of Thy Law	Psalm 119:18
I am a stranger in the earth: hide not Thy Commandments from me	Psalm 119:19
My soul breaketh for the longing that it hath unto Thy Judgments at all times	Psalm 119:20
Thou hast rebuked the proud that are cursed, which do err from Thy Commandments	Psalm 119:21
Remove from me reproach and contempt; for I have kept Thy Testimonies	Psalm 119:22
Princes also did sit and speak against me: but Thy Servant did meditate in Thy Statutes	Psalm 119:23
Thy Testimonies also are my delight and my counsellors	Psalm 119:24

My soul cleaveth unto the dust: quicken Thou
me according to Thy Word

Psalm 119:25

I have declared my ways, and Thou heardest
me: teach me Thy Statutes

Psalm 119:26

Make me to understand the way of Thy
Precepts: so shall I talk of Thy Wondrous
Works

Psalm 119:27

My soul melteth for heaviness: strengthen Thou
me according unto Thy Word

Psalm 119:28

Remove from me the way of lying: and grant
me Thy Law graciously

Psalm 119:29

I have chosen the Way of Truth: Thy
Judgments have I laid before me

Psalm 119:30

I have stuck unto Thy Testimonies: O LORD,
put me not to shame

Psalm 119:31

I will run the way of Thy Commandments,
when Thou shalt enlarge my heart

Psalm 119:32

Teach me, O LORD, the way of Thy Statutes;
and I shall keep it unto the end

Psalm 119:33

Give me understanding, and I shall keep Thy
Law; yea, I shall observe it with my whole heart

Psalm 119:34

Make me to go in the path of Thy
Commandments; for therein do I delight

Psalm 119:35

Incline my heart unto Thy Testimonies, and
not to covetousness

Psalm 119:36

Turn away mine eyes from beholding vanity;
and quicken Thou me in Thy Way

Psalm 119:37

Stablish Thy Word unto Thy Servant, who is devoted to Thy Fear | Psalm 119:38

Turn away my reproach which I fear: for Thy Judgments are good | Psalm 119:39

Behold, I have longed after Thy Precepts: quicken me in Thy Righteousness | Psalm 119:40

Let Thy Mercies come also unto me, O LORD, even Thy Salvation, according to Thy Word. So shall I have wherewith to answer him that reproacheth me: for I trust in Thy Word | Psalm 119:41-42

And take not the Word of Truth utterly out of my mouth; for I have hoped in Thy Judgments | Psalm 119:43

So shall I keep Thy Law continually for ever and ever | Psalm 119:44

And I will walk at liberty: for I seek Thy Precepts | Psalm 119:45

I will speak of Thy Testimonies also before kings, and will not be ashamed | Psalm 119:46

And I will delight myself in Thy Commandments, which I have loved | Psalm 119:47

My hands also will I lift up unto Thy Commandments, which I have loved; and I will meditate in Thy Statutes | Psalm 119:48

Remember the Word unto Thy Servant, upon which Thou hast caused me to hope | Psalm 119:49

This is my comfort in my affliction: for Thy Word hath quickened me | Psalm 119:50

The proud have had me greatly in derision: yet   Psalm 119:51
have I not declined from Thy Law

I remembered Thy Judgments of old, O   Psalm 119:52
LORD; and have comforted myself

Horror hath taken hold upon me because of the   Psalm 119:53
wicked that forsake Thy Law

Thy Statutes have been my songs in the house   Psalm 119:54
of my pilgrimage

I have remembered Thy Name, O LORD, in   Psalm 119:55
the night, and have kept Thy Law

This I had, because I kept Thy Precepts   Psalm 119:56

Thou art my portion, O LORD: I have said   Psalm 119:57
that I would keep Thy Words

I entreated Thy Favour with my whole heart: Psalm 119:58
be merciful unto me according to Thy Word

I thought on my ways, and turned my feet unto   Psalm 119:59
Thy Testimonies

I made haste, and delayed not to keep Thy   Psalm 119:60
Commandments

The bands of the wicked have robbed me: but I   Psalm 119:61
have not forgotten Thy Law

At midnight I will rise to give thanks unto   Psalm 119:62
Thee because of Thy Righteous Judgments

I am a companion of all them that fear Thee,   Psalm 119:63
and of them that keep Thy Precepts

The earth, O LORD, is full of Thy Mercy: Psalm 119:64
teach me Thy Statutes

Thou hast dealt well with Thy Servant, O   Psalm 119:65
LORD, according unto Thy Word

Teach me good judgment and knowledge: for I   Psalm 119:66
have believed Thy Commandments

Before I was afflicted I went astray: but now   Psalm 119:67
have I kept Thy Word

Thou art good, and doest good; teach me Thy   Psalm 119:68
Statutes

The proud have forged a lie against me: but I   Psalm 119:69
will keep Thy Precepts with my whole heart

Their heart is as fat as grease; but I delight in   Psalm 119:70
Thy Law

It is good for me that I have been afflicted; that   Psalm 119:71
I might learn Thy Statutes

The Law of Thy Mouth is better unto me than   Psalm 119:72
thousands of gold and silver

Thy Hands have made me and fashioned me: Psalm 119:73
give me understanding, that I may learn Thy
Commandments

They that fear Thee will be glad when they see   Psalm 119:74
me; because I have hoped in Thy Word

I know, O LORD, that Thy Judgments are   Psalm 119:75
right, and that Thou in faithfulness hast
afflicted me

Let, I pray Thee, Thy Merciful Kindness be for my comfort, according to Thy Word unto Thy Servant
Psalm 119:76

Let Thy Tender Mercies come unto me, that I may live: for Thy Law is my delight
Psalm 119:77

Let the proud be ashamed; for they dealt perversely with me without a cause: but I will meditate in Thy Precepts
Psalm 119:78

Let those that fear Thee turn unto me, and those that have known Thy Testimonies
Psalm 119:79

Let my heart be sound in Thy Statutes; that I be not ashamed
Psalm 119:80

My soul fainteth for Thy Salvation: but I hope in Thy Word
Psalm 119:81

Mine eyes fail for Thy Word, saying, When wilt Thou comfort me?
Psalm 119:82

For I am become like a bottle in the smoke; yet do I not forget Thy Statutes
Psalm 119:83

How many are the days of Thy Servant? when wilt Thou execute judgment on them that persecute me?
Psalm 119:84

The proud have digged pits for me, which are not after Thy Law
Psalm 119:85

All Thy Commandments are faithful: they persecute me wrongfully; help Thou me
Psalm 119:86

They had almost consumed me upon earth; but I forsook not Thy Precepts
Psalm 119:87

Quicken me after Thy Lovingkindness; so shall I keep the Testimony of Thy Mouth	Psalm 119:88
For ever, O LORD, Thy Word is settled in heaven	Psalm 119:89
Thy Faithfulness is unto all generations: Thou hast established the earth, and it abideth	Psalm 119:90
They continue this day according to Thine Ordinances: for all are Thy Servants	Psalm 119:91
Unless Thy Law had been my delights, I should then have perished in mine affliction	Psalm 119:92
I will never forget Thy Precepts: for with Them Thou hast quickened me	Psalm 119:93
I am Thine, save me; for I have sought Thy Precepts	Psalm 119:94
Wicked, the wicked have waited for me to destroy me: but I will consider Thy Testimonies	Psalm 119:95
I have seen an end of all perfection: but Thy Commandment is exceeding broad	Psalm 119:96
O how love I Thy Law! It is my meditation all the day	Psalm 119:97
Thou through Thy Commandments hast made me wiser than mine enemies: for They are ever with me	Psalm 119:98
I have more understanding than all my teachers: for Thy Testimonies are my meditation	Psalm 119:99
I understand more than the ancients, because I keep Thy Precepts	Psalm 119:100

I have refrained my feet from every evil way,   Psalm 119:101
that I might keep Thy Word

I have not departed from Thy Judgments: for   Psalm 119:102
Thou hast taught me

How sweet are Thy Words unto my taste! yea,   Psalm 119:103
sweeter than honey to my mouth!

Through Thy Precepts I get understanding: Psalm 119:104
therefore I hate every false way

Thy Word is a lamp unto my feet, and a light   Psalm 119:105
unto my path

I have sworn, and I will perform it, that I will   Psalm 119:106
keep Thy Righteous Judgments

I am afflicted very much: quicken me, O   Psalm 119:107
LORD, according unto Thy Word

Accept, I beseech Thee, the freewill offerings   Psalm 119:108
of my mouth, O LORD, and teach me Thy
Judgments

My soul is continually in my hand: yet do I not   Psalm 119:109
forget Thy Law

The wicked have laid a snare for me: yet I erred   Psalm 119:110
not from Thy Precepts

Thy Testimonies have I taken as an heritage for   Psalm 119:111
ever: for They are the rejoicing of my heart

I have inclined mine heart to perform Thy   Psalm 119:112
Statutes always, even unto the end

I hate vain thoughts: but Thy Law do I love   Psalm 119:113

Thou art my hiding place and my shield: I hope in Thy Word	Psalm 119:114
Depart from me, ye evildoers: for I will keep the Commandments of my God	Psalm 119:115
Uphold me according unto Thy Word, that I may live: and let me not be ashamed of my hope	Psalm 119:116
Hold Thou me up, and I shall be safe: and I will have respect unto Thy Statutes continually	Psalm 119:117
Thou hast trodden down all them that err from Thy Statutes: for their deceit is falsehood	Psalm 119:118
Thou puttest away all the wicked of the earth like dross: therefore I love Thy Testimonies	Psalm 119:119
My flesh trembleth for fear of Thee; and I am afraid of Thy Judgments	Psalm 119:120
I have done judgment and justice: leave me not to mine oppressors	Psalm 119:121
Be surety for Thy Servant for good: let not the proud oppress me	Psalm 119:122
Mine eyes fail for Thy Salvation, and for the Word of Thy Righteousness	Psalm 119:123
Deal with Thy Servant according unto Thy Mercy, and teach me Thy Statutes	Psalm 119:124
I am Thy Servant; give me understanding, that I may know Thy Testimonies	Psalm 119:125
It is time for Thee, LORD, to work: for they have made void Thy Law	Psalm 119:126

Therefore I love Thy Commandments above
gold; yea, above fine gold. Therefore I esteem
all Thy Precepts concerning all things to be
right; and I hate every false way

Psalm 119:127-
128

Thy Testimonies are wonderful: therefore doth
my soul keep Them

Psalm 119:129

The entrance of Thy Words giveth light; it
giveth understanding unto the simple

Psalm 119:130

I opened my mouth, and panted: for I longed
for Thy Commandments

Psalm 119:131

Look Thou upon me, and be merciful unto me,
as Thou usest to do unto those that love Thy
Name

Psalm 119:132

Order my steps in Thy Word: and let not any
iniquity have dominion over me

Psalm 119:133

Deliver me from the oppression of man: so will
I keep Thy Precepts

Psalm 119:134

Make Thy Face to shine upon Thy Servant; and
teach me Thy Statutes

Psalm 119:135

Rivers of waters run down mine eyes, because
they keep not Thy Law

Psalm 119:136

Righteous art Thou, O LORD, and upright are
Thy Judgments

Psalm 119:137

Thy Testimonies that Thou hast commanded
are righteous and very faithful

Psalm 119:138

My zeal hath consumed me, because mine
enemies have forgotten Thy Words

Psalm 119:139

Thy Word is very pure: therefore Thy Servant   Psalm 119:140
loveth It

I am small and despised: yet do not I forget Thy   Psalm 119:141
Precepts

Thy Righteousness is an everlasting   Psalm 119:142
righteousness, and Thy Law is the truth

Trouble and anguish have taken hold on me: Psalm 119:143
yet Thy Commandments are my delights

The righteousness of Thy Testimonies is   Psalm 119:144
everlasting: give me understanding, and I shall
live

I cried with my whole heart; hear me, O   Psalm 119:145
LORD: I will keep Thy Statutes

I cried unto Thee; save me, and I shall keep   Psalm 119:146
Thy Testimonies

I prevented the dawning of the morning, and   Psalm 119:147
cried: I hoped in Thy Word

Mine eyes prevent the night watches, that I   Psalm 119:148
might meditate in Thy Word

Hear my voice according unto Thy   Psalm 119:149
Lovingkindness: O LORD, quicken me
according to Thy Judgment

They draw nigh that follow after mischief: they   Psalm 119:150
are far from Thy Law

Thou art near, O LORD; and all Thy   Psalm 119:151
Commandments are truth

Concerning Thy Testimonies, I have known of old that Thou hast founded Them for ever	Psalm 119:152
Consider mine affliction, and deliver me: for I do not forget Thy Law	Psalm 119:153
Plead my cause, and deliver me: quicken me according to Thy Word	Psalm 119:154
Salvation is far from the wicked: for they seek not Thy Statutes	Psalm 119:155
Great are Thy Tender Mercies, O LORD: quicken me according to Thy Judgments	Psalm 119:156
Many are my persecutors and mine enemies; yet do I not decline from Thy Testimonies	Psalm 119:157
I beheld the transgressors, and was grieved; because they kept not Thy Word	Psalm 119:158
Consider how I love Thy Precepts: quicken me, O LORD, according to Thy Lovingkindness	Psalm 119:159
Thy Word is true from the beginning: and every one of Thy Righteous Judgments endureth for ever	Psalm 119:160
Princes have persecuted me without a cause: but my heart standeth in awe of Thy Word	Psalm 119:161
I rejoice at Thy Word, as one that findeth great spoil	Psalm 119:162
I hate and abhor lying: but Thy Law do I love	Psalm 119:163
Seven times a day do I praise Thee because of Thy Righteous Judgments	Psalm 119:164

Great peace have they which love Thy Law: and nothing shall offend them	Psalm 119:165
LORD, I have hoped for Thy Salvation, and done Thy Commandments	Psalm 119:166
My soul hath kept Thy Testimonies; and I love Them exceedingly	Psalm 119:167
I have kept Thy Precepts and Thy Testimonies: for all my ways are before Thee	Psalm 119:168
Let my cry come near before Thee, O LORD: give me understanding according to Thy Word	Psalm 119:169
Let my supplication come before Thee: deliver me according to Thy Word	Psalm 119:170
My lips shall utter praise, when Thou hast taught me Thy Statutes	Psalm 119:171
My tongue shall speak of Thy Word: for all Thy Commandments are righteousness	Psalm 119:172
Let Thine Hand help me; for I have chosen Thy Precepts	Psalm 119:173
I have longed for Thy Salvation, O LORD; and Thy Law is my delight	Psalm 119:174
Let my soul live, and it shall praise Thee; and let Thy Judgments help me	Psalm 119:175
I have gone astray like a lost sheep; seek Thy Servant; for I do not forget Thy Commandments	Psalm 119:176
Unto Thee lift I up mine eyes, O Thou that dwellest in the heavens	Psalm 123:1

Behold, as the eyes of servants look unto the hand of their masters, and as the eyes of a maiden unto the hand of her mistress; so our eyes wait upon The LORD our God, until that He have mercy upon us	Psalm 123:2
Have mercy upon us, O LORD, have mercy upon us: for we are exceedingly filled with contempt. Our soul is exceedingly filled with the scorning of those that are at ease, and with the contempt of the proud	Psalm 123:3-4
LORD, my heart is not haughty, nor mine eyes lofty: neither do I exercise myself in great matters, or in things too high for me	Psalm 131:1
Surely I have behaved and quieted myself, as a child that is weaned of his mother: my soul is even as a weaned child	Psalm 131:2
O LORD, Thou hast searched me, and known me	Psalm 139:1
Thou knowest my downsitting and mine uprising, Thou understandest my thought afar off	Psalm 139:2
Thou compassest my path and my lying down, and art acquainted with all my ways	Psalm 139:3
For there is not a word in my tongue, but, lo, O LORD, Thou knowest it altogether	Psalm 139:4
Thou hast beset me behind and before, and laid Thine Hand upon me. Such knowledge is too wonderful for me; it is high, I cannot attain unto it	Psalm 139:5-6

Whither shall I go from Thy Spirit? or whither shall I flee from Thy Presence? If I ascend up into heaven, Thou art there: if I make my bed in hell, behold, Thou art there — Psalm 139:7-8

If I take the wings of the morning, and dwell in the uttermost parts of the sea; Even there shall Thy Hand lead me, and Thy Right Hand shall hold me — Psalm 139:9-10

If I say, Surely the darkness shall cover me; even the night shall be light about me. Yea, the darkness hideth not from Thee; but the night shineth as the day: the darkness and the light are both alike to Thee — Psalm 139:11-12

For Thou hast possessed my reins: Thou hast covered me in my mother's womb — Psalm 139:13

I will praise Thee; for I am fearfully and wonderfully made: marvellous are Thy Works; and that my soul knoweth right well — Psalm 139:14

My substance was not hid from Thee, when I was made in secret, and curiously wrought in the lowest parts of the earth. Thine Eyes did see my substance, yet being unperfect; and in Thy Book all my members were written, which in continuance were fashioned, when as yet there was none of them — Psalm 139:15-16

How precious also are Thy Thoughts unto me, O God! how great is the sum of Them! If I should count Them, they are more in number than the sand: when I awake, I am still with Thee — Psalm 139:17-18

Surely Thou wilt slay the wicked, O God: depart from me therefore, ye bloody men — Psalm 139:19

For they speak against Thee wickedly, and Thine Enemies take Thy Name in vain	Psalm 139:20
Do not I hate them, O LORD, that hate Thee? and am not I grieved with those that rise up against Thee? I hate them with perfect hatred: I count them mine enemies	Psalm 139:21-22
Search me, O God, and know my heart: try me, and know my thoughts: And see if there be any wicked way in me, and lead me in the way everlasting	Psalm 139:23-24

We have a strong city; salvation will God appoint for walls and bulwarks. Open ye the gates, that the righteous nation which keepeth the truth may enter in	Isaiah 26:1b-2
Thou wilt keep him in perfect peace, whose mind is stayed on Thee: because he trusteth in Thee	Isaiah 26:3
Trust ye in The LORD for ever: for in The LORD JEHOVAH is Everlasting Strength	Isaiah 26:4
For He bringeth down them that dwell on high; the lofty city, He layeth it low; He layeth it low, even to the ground; He bringeth it even to the dust. The foot shall tread it down, even the feet of the poor, and the steps of the needy	Isaiah 26:5-6
The way of the just is uprightness: Thou, most upright, dost weigh the path of the just	Isaiah 26:7
Yea, in the way of Thy Judgments, O LORD, have we waited for Thee; the desire of our soul is to Thy Name, and to the remembrance of Thee	Isaiah 26:8

With my soul have I desired Thee in the night;   Isaiah 26:9
yea, with my spirit within me will I seek Thee
early: for when Thy Judgments are in the
earth, the inhabitants of the world will learn
righteousness

Let favour be shown to the wicked, yet will   Isaiah 26:10
he not learn righteousness: in the land of
uprightness will he deal unjustly, and will not
behold The Majesty of The LORD

LORD, when Thy Hand is lifted up, they will   Isaiah 26:11
not see: but they shall see, and be ashamed for
their envy at the people; yea, the fire of Thine
Enemies shall devour them

LORD, Thou wilt ordain peace for us: for   Isaiah 26:12
Thou also hast wrought all our works in us

O LORD our God, other lords beside Thee have   Isaiah 26:13-14
had dominion over us: but by Thee only will we
make mention of Thy Name. They are dead, they
shall not live; they are deceased, they shall not
rise: therefore hast Thou visited and destroyed
them, and made all their memory to perish

Thou hast increased the nation, O LORD,   Isaiah 26:15
Thou hast increased the nation: Thou art
Glorified: Thou hadst removed it far unto all
the ends of the earth

Lord, in trouble have they visited Thee, they   Isaiah 26:16
poured out a prayer when Thy Chastening was
upon them

Like as a woman with child, that draweth near   Isaiah 26:17
the time of her delivery, is in pain, and crieth
out in her pangs; so have we been in Thy Sight,
O LORD

We have been with child, we have been in   Isaiah 26:18
pain, we have as it were brought forth wind;
we have not wrought any deliverance in the
earth; neither have the inhabitants of the
world fallen

I said in the cutting off of my days, I shall   Isaiah 38:10-14
go to the gates of the grave: I am deprived of
the residue of my years. I said, I shall not see
The LORD, even The LORD, in the land
of the living: I shall behold man no more
with the inhabitants of the world. Mine age
is departed, and is removed from me as a
shepherd's tent: I have cut off like a weaver
my life: He will cut me off with pining
sickness: from day even to night wilt Thou
make an end of me. I reckoned till morning,
that, as a lion, so will He break all my bones:
from day even to night wilt Thou make an
end of me. Like a crane or a swallow, so did
I chatter: I did mourn as a dove: mine eyes
fail with looking upward: O LORD, I am
oppressed; undertake for me

What shall I say? He hath both spoken unto   Isaiah 38:15-16
me, and Himself hath done it: I shall go softly
all my years in the bitterness of my soul. O
LORD, by these things men live, and in all
these things is the life of my spirit: so wilt
Thou recover me, and make me to live

Behold, for peace I had great bitterness: but Thou hast in love to my soul delivered it from the pit of corruption: for Thou hast cast all my sins behind Thy Back. For the grave cannot praise Thee, death can not celebrate Thee: they that go down into the pit cannot hope for Thy Truth. The living, the living, he shall praise Thee, as I do this day: the father to the children shall make known Thy Truth. The LORD was ready to save me: therefore we will sing my songs to the stringed instruments all the days of our life in the House of The LORD

Isaiah 38:17-20

Ah, Lord GOD! surely Thou hast greatly deceived this people, and Jerusalem, saying, Ye shall have peace; whereas the sword reacheth unto the soul

Jeremiah 4:10

O LORD, are not Thine Eyes upon the truth? Thou hast stricken them, but they have not grieved; Thou hast consumed them, but they have refused to receive correction: they have made their faces harder than a rock; they have refused to return

Jeremiah 5:3

then Thou showedst me their doings

Jeremiah 11:18b

Righteous art Thou, O LORD, when I plead with Thee: yet let me talk with Thee of Thy Judgments: Wherefore doth the way of the wicked prosper? wherefore are all they happy that deal very treacherously? Thou hast planted them, yea, they have taken root: they grow, yea, they bring forth fruit: Thou art near in their mouth, and far from their reins

Jeremiah 12:1-2

But Thou, O LORD, knowest me: Thou hast seen me, and tried mine heart toward Thee: pull them out like sheep for the slaughter, and prepare them for the day of slaughter	Jeremiah 12:3
How long shall the land mourn, and the herbs of every field wither, for the wickedness of them that dwell therein? the beasts are consumed, and the birds; because they said, He shall not see our last end	Jeremiah 12:4
Ah, Lord GOD! behold, the prophets say unto them, Ye shall not see the sword, neither shall ye have famine; but I will give you assured peace in this place	Jeremiah 14:13
O LORD, my strength, and my fortress, and my refuge in the day of affliction, the Gentiles shall come unto Thee from the ends of the earth, and shall say, Surely our fathers have inherited lies, vanity, and things wherein there is no profit	Jeremiah 16:19
Shall a man make gods unto himself, and they are no gods?	Jeremiah 16:20
O LORD, Thou hast deceived me, and I was deceived; Thou art stronger than I, and hast prevailed: I am in derision daily, every one mocketh me	Jeremiah 20:7
For since I spake, I cried out, I cried violence and spoil; because The Word of The LORD was made a reproach unto me, and a derision, daily	Jeremiah 20:8

Then I said, I will not make mention of Him, nor speak any more in His Name. But His Word was in mine heart as a burning fire shut up in my bones, and I was weary with forbearing, and I could not stay	Jeremiah 20:9
For I heard the defaming of many, fear on every side. Report, say they, and we will report it. All my familiars watched for my halting, saying, Peradventure he will be enticed, and we shall prevail against him, and we shall take our revenge on him	Jeremiah 20:10
But The LORD is with me as a Mighty Terrible One: therefore my persecutors shall stumble, and they shall not prevail: they shall be greatly ashamed; for they shall not prosper: their everlasting confusion shall never be forgotten	Jeremiah 20:11
But, O LORD of Hosts, that triest the righteous, and seest the reins and the heart, let me see Thy Vengeance on them: for unto Thee have I opened my cause	Jeremiah 20:12; 17:10a [Revelation 2:23b]
Behold, O LORD; for I am in distress: my bowels are troubled; mine heart is turned within me; for I have grievously rebelled: abroad the sword bereaveth, at home there is as death	Lamentations 1:20
They have heard that I sigh: there is none to comfort me: all mine enemies have heard of my trouble; they are glad that Thou hast done it: Thou wilt bring the day that Thou hast called, and they shall be like unto me	Lamentations 1:21

Let all their wickedness come before Thee; and do unto them, as Thou hast done unto me for all my transgressions: for my sighs are many, and my heart is faint	Lamentations 1:22
We have transgressed and have rebelled: Thou hast not pardoned	Lamentations 3:42
Thou hast covered with anger, and persecuted us: Thou hast slain, Thou hast not pitied	Lamentations 3:43
Thou hast covered Thyself with a cloud, that our prayer should not pass through	Lamentations 3:44
Thou hast made us as the offscouring and refuse in the midst of the people	Lamentations 3:45
All our enemies have opened their mouths against us	Lamentations 3:46
Fear and a snare is come upon us, desolation and destruction	Lamentations 3:47
Mine eye runneth down with rivers of water for the destruction of the daughter of my people	Lamentations 3:48
Mine eye trickleth down, and ceaseth not, without any intermission. Till The LORD look down, and behold from heaven	Lamentations 3:49-50
Mine eye affecteth mine heart because of all the daughters of my city	Lamentations 3:51
Mine enemies chased me sore, like a bird, without cause	Lamentations 3:52
They have cut off my life in the dungeon, and cast a stone upon me. Waters flowed over mine head; then I said, I am cut off	Lamentations 3:53-54

I called upon Thy Name, O LORD, out of the low dungeon	Lamentations 3:55
Thou hast heard my voice: hide not Thine Ear at my breathing, at my cry	Lamentations 3:56
Thou drewest near in the day that I called upon Thee: Thou saidst, Fear not	Lamentations 3:57
O Lord, Thou hast pleaded the causes of my soul; Thou hast redeemed my life	Lamentations 3:58
O LORD, Thou hast seen my wrong: judge Thou my cause	Lamentations 3:59
Thou hast seen all their vengeance and all their imaginations against me	Lamentations 3:60
Thou hast heard their reproach, O LORD, and all their imaginations against me; The lips of those that rose up against me, and their device against me all the day	Lamentations 3:61-62
Behold their sitting down, and their rising up; I am their music	Lamentations 3:63
Render unto them a recompence, O LORD, according to the work of their hands	Lamentations 3:64
Give them sorrow of heart, Thy Curse unto them	Lamentations 3:65
Persecute and destroy them in anger from under the heavens of The LORD	Lamentations 3:66
Remember, O LORD, what is come upon us: consider, and behold our reproach	Lamentations 5:1

Our inheritance is turned to strangers, our houses to aliens	Lamentations 5:2
We are orphans and fatherless, our mothers are as widows	Lamentations 5:3
We have drunken our water for money; our wood is sold unto us	Lamentations 5:4
Our necks are under persecution: we labour, and have no rest	Lamentations 5:5
We have given the hand to the Egyptians, and to the Assyrians, to be satisfied with bread	Lamentations 5:6
Our fathers have sinned, and are not; and we have borne their iniquities	Lamentations 5:7
Servants have ruled over us: there is none that doth deliver us out of their hand	Lamentations 5:8
We gat our bread with the peril of our lives because of the sword of the wilderness	Lamentations 5:9
Our skin was black like an oven because of the terrible famine	Lamentations 5:10
They ravished the women in Zion, and the maids in the cities of Judah	Lamentations 5:11
Princes are hanged up by their hand: the faces of elders were not honoured	Lamentations 5:12
They took the young men to grind, and the children fell under the wood	Lamentations 5:13
The elders have ceased from the gate, the young men from their music	Lamentations 5:14

The joy of our heart is ceased; our dance is turned into mourning	Lamentations 5:15
The crown is fallen from our head: woe unto us, that we have sinned!	Lamentations 5:16
For this our heart is faint; for these things our eyes are dim. Because of the mountain of Zion, which is desolate, the foxes walk upon it	Lamentations 5:17-18
Thou, O LORD, remainest for ever; Thy Throne from generation to generation	Lamentations 5:19
Wherefore dost Thou forget us for ever, and forsake us so long time?	Lamentations 5:20
Turn Thou us unto Thee, O LORD, and we shall be turned; renew our days as of old. But Thou hast utterly rejected us; Thou art very wroth against us	Lamentations 5:21-22
Ah Lord GOD! wilt Thou make a full end of the remnant of Israel?	Ezekiel 11:13b
O my Lord, by the vision my sorrows are turned upon me, and I have retained no strength. For how can the servant of this my Lord talk with this my Lord? for as for me, straightway there remained no strength in me, neither is there breath left in me	Daniel 10:16b-17
my God, we know Thee	Hosea 8:2
Give them, O LORD: what wilt Thou give? give them a miscarrying womb and dry breasts	Hosea 9:14
O LORD, to Thee will I cry: for the fire hath devoured the pastures of the wilderness, and the flame hath burned all the trees of the field	Joel 1:19

The beasts of the field cry also unto Thee: for Joel 1:20
the rivers of waters are dried up, and the fire
hath devoured the pastures of the wilderness

Spare Thy People, O LORD, and give not Joel 2:17b
Thine Heritage to reproach, that the heathen
should rule over them: wherefore should they
say among the people, Where is their God?

We beseech Thee, O LORD, we beseech Thee, Jonah 1:14
let us not perish for this man's life, and lay not
upon us innocent blood: for Thou, O LORD,
hast done as it pleased Thee

I cried by reason of mine affliction unto The Jonah 2:2
LORD, and He heard me; out of the belly of [Psalm 18:4-6;
hell cried I, and Thou heardest my voice 22:23-24; 88 &
89 throughout
this prayer]

For Thou hadst cast me into the deep, in the Jonah 2:3
midst of the seas; and the floods compassed me [Psalm 42:7]
about: all Thy Billows and Thy Waves passed
over me

Then I said, I am cast out of Thy Sight; yet I Jonah 2:4
will look again toward Thy Holy Temple

The waters compassed me about, even to the Jonah 2:5-6
soul: the depth closed me round about, the
weeds were wrapped about my head. I went
down to the bottoms of the mountains; the
earth with her bars was about me for ever: yet
hast Thou brought up my life from corruption,
O LORD my God

When my soul fainted within me I remembered Jonah 2:7
The LORD: and my prayer came in unto
Thee, into Thine Holy Temple

They that observe lying vanities forsake their own mercy. But I will sacrifice unto Thee with the voice of thanksgiving; I will pay that that I have vowed. Salvation is of The LORD	Jonah 2:8-9
I pray Thee, O LORD, was not this my saying, when I was yet in my country? Therefore I fled before unto Tarshish: for I knew that Thou art A Gracious God, and merciful, slow to anger, and of great kindness, and repentest Thee of the evil	Jonah 4:2
Therefore now, O LORD, take, I beseech Thee, my life from me; for it is better for me to die than to live	Jonah 4:3
I will stand upon my watch, and set me upon the tower, and will watch to see what he will say unto me, and what I shall answer when I am reproved	Habakkuk 2:1
The LORD is my God	Zechariah 13:9b
Lord, I am not worthy that Thou shouldest come under my roof: but speak the Word only, and my servant shall be healed	Matthew 8:8; Luke 7:6b-7
My daughter is even now dead: but come and lay Thy Hand upon her, and she shall live	Matthew 9:18b
I thank Thee, O Father, Lord of heaven and earth, because Thou hast hid these things from the wise and prudent, and hast revealed them unto babes. Even so, Father: for so it seemed good in Thy Sight	Matthew 11:25-26; Luke 10:21
Send her away; for she crieth after us	Matthew 15:23b

Thou art the Christ, the Son of the Living God	Matthew 16:16; Luke 9:20b
Lord, have mercy on my son: for he is lunatic, and sore vexed: for ofttimes he falleth into the fire, and oft into the water. And I brought him to Thy Disciples, and they could not cure him	Matthew 17:15–16; Mark 9:17b–22; Luke 9:38b–40
All these things have I kept from my youth up: what lack I yet?	Matthew 19:20
Behold, we have forsaken all, and followed Thee; what shall we have therefore?	Matthew 19:27
O My Father, if it be possible, let this cup pass from Me: nevertheless not as I will, but as Thou wilt	Matthew 26:39, 44; Mark 14:36; Luke 22:42
O My Father, if this cup may not pass away from Me, except I drink it, Thy Will be done	Matthew 26:42, 44; Mark 14:36; Luke 22:42
If Thou wilt, Thou canst make me clean	Mark 1:40b
My little daughter lieth at the point of death: I pray Thee, come and lay Thy Hands on her, that she may be healed; and she shall live	Mark 5:23
If I may touch but His Clothes, I shall be whole	Mark 5:28
Master, I have brought unto Thee my son, which hath a dumb spirit; And wheresoever he taketh him, he teareth him: and he foameth, and gnasheth with his teeth, and pineth away: and I spake to Thy Disciples that they should cast him out; and they could not	Mark 9:17b–18; Matthew 17:15–16; Luke 9:38b–40
Lord, I believe; help Thou mine unbelief	Mark 9:24b

Abba, Father, all things are possible unto Thee; take away this cup from Me: nevertheless not what I will, but what Thou wilt	Mark 14:36; Matthew 26:39, 44; Luke 22:42
Lord, now lettest Thou Thy Servant depart in peace, according to Thy Word: For mine eyes have seen Thy Salvation, Which Thou hast prepared before the face of all people; A light to lighten the Gentiles, and the glory of Thy People Israel	Luke 2:29-32
That he was worthy for whom he should do this: For he loveth our nation, and he hath built us a synagogue	Luke 7:4b-5
Lord, trouble not Thyself: for I am not worthy that Thou shouldest enter under my roof: Wherefore neither thought I myself worthy to come unto Thee: but say in a Word, and my servant shall be healed	Luke 7:6b-7; Matthew 8:8
The Christ of God	Luke 9:20b; Matthew 16:16
Master, I beseech Thee, look upon my son: for he is mine only child. And, lo, a spirit taketh him, and he suddenly crieth out; and it teareth him that he foameth again, and bruising him hardly departeth from him. And I besought Thy Disciples to cast him out; and they could not	Luke 9:38b-40; Matthew 17:15-16; Mark 9:17b-22
I thank Thee, O Father, Lord of heaven and earth, that Thou hast hid these things from the wise and prudent, and hast revealed them unto babes: even so, Father; for so it seemed good in Thy Sight	Luke 10:21; Matthew 11:25-26

Father, I have sinned against heaven, and [before Thee] in Thy Sight, and am no more worthy to be called Thy Son: [make me as one of Thy Hired Servants]	Luke 15:18b–19[21]
Father, I have sinned against heaven, and [before Thee] in Thy Sight, and am no more worthy to be called Thy Son[: make me as one of Thy Hired Servants]	Luke 15:21[18b–19]
Behold, Lord, the half of my goods I give to the poor; and if I have taken any thing from any man by false accusation, I restore him fourfold	Luke 19:8
Father, if Thou be willing, remove this cup from me: nevertheless not my will, but Thine, be done	Luke 22:42; Matthew 26:39, 44; Mark 14:36
Father, forgive them; for they know not what they do	Luke 23:34a
Father, into Thy Hands I commend my spirit	Luke 23:46 [Psalm 31:5a]
Rabbi, Thou art the Son of God; Thou art the King of Israel	John 1:49
The zeal of Thine House hath eaten Me up	John 2:17b [Psalm 69:9]
Lord, evermore give us This Bread	John 6:34
Lord, to whom shall we go? Thou hast the Words of eternal life. And we believe and are sure that Thou art That Christ, the Son of the Living God	John 6:68-69
Lord, behold, he whom Thou lovest is sick	John 11:3

Lord, if Thou hadst been here, my brother had not died. But I know, that even now, whatsoever Thou wilt ask of God, God will give it Thee	John 11:21-22
Father, I thank Thee that Thou hast heard Me. And I knew that Thou hearest Me always: but because of the people which stand by I said it, that they may believe that Thou hast sent Me	John 11:41b-42
Lord, not my feet only, but also my hands and my head	John 13:9
Lord, why cannot I follow Thee now? I will lay down my life for Thy Sake	John 13:37
Lord, show us The Father, and it sufficeth us	John 14:8
Father, the hour is come; glorify Thy Son, that Thy Son also may glorify Thee:	John 17:1
And this is life eternal, that they might know Thee The Only True God, and Jesus Christ, Whom Thou hast sent	John 17:3
I have glorified Thee on the earth: I have finished the work which Thou gavest Me to do	John 17:4
I have manifested Thy Name unto the men which Thou gavest me out of the world: Thine they were, and Thou gavest them Me; and they have kept Thy Word	John 17:6
Now they have known that all things whatsoever Thou hast given Me are of Thee. For I have given unto them the Words which Thou gavest Me; and they have received Them, and have known surely that I came out from Thee, and they have believed that Thou didst send Me	John 17:7-8

I pray for them: I pray not for the world, but for them which Thou hast given Me; for they are Thine. And all Mine are Thine, and Thine are Mine; and I am glorified in them	John 17:9-10
And now I am no more in the world, but these are in the world, and I come to Thee. Holy Father, keep through Thine Own Name those whom Thou hast given Me, that they may be one, as We are	John 17:11
While I was with them in the world, I kept them in Thy Name: those that Thou gavest Me I have kept, and none of them is lost, but the son of perdition; that the Scripture might be fulfilled	John 17:12; 18:9b
And now come I to Thee; and these things I speak in the world, that they might have My Joy fulfilled in themselves	John 17:13
I have given them Thy Word; and the world hath hated them, because they are not of the world, even as I am not of the world	John 17:14
I pray not that Thou shouldest take them out of the world, but that Thou shouldest keep them from the evil. They are not of the world, even as I am not of the world	John 17:15-16
Sanctify them through Thy Truth: Thy Word is Truth	John 17:17
As Thou hast sent Me into the world, even so have I also sent them into the world	John 17:18
And for their sakes I sanctify Myself, that they also might be sanctified through the Truth	John 17:19

Neither pray I for these alone, but for them also which shall believe on Me through their word	John 17:20
I in them, and Thou in Me, that they may be made perfect in One; and that the world may know that Thou hast sent Me, and hast loved them, as Thou hast loved Me	John 17:23
Of them which Thou gavest Me have I lost none	John 18:9b; 6:39; 17:12b
Lord, Thou knowest all things; Thou knowest that I love Thee	John 21:17b
Lord, Thou art God, which hast made heaven, and earth, and the sea, and all that in them is: Who by the mouth of Thy Servant David hast said, Why did the heathen rage, and the people imagine vain things? The kings of the earth stood up, and the rulers were gathered together against The Lord, and against His Christ	Acts 4:24-26 [Psalm 2:1-2]
For of a truth against Thy Holy Child Jesus, Whom Thou hast anointed, both Herod, and Pontius Pilate, with the Gentiles, and the people of Israel, were gathered together, for to do whatsoever Thy Hand and Thy Counsel determined before to be done	Acts 4:27-28
And now, Lord, behold their threatenings: and grant unto Thy Servants, that with all boldness they may speak Thy Word, by stretching forth Thine Hand to heal; and that signs and wonders may be done by The Name of Thy Holy Child Jesus	Acts 4:29-30

Lord, I have heard by many of this man, how much evil he hath done to Thy Saints at Jerusalem: and here he hath authority from the chief priests to bind all that call on Thy Name	Acts 9:13-14
Abba, Father	Romans 8:15b [Galatians 4:6b]
Lord, they have killed Thy Prophets, and digged down Thine Altars; and I am left alone, and they seek my life	Romans 11:3 [1 Kings 19:10,14]
Now to Him that is of power to stablish you according to my gospel, and the preaching of Jesus Christ, according to the revelation of the mystery, which was kept secret since the world began, But now is made manifest, and by the scriptures of the prophets, according to the commandment of the everlasting God, made known to all nations for the obedience of faith: To God only wise, be glory through Jesus Christ for ever. Amen	Romans 16:25-27
Abba, Father	Galatians 4:6b [Romans 8:15b]
Jesus Christ is Lord	Philippians 2:11
Thy Throne, O God, is for ever and ever: [the] a sceptre of [Thy Kingdom] righteousness is the [a right] sceptre of Thy Kingdom. Thou hast loved [lovest] righteousness, and hated iniquity [hatest wickedness]; therefore God, [even] Thy God, hath anointed Thee with the oil of gladness above Thy Fellows	Hebrews 1:8-9 [Psalm 45:6-7]

317

And, Thou, Lord, in the beginning [of old] hast [Thou] laid the foundation of the earth: and the heavens are the Work[s] of Thine [Thy] Hands. They shall perish, but Thou remainest [shalt endure: yea], they all [all of them] shall wax old as doth [like] a garment; and as a vesture shalt Thou fold [change] them up, and they shall be changed: but Thou art the same, and Thy Years shall not fail [have no end]	Hebrews 1:10-12 [Psalm 102:25-27]
What is man, that Thou art mindful of him? or [and] the son of man, that Thou visitest him? [For] Thou madest [hast made] him a little lower than the angels, [and] Thou crownedest [hast crowned] him with glory and honour, and didst set him over the Works of Thy Hands	Hebrews 2:6b-7 [Psalm 8:4-6a]
Thou hast put all things in subjection under his feet	Hebrews 2:8a [Psalm 8:6b]
I will declare Thy Name unto my brethren, in the midst of the church [congregation] will I [sing] praise [unto] Thee	Hebrews 2:12 [Psalm 22:22]
Sacrifice and offering Thou wouldest not, but a body hast Thou prepared Me: In burnt offerings and sacrifices for sin Thou hast had no pleasure. Then said I, Lo, I come (in the Volume of the Book it is written of me,) to do Thy Will, O God	Hebrews 10:5b-8 [Psalm 40:5-8]
Lo, I come to do Thy Will, O God	Hebrews 10:9a [Psalm 40:8a]

Now The God of Peace, that brought again from the dead our Lord Jesus, That Great Shepherd of the sheep, through the blood of the everlasting covenant, Make you perfect in every good work to do His Will, working in you that which is wellpleasing in His Sight, through Jesus Christ; to Whom be glory for ever and ever. Amen	Hebrews 13:20-21
But The God of All Grace, Who hath called us unto His Eternal Glory by Christ Jesus, after that ye have suffered a while, make you perfect, stablish, strengthen, settle you. To Him be glory and dominion for ever and ever. Amen	1 Peter 5:10-11
Thou art worthy to take the book, and to open the seals thereof: for Thou wast slain, and hast redeemed us to God by Thy Blood out of every kindred, and tongue, and people, and nation; And hast made us unto our God kings and priests: and we shall reign on the earth	Revelation 5:9-10
Amen	Revelation 5:14a
Alleluia: for The Lord God Omnipotent reigneth. Let us be glad and rejoice, and give honour to Him: for the marriage of The Lamb is come, and His Wife hath made herself ready. And to her was granted that she should be arrayed in fine linen, clean and white: for the fine linen is the righteousness of saints	Revelation 19:6-8

Prayer portions that contain Statements in them

Genesis 9:26-27	2 Samuel 7:19-21 [1 Chron 17:17-19]
Genesis 18:25	2 Samuel 7:24 [1 Chron 17:22]
Genesis 18:27-28a	2 Samuel 7:27-29 [1 Chron 17:25-27]
Genesis 18:29a	2 Samuel 22:16-46 [Psalm 18]
Genesis 18:30a	2 Samuel 22:48-51 [Psalm 18]
Genesis 18:31a	2 Samuel 24:10 [1 Chron 21:8]
Genesis 18:32a	1 Kings 8:37-43 [2 Chron 6:14-42]
Genesis 24:12-14	1 Kings 8:46-53 [2 Chron 6:14-42]
Genesis 24:42-44	1 Kings 8:56
Genesis 28:22	1 Kings 8:59-61
Genesis 32:9-10	2 Kings 19:17-19 [Isaiah 37:18-20]
Genesis 32:12	1 Chron 17:17-19 [2 Sam 7:19-21]
Genesis 32:26b	1 Chron 17:21-22 [2 Sam 7:23-24]
Exodus 5:23	1 Chron 17:25-27 [2 Sam 7:27-29]
Exodus 15:9-10	1 Chron 21:8 [2 Samuel 24:10]
Exodus 15:12-18	1 Chronicles 22:13
Numbers 14:13-18	1 Chronicles 29:14-18
Deuteronomy 3:24	2 Chron 6:28-33 [1 Kings 8:23-53]
Deuteronomy 9:27-29	2 Chron 6:36-39 [1 Kings 8:23-53]
Deuteronomy 26:13-14	2 Chronicles 20:10-12
Deuteronomy 33:3-4	Nehemiah 1:8-10
Deuteronomy 33:8-25	Nehemiah 9:7-38
Judges 10:10	Job 1:21
Judges 15:18	Psalm 3:1-7
Joshua 7:7-9	Psalm 6:4-9
1 Samuel 2:3-10	Psalm 8:2
1 Samuel 16:2a	Psalm 8:3-5 [Hebrews 2:6b-7a]

Psalm 8:6-8 [Hebrews 2:7b-8a]

Psalm 9:1-12

Psalm 9:15-18

Psalm 10:13-14

Psalm 12:1-8

Psalm 13:3-5

Psalm 16:1-11

Psalm 18:15-45 [2 Samuel 22]

Psalm 18:47-50 [2 Samuel 22]

Psalm 20:1-5

Psalm 21:1-12

Psalm 22:2-21

Psalm 22:22 [Hebrews 2:12]

Psalm 22:23-31

Psalm 25:4-5

Psalm 25:8-22

Psalm 28:1

Psalm 28:3-5

Psalm 30:2-12

Psalm 32:1-7

Psalm 33:22

Psalm 35:4-23

Psalm 35:27-28

Psalm 36:5-9

Psalm 36:12

Psalm 40:6 [Hebrews 10:5b-8a]

Psalm 40:7-8 [Hebrews 10:7,9a]

Psalm 40:9-10

Psalm 40:12

Psalm 40:16-17

Psalm 41:1-3

Psalm 41:5-12

Psalm 43:4

Psalm 44:1-2

Psalm 44:5-6

Psalm 45:1

Psalm 45:6-7 [Hebrews 1:8-9]

Psalm 45:13-17

Psalm 48:4-11

Psalm 51:1-8

Psalm 51:13-19

Psalm 54:6

Psalm 57:1-4

Psalm 57:6-10

Psalm 59:3-17

Psalm 61:2-8

Psalm 65:1-13

Psalm 66:10-14

Psalm 67:1-7

Psalm 68:7-10

Psalm 68:29

Psalm 70:4-5

Psalm 71:1

Psalm 71:3-8

Psalm 71:10-11

Psalm 71:13-24

Psalm 75:1-5

Psalm 76:5-10

Statement Prayers

Psalm 77:3-6	Psalm 132:10
Psalm 77:10-13	Psalm 138:1
Psalm 79:1-4	Psalm 138:4-8
Psalm 79:6-13	Psalm 140:1-8
Psalm 83:2-18	Psalm 140:11-13
Psalm 84:1-7	Psalm 141:5-8
Psalm 84:10-12	Psalm 142:1-7
Psalm 85:1-3	Psalm 143:2-9
Psalm 85:8-13	Psalm 143:12
Psalm 86:1-5	Psalm 144:4-5
Psalm 86:7	Psalm 144:7-8
Psalm 86:9-15	Psalm 144:11-15
Psalm 86:17-19 (20-45)	Psalm 145:14-21
Psalm 89:50-51	Proverbs 30:7-9
Psalm 90:2-14	Isaiah 25:5
Psalm 99:1-9	Isaiah 33:2-3
Psalm 106:4-7	Isaiah 37:18-20 [2 Kings 19:17-19]
Ps 106:47-48 [1 Chron 16:35-36]	Isaiah 63:15-16
Psalm 108:1-2	Isaiah 63:18-19
Psalm 108:6	Isaiah 64:3-11
Psalm 108:10-11	Jeremiah 10:23-25
Psalm 108:12-13; 60:11-12	Jeremiah 11:20
Psalm 116:8-9	Jeremiah 14:19
Psalm 116:16-17	Jeremiah 14:22
Psalm 118:26 [Matthew 21:9;	Jeremiah 15:15-17
23:39b; Mark 11:9-10; Luke	Jeremiah 17:12-13
13:35b; 19:38; John 12:13]	Jeremiah 17:15-16
Psalm 118:28	Jeremiah 18:20
Psalm 130:1	Jeremiah 18:22-23
Psalm 130:3-4	Jeremiah 31:18b-19

Jeremiah 32:22-25

Lamentations 1:9b

Lamentations 1:11b

Lamentations 2:21-22

Ezekiel 4:14

Daniel 9:6-16

Daniel 9:19

Hosea 14:2b-3

Micah 7:18-20

Habakkuk 1:2-4

Habakkuk 1:12-17

Habakkuk 3:7-18

Matt 8:25b; Mark 4:38b; Luke 8:24a

Mark 4:38b; Matt 8:25b; Luke 8:24a

Luke 8:24a; Matt 8:25b; Mark 4:38b

John 14:5

Revelation 11:18

Prayers of Thanks

The king shall joy in Thy Strength, O
LORD; and in Thy Salvation how greatly
shall he rejoice! Thou hast given him his
heart's desire, and hast not withholden the
request of his lips. Selah. For Thou preventest
him with the blessings of goodness: Thou
settest a crown of pure gold on his head. He
asked life of Thee, and Thou gavest it him,
even length of days for ever and ever. His
glory is great in Thy Salvation: honour and
majesty hast Thou laid upon him. For Thou
hast made him most blessed for ever: Thou
hast made him exceeding glad with Thy
Countenance. For the king trusteth in The
LORD, and through the mercy of The Most
High he shall not be moved

Psalm 21:1-7

Thine Hand shall find out all Thine Enemies: Psalm 21:8-12
Thy Right Hand shall find out those that
hate Thee. Thou shalt make them as a fiery
oven in the Time of Thine Anger: The
LORD shall swallow them up in His Wrath,
and the fire shall devour them. Their fruit
shalt Thou destroy from the earth, and
their seed from among the children of men.
For they intended evil against Thee: they
imagined a mischievous device, which they
are not able to perform. Therefore shalt Thou
make them turn their back, when Thou shalt
make ready Thine Arrows upon Thy Strings
against the face of them

Be Thou exalted, LORD, in Thine Own   Psalm 21:13
Strength: so will we sing and praise Thy
Power

I will extol Thee, O LORD; for Thou hast   Psalm 30:1
lifted me up, and hast not made my foes to
rejoice over me

O LORD my God, I cried unto Thee, and   Psalm 30:2
Thou hast healed me

O LORD, Thou hast brought up my soul   Psalm 30:3
from the grave: Thou hast kept me alive, that
I should not go down to the pit

Sing unto The LORD, O ye saints of His,   Psalm 30:4-5
and give thanks at the remembrance of His
Holiness. For His Anger endureth but a
moment; in His Favour is life: weeping may
endure for a night, but joy cometh in the
morning

And in my prosperity I said, I shall never be
moved. LORD, by Thy Favour Thou hast
made my mountain to stand strong: Thou
didst hide Thy Face, and I was troubled

Psalm 30:6-7

I cried to Thee, O LORD; and unto The
LORD I made supplication. What profit is
there in my blood, when I go down to the
pit? Shall the dust praise Thee? shall it declare
Thy Truth? Hear, O LORD, and have mercy
upon me: LORD, be Thou my helper

Psalm 30:8-10

Thou hast turned for me my mourning into
dancing: Thou hast put off my sackcloth, and
girded me with gladness; To the end that my
glory may sing praise to Thee, and not be
silent. O LORD my God, I will give thanks
unto Thee for ever

Psalm 30:11-12

Unto Thee, O God, do we give thanks, unto
Thee do we give thanks: for that Thy Name
is near Thy Wondrous Works declare

Psalm 75:1

When I shall receive the congregation I
will judge uprightly. The earth and all the
inhabitants thereof are dissolved: I bear up
the pillars of it

Psalm 75:2-3

I said unto the fools, Deal not foolishly: and
to the wicked, Lift not up the horn: Lift not
up your horn on high: speak not with a stiff
neck

Psalm 75:4-5

For Thou hast delivered my soul from death,
mine eyes from tears, and my feet from
falling. I will walk before The LORD in the
land of the living

Psalm 116:8-9

O LORD, truly I am Thy Servant; I am Thy   Psalm 116:16
Servant, and the son of Thine Handmaid:
Thou hast loosed my bonds

I will offer to Thee the sacrifice of   Psalm 116:17
thanksgiving, and will call upon the Name of
The LORD

I will praise Thee: for Thou hast heard me,   Psalm 118:21
and art become my salvation

Save now, I beseech Thee, O LORD: O   Psalm 118:25
LORD, I beseech Thee, send now prosperity

Blessed be He that cometh in The Name of   Psalm 118:26
the LORD: we have blessed you out of the   [Matthew 21:9;
House of The LORD   23:39b; Mark
    11:9-10; Luke
    13:35b; 19:38;
    John 12:13]

Thou art my God, and I will praise Thee: Psalm 118:28
Thou art my God, I will exalt Thee

I thank Thee, and praise Thee, O Thou God   Daniel 2:23
of my fathers, Who hast given me wisdom
and might, and hast made known unto me
now what we desired of Thee: for Thou hast
now made known unto us the king's matter

I thank Thee, O Father, Lord of heaven and   Matthew
earth, because Thou hast hid these things   11:25-26; Luke
from the wise and prudent, and hast revealed   10:21
them unto babes. Even so, Father: for so it
seemed good in Thy Sight

I thank Thee, O Father, Lord of heaven and earth, that Thou hast hid these things from the wise and prudent, and hast revealed them unto babes: even so, Father; for so it seemed good in Thy Sight	Luke 10:21; Matthew 11:25-26
Father, I thank Thee that Thou hast heard Me. And I knew that Thou hearest Me always: but because of the people which stand by I said it, that they may believe that Thou hast sent Me	John 11:41b-42
We give Thee thanks, O Lord God Almighty, Which art, and wast, and art to come; because Thou hast taken to Thee Thy Great Power, and hast reigned	Revelation 11:17
And the nations were angry, and Thy Wrath is come, and the time of the dead, that they should be judged, and that Thou shouldest give reward unto Thy Servants the prophets, and to the saints, and them that fear Thy Name, small and great; and shouldest destroy them which destroy the earth	Revelation 11:18

Prayer portions that contain Thanks in them

2 Samuel 22:48-50 [Psalm 18]	Psalm 92:1-5
1 Chronicles 16:35 [Psalm 106:47]	Psalm 106:47 [1 Chronicles 16:35]
1 Chronicles 29:13	Psalm 119:62
Psalm 18:47-49 [2 Samuel 22]	Psalm 140:13
Psalm 26:1-7	Isaiah 38:17-20
Psalm 35:18	Jonah 2:8-9
Psalm 79:13	Revelation 7:12

Prayers of Worship

Blessed be The LORD God of Shem; and Canaan shall be his servant. God shall enlarge Japheth, and he shall dwell in the tents of Shem; and Canaan shall be his servant	Genesis 9:26-27
Blessed be The LORD God of Israel for ever and ever	1 Chronicles 16:36a [Psalm 106:48]
Blessed be Thou, LORD God of Israel our father, for ever and ever	1 Chronicles 29:10
Thine, O LORD is the greatness, and the power, and the glory, and the victory, and the majesty: for all that is in the heaven and in the earth is Thine; Thine is the Kingdom, O LORD, and Thou art exalted as Head above all. Both riches and honour come of Thee, and Thou reignest over all; and in Thine Hand is power and might; and in Thine Hand it is to make great, and to give strength unto all	1 Chronicles 29:11-12
Now therefore, our God, we thank Thee, and praise Thy Glorious Name	1 Chronicles 29:13

But who am I, and what is my people, that we should be able to offer so willingly after this sort? for all things come of Thee, and of Thine Own have we given Thee. For we are strangers before Thee, and sojourners, as were all our fathers: our days on the earth are as a shadow, and there is none abiding	1 Chronicles 29:14-15
O LORD our God, all this store that we have prepared to build Thee an house for Thine Holy Name cometh of Thine Hand, and is All Thine Own	1 Chronicles 29:16
I know also, my God, that Thou triest the heart, and hast pleasure in uprightness. As for me, in the uprightness of mine heart I have willingly offered all these things: and now have I seen with joy Thy People, which are present here, to offer willingly unto Thee	1 Chronicles 29:17
O LORD God of Abraham, Isaac, and of Israel, our fathers, keep this for ever in the imagination of the thoughts of the heart of Thy People, and prepare their heart unto Thee	1 Chronicles 29:18
And give unto Solomon my son a perfect heart, to keep Thy Commandments, Thy Testimonies, and Thy Statutes, and to do all these things, and to build the palace, for the which I have made provision	1 Chronicles 29:19

The Law of the LORD is perfect, converting   Psalm 19:7-13
the soul: the Testimony of The LORD is
sure, making wise the simple. The Statutes
of The LORD are right, rejoicing the heart:
the Commandment of The LORD is pure,
enlightening the eyes. The fear of The LORD
is clean, enduring for ever: the Judgments of
The LORD are true and righteous altogether.
More to be desired are They than gold, yea,
than much fine gold: sweeter also than honey
and the honeycomb. Moreover by Them is Thy
Servant warned: and in keeping of Them there
is great reward. Who can understand his errors?
cleanse Thou me from secret faults. Keep back
Thy Servant also from presumptuous sins; let
them not have dominion over me: then shall
I be upright, and I shall be innocent from the
great transgression

Let the words of my mouth, and the meditation   Psalm 19:14
of my heart, be acceptable in Thy Sight, O
LORD, my strength, and my redeemer

My heart is inditing a good matter: I speak of   Psalm 45:1
the things which I have made touching The
King: my tongue is the pen of a ready writer

Thou art fairer than the children of men: grace   Psalm 45:2
is poured into Thy Lips: therefore God hath
blessed Thee for ever

Gird Thy Sword upon Thy Thigh, O Most   Psalm 45:3-5
Mighty, with Thy Glory and Thy Majesty. And
in Thy Majesty ride prosperously because of
truth and meekness and righteousness; and Thy
Right Hand shall teach Thee terrible things.
Thine Arrows are sharp in the heart of The
King's Enemies; whereby the people fall under
Thee

Thy Throne, O God, is for ever and ever: [the] a sceptre of [Thy Kingdom] righteousness is the [a right] sceptre of Thy Kingdom. Thou hast loved [lovest] righteousness, and hated iniquity [hatest wickedness]; therefore God, [even] Thy God, hath anointed Thee with the oil of gladness above Thy Fellows	Psalm 45:6-7 [Hebrews 1:8-9]
All Thy Garments smell of myrrh, and aloes, and cassia, out of the ivory palaces, whereby they have made Thee glad	Psalm 45:8
Kings' daughters were among Thy Honourable Women: upon Thy Right Hand did stand the queen in gold of Ophir	Psalm 45:9
Be merciful unto me, O God, be merciful unto me: for my soul trusteth in Thee: yea, in the shadow of Thy Wings will I make my refuge, until these calamities be overpast	Psalm 57:1
Be Thou exalted, O God, above the heavens; let Thy Glory be above all the earth	Psalm 57:5,11
They have prepared a net for my steps; my soul is bowed down: they have digged a pit before me, into the midst whereof they are fallen themselves	Psalm 57:6
My heart is fixed, O God, my heart is fixed: I will sing and give praise	Psalm 57:7
Awake up, my glory; awake, psaltery and harp: I myself will awake early. I will praise Thee, O Lord, among the people: I will sing unto Thee among the nations. For Thy Mercy is great unto the heavens, and Thy Truth unto the clouds	Psalm 57:8-10

Be Thou exalted, O God, above the heavens;   Psalm 57:11,5
let Thy Glory be above all the earth

God hath spoken once; twice have I heard this;   Psalm 62:11-12
that power belongeth unto God. Also unto
Thee, O Lord, belongeth mercy: for Thou
renderst to every man according to his work

O God, Thou art my God, early will I seek   Psalm 63:1-2
Thee: my soul thirsteth for Thee, my flesh
longeth for Thee in a dry and thirsty land,
where no water is; To see Thy Power and Thy
Glory, so as I have seen Thee in the sanctuary

Because Thy Lovingkindness is better than life,   Psalm 63:3-4
my lips shall praise Thee. Thus will I bless Thee
while I live: I will lift up my hands in Thy
Name

My soul shall be satisfied as with marrow and   Psalm 63:5-6
fatness; and my mouth shall praise Thee with
joyful lips: When I remember Thee upon my
bed, and meditate on Thee in the night watches

Because Thou hast been my help, therefore in   Psalm 63:7
the shadow of Thy Wings will I rejoice

My soul followeth hard after Thee: Thy Right   Psalm 63:8
Hand upholdeth me

How terrible art Thou in Thy Works! through   Psalm 66:3-4
the greatness of Thy Power shall Thine
Enemies submit themselves unto Thee. All the
earth shall worship Thee, and shall sing unto
Thee; they shall sing to Thy Name

For Thou, O God, hast proved us: Thou hast tried us, as silver is tried. Thou broughtest us into the net; Thou laidest affliction upon our loins. Thou hast caused men to ride over our heads; we went through fire and through water: but Thou broughtest us out into a wealthy place	Psalm 66:10-12
I will go into Thy House with burnt offerings: I will pay Thee my vows, Which my lips have uttered, and my mouth hath spoken, when I was in trouble	Psalm 66:13-14
I will offer unto Thee burnt sacrifices of fatlings, with the incense of rams; I will offer bullocks with goats	Psalm 66:15
Blessed be The LORD God, The God of Israel, Who only doeth wondrous things. And blessed be His Glorious Name for ever: and let the whole earth be filled with His Glory; Amen, and Amen	Psalm 72:18-19
Thou art more glorious and excellent than the mountains of prey	Psalm 76:4
The stout-hearted are spoiled, they have slept their sleep: and none of the men of might have found their hands	Psalm 76:5
At Thy Rebuke, O God of Jacob, both the chariot and horse are cast into a dead sleep. Thou, even Thou, art to be feared: and who may stand in Thy Sight when once Thou art angry?	Psalm 76:6-7
Thou didst cause judgment to be heard from heaven; the earth feared, and was still. When God arose to judgment, to save all the meek of the earth	Psalm 76:8-9

Surely the wrath of man shall praise Thee: the   Psalm 76:10
remainder of wrath shalt Thou restrain

How amiable are Thy Tabernacles, O LORD   Psalm 84:1-2
of Hosts! My soul longeth, yea, even fainteth
for the courts of The LORD: my heart and my
flesh crieth out for The Living God

Yea, the sparrow hath found an house, and   Psalm 84:3-4
the swallow a nest for herself, where she may
lay her young, even Thine Altars, O LORD
of Hosts, my King, and my God. Blessed are
they that dwell in Thy House: they will be still
praising Thee

Blessed is the man whose strength is in Thee;   Psalm 84:5-7
in whose heart are the Ways of Them. Who
passing through the valley of Baca make it a
well: the rain also filleth the pools. They go
from strength to strength, every one of them in
Zion appeareth before God

O LORD God of Hosts, hear my prayer: give   Psalm 84:8
ear, O God of Jacob

Behold, O God our Shield, and look upon the   Psalm 84:9
face of Thine Anointed

For a day in Thy Courts is better than a   Psalm 84:10
thousand. I had rather be a doorkeeper in the
house of my God, than to dwell in the tents of
wickedness

For The LORD God is a sun and shield: The   Psalm 84:11
LORD will give grace and glory: no good
thing will He withhold from them that walk
uprightly

O LORD of Hosts, blessed is the man that trusteth in Thee   Psalm 84:12

I will sing of the Mercies of The LORD for ever: with my mouth will I make known Thy Faithfulness to all generations. For I have said, Mercy shall be built up for ever: Thy Faithfulness shalt Thou establish in the very heavens   Psalm 89:1-2 [some of Jonah 2 throughout this Psalm]

And the heavens shall praise Thy Wonders, O LORD: Thy Faithfulness also in the congregation of the saints   Psalm 89:5

For who in the heaven can be compared unto The LORD? who among the sons of the mighty can be likened unto The LORD? God is greatly to be feared in the assembly of the saints, and to be had in reverence of all them that are about Him   Psalm 89:6-7

O LORD God of Hosts, who is a Strong LORD like unto Thee? or to Thy Faithfulness round about Thee? Thou rulest the raging of the sea: when the waves thereof arise, Thou stillest them   Psalm 89:8-9

Thou hast broken Rahab in pieces, as one that is slain: Thou hast scattered Thine Enemies with Thy Strong Arm   Psalm 89:10

The heavens are Thine, the earth also is Thine: as for the world and the fulness thereof, Thou hast founded them. The north and the south Thou hast created them: Tabor and Hermon shall rejoice in Thy Name   Psalm 89:11-12

Thou hast a Mighty Arm: strong is Thy Hand, and high is Thy Right Hand. Justice and judgment are the habitation of Thy Throne: mercy and truth shall go before Thy Face

Psalm 89:13-14

Blessed is the people that know the joyful sound: they shall walk, O LORD, in the light of Thy Countenance. In Thy Name shall they rejoice all the day: and in Thy Righteousness shall they be exalted. For Thou art the Glory of their strength: and in Thy Favour our horn shall be exalted

Psalm 89:15-17

For The LORD is our Defence; and the Holy One of Israel is our King. Then Thou spakest in vision to Thy Holy One, and saidst, I have laid help upon one that is mighty; I have exalted one chosen out of the people....

Psalm 89:18-19 (20-45)

Thou art my Father, my God, and the rock of my salvation

Psalm 89:26b

It is a good thing to give thanks unto The LORD, and to sing praises unto Thy Name, O Most High: To show forth Thy Lovingkindness in the morning, and Thy Faithfulness every night, Upon an instrument of ten strings, and upon the psaltery; upon the harp with a solemn sound

Psalm 92:1-3

For Thou, LORD, hast made me glad through Thy Work: I will triumph in the works of Thy Hands

Psalm 92:4

O LORD, how great are Thy Works! and Thy Thoughts are very deep

Psalm 92:5

A brutish man knoweth not; neither doth a fool
understand this. When the wicked spring as
the grass, and when all the workers of iniquity
do flourish; it is that they shall be destroyed
for ever: But Thou, LORD, art Most High for
evermore

Psalm 92:6-8

For, lo, Thine Enemies, O LORD, for, lo,
Thine Enemies shall perish; all the workers of
iniquity shall be scattered. But my horn shalt
Thou exalt like the horn of an unicorn: I shall
be anointed with fresh oil

Psalm 92:9-10

Mine eye also shall see my desire on mine
enemies, and mine ears shall hear my desire of
the wicked that rise up against me

Psalm 92:11

The righteous shall flourish like the palm tree:
he shall grow like a cedar in Lebanon. Those
that be planted in the House of The LORD
shall flourish in the courts of our God. They
shall still bring forth fruit in old age; they
shall be fat and flourishing; To show that The
LORD is upright: He is my rock, and there is
no unrighteousness in Him

Psalm 92:12-15

The LORD reigneth, He is clothed with
majesty; the LORD is clothed with strength,
wherewith He hath girded himself: the world
also is stablished, that it cannot be moved. Thy
Throne is established of old: Thou art from
everlasting

Psalm 93:1-2

The floods have lifted up, O LORD, the floods
have lifted up their voice; the floods lift up
their waves. The LORD on high is mightier
than the noise of many waters, yea, than the
mighty waves of the sea

Psalm 93:3-4

Thy Testimonies are very sure: holiness becometh Thine House, O LORD, for ever	Psalm 93:5
Zion heard, and was glad; and the daughters of Judah rejoiced because of Thy Judgments, O LORD	Psalm 97:8
For Thou, LORD, art High above all the earth: Thou art exalted far above all gods	Psalm 97:9
The LORD reigneth; let the people tremble: he sitteth between the cherubims; let the eath be moved. The LORD is great in Zion; and He is High above all the people. Let them praise Thy Great and Terrible Name; for It is Holy	Psalm 99:1-3
The King's Strength also loveth judgment; Thou dost establish equity, Thou executest judgment and righteousness in Jacob	Psalm 99:4
Exalt ye The LORD our God, and worship at His Footstool; for He is Holy	Psalm 99:5
Moses and Aaron among His Priests, and Samuel among them that call upon His Name; they called upon The LORD, and He answered them. He spake unto them in the cloudy pillar: they kept His Testimonies, and the ordinance that He gave them	Psalm 99:6-7
Thou answeredst them, O LORD our God: Thou wast A God that forgavest them, though Thou tookest vengeance of their inventions	Psalm 99:8
Exalt The LORD our God, and worship at His Holy Hill; for The LORD our God is Holy	Psalm 99:9

Bless The LORD, O my soul, O LORD my   Psalm 104:1
God, Thou art Very Great, Thou art Clothed
with Honour and Majesty

Who coverest Thyself with light as with a   Psalm 104:2-3
garment: Who stretchest out the heavens
like a curtain: Who layeth the beams of His
Chambers in the waters: Who maketh the
clouds His Chariot: Who walketh upon the
wings of the wind

Who maketh His Angels spirits; His Ministers a   Psalm 104:4
flaming fire

Who laid the foundations of the earth, that it   Psalm 104:5-6
should not be removed for ever. Thou coveredst
it with the deep as with a garment: the waters
stood above the mountains

At Thy Rebuke they fled; at the voice of Thy   Psalm 104:7-9
Thunder they hasted away. They go up by the
mountains; they go down by the valleys unto
the place which Thou hast founded for them.
Thou hast set a bound that they may not pass
over; that they turn not again to cover the earth

He sendeth the springs into the valleys, which   Psalm 104:10-12
run among the hills. They give drink to every
beast of the field: the wild asses quench their
thirst. By them shall the fowls of the heaven
have their habitation, which sing among the
branches

He watereth the hills from His Chambers: the   Psalm 104:13
earth is satisfied with the fruit of Thy Works

He causeth the grass to grow for the cattle, and herb for the service of man: that he may bring forth food out of the earth; And wine that maketh glad the heart of man, and oil to make his face to shine, and bread which strengtheneth man's heart

Psalm 104:14-15

The trees of The LORD are full of sap; the cedars of Lebanon, which He hath planted; Where the birds make their nests: as for the stork, the fir trees are her house

Psalm 104:16-17

The high hills are a refuge for the wild goats; and the rocks for the conies. He appointed the moon for seasons: the sun knoweth his going down

Psalm 104:18-19

Thou makest darkness, and it is night: wherein all the beasts of the forest do creep forth

Psalm 104:20

The young lions roar after their prey, and seek their meat from God. The sun ariseth, they gather themselves together, and lay them down in their dens. Man goeth forth unto his work and to his labour until the evening

Psalm 104:21-23

O LORD, how manifold are Thy Works! In wisdom hast Thou made them all: the earth is full of Thy Riches. So is this great and wide sea, wherein are things creeping innumerable, both small and great beasts

Psalm 104:24-25

There go the ships: there is that leviathan, whom Thou hast made to play therein

Psalm 104:26

These wait all upon Thee; that Thou mayest give them their meat in due season. That Thou givest them they gather: Thou openest Thine Hand, they are filled with good

Psalm 104:27-28

Thou hidest Thy Face, they are troubled: Thou takest away their breath, they die, and return to their dust

Psalm 104:29

Thou sendest forth Thy Spirit, they are created: and Thou renewest the face of the earth

Psalm 104:30

O GOD, my heart is fixed; I will sing and give praise, even with my glory. Awake, psaltery and harp: I myself will awake early

Psalm 108:1-2

I will praise Thee, O LORD, among the people: and I will sing praises unto Thee among the nations. For Thy Mercy is great above the heavens: and Thy Truth reacheth unto the clouds

Psalm 108:3-4

Be Thou exalted, O God, above the heavens: and Thy Glory above the earth

Psalm 108:5

Not unto us, O LORD, not unto us, but unto Thy Name give glory, for Thy Mercy, and for Thy Truth's Sake

Psalm 115:1

Thy Name, O LORD, endureth for ever; and Thy Memorial, O LORD, throughout all generations

Psalm 135:13

Forasmuch as there is none like unto Thee, O LORD; Thou art great, and Thy Name is great in might

Jeremiah 10:6

Who would not fear Thee, O King of nations? for to Thee doth it appertain: forasmuch as among all the wise men of the nations, and in all their kingdoms, there is none like unto Thee

Jeremiah 10:7

Our Father Which art in heaven, Hallowed by Thy Name. Thy Kingdom come. Thy Will be done in earth, as it is in heaven. Give us this day our daily bread. And forgive us our debts, as we forgive our debtors. And lead us not into temptation, but deliver us from evil: For Thine is the kingdom, and the power, and the glory, for ever. Amen	Matthew 6:9-13; Luke 11:2-4
Hosanna to the Son of David: Blessed is He that cometh in the Name of the Lord; Hosanna in the highest	Matthew 21:9; 23:39b; Mark 11:9-10; Luke 13:35b; 19:38; John 12:13 [Psalm 118:26]
Blessed is He that cometh in the Name of the Lord	Matthew 23:39b; 21:9; Mark 11:9-10; Luke 13:35b; 19:38; John 12:13 [Psalm 118:26]
Hosanna; Blessed is He that cometh in the Name of the Lord: Blessed be the kingdom of our father David, that cometh in the Name of the Lord: Hosanna in the highest	Mark 11:9-10; Matthew 21:9; 23:39b; Luke 13:35b; 19:38; John 12:13 [Psalm 118:26]
Our Father Which art in heaven, Hallowed be Thy Name. Thy Kingdom come. Thy Will be done, as in heaven, so in earth. Give us day by day our daily bread. And forgive us our sins; for we also forgive every one that is indebted to us. And lead us not into temptation; but deliver us from evil	Luke 11:2-4; Matthew 6:9-13

Blessed is the womb that bare Thee, and the paps which Thou hast sucked	Luke 11:27b
Blessed is He that cometh in the Name of the Lord	Luke 13:35b; 19:38; Matthew 21:9; 23:39b; Mark 11:9-10; John 12:13 [Psalm 118:26]
Blessed be the King that cometh in the Name of the Lord: peace in heaven, and glory in the highest	Luke 19:38; 13:35b; Matthew 21:9; 23:39b; Mark 11:9-10; John 12:13 [Psalm 118:26]
Lord, to whom shall we go? Thou hast the Words of eternal life. And we believe and are sure that Thou art That Christ, the Son of the Living God	John 6:68-69
Yea, Lord: I believe that Thou art The Christ, The Son of God, which should come into the world	John 11:27
Hosanna: Blessed is the King of Israel that cometh in the Name of the Lord	John 12:13; Matthew 21:9; 23:39b; Mark 11:9-10; Luke 13:35b; 19:38 [Psalm 118:26]
My Lord and my God	John 20:28

Now to Him that is of power to stablish you according to my gospel, and the preaching of Jesus Christ, according to the revelation of the mystery, which was kept secret since the world began, But now is made manifest, and by the scriptures of the prophets, according to the commandment of the everlasting God, made known to all nations for the obedience of faith: To God only wise, be glory through Jesus Christ for ever. Amen — Romans 16:25–27

Jesus Christ is Lord — Philippians 2:11

Now unto the King eternal, immortal, invisible, the only wise God, be honour and glory for ever and ever. Amen — 1 Timothy 1:17

Thy Throne, O God, is for ever and ever: [the] a sceptre of [Thy Kingdom] righteousness is the [a right] sceptre of Thy Kingdom. Thou hast loved [lovest] righteousness, and hated iniquity [hatest wickedness]; therefore God, [even] Thy God, hath anointed Thee with the oil of gladness above Thy Fellows — Hebrews 1:8-9 [Psalm 45:6-7]

And, Thou, Lord, in the beginning [of old] hast [Thou] laid the foundation of the earth: and the heavens are the Work[s] of Thine [Thy] Hands. They shall perish, but Thou remainest [shalt endure: yea], they all [all of them] shall wax old as doth [like] a garment; and as a vesture shalt Thou fold [change] them up, and they shall be changed: but Thou art the same, and Thy Years shall not fail [have no end] — Hebrews 1:10-12 [Psalm 102:25-27]

Now The God of Peace, that brought again from the dead our Lord Jesus, That Great Shepherd of the sheep, through the blood of the everlasting covenant, Make you perfect in every good work to do His Will, working in you that which is wellpleasing in His Sight, through Jesus Christ; to Whom be glory for ever and ever. Amen	Hebrews 13:20-21
But The God of All Grace, Who hath called us unto His Eternal Glory by Christ Jesus, after that ye have suffered a while, make you perfect, stablish, strengthen, settle you. To Him be glory and dominion for ever and ever. Amen	1 Peter 5:10-11
Holy, Holy, Holy, Lord God Almighty, Which was, and is, and is to come	Revelation 4:8b
Thou art worthy, O Lord, to receive glory and honour and power: for Thou hast created all things, and for Thy Pleasure they are and were created	Revelation 4:11
Thou art worthy to take the book, and to open the seals thereof: for Thou wast slain, and hast redeemed us to God by Thy Blood out of every kindred, and tongue, and people, and nation; And hast made us unto our God kings and priests: and we shall reign on the earth	Revelation 5:9-10
Worthy is The Lamb that was slain to receive power, and riches, and wisdom, and strength, and honour, and glory, and blessing	Revelation 5:12
Blessing, and honour, and glory, and power, be unto Him that sitteth upon the throne, and unto the Lamb for ever and ever	Revelation 5:13b
Amen	Revelation 5:14a

Salvation to our God which sitteth upon the throne, and unto the Lamb	Revelation 7:10
Amen: Blessing, and glory, and wisdom, and thanksgiving, and honour, and power, and might, be unto our God for ever and ever. Amen	Revelation 7:12
We give Thee thanks, O Lord God Almighty, Which art, and wast, and art to come; because Thou hast taken to Thee Thy Great Power, and hast reigned	Revelation 11:17
And the nations were angry, and Thy Wrath is come, and the time of the dead, that they should be judged, and that Thou shouldest give reward unto Thy Servants the prophets, and to the saints, and them that fear Thy Name, small and great; and shouldest destroy them which destroy the earth	Revelation 11:18
Great and Marvellous are Thy Works, Lord God Almighty; just and true are Thy Ways, Thou King of Saints. Who shall not fear Thee, O Lord, and glorify Thy Name? for Thou Only art Holy: for all nations shall come and worship before Thee; for Thy Judgments are made manifest	Revelation 15:3b-4
Alleluia; Salvation, and glory, and honour, and power, unto The Lord our God: For true and righteous are His Judgments: for He hath judged the great whore, which did corrupt the earth with her fornication, and hath avenged the blood of His Servants at her hand	Revelation 19:1b-2
Alleluia	Revelation 19:3a

347

Amen; Alleluia	Revelation 19:4b

Alleluia: for The Lord God Omnipotent reigneth. Let us be glad and rejoice, and give honour to Him: for the marriage of The Lamb is come, and His Wife hath made herself ready. And to her was granted that she should be arrayed in fine linen, clean and white: for the fine linen is the righteousness of saints	Revelation 19:6-8

Prayer portions that contain Worship in them

Exodus 15:11	2 Chron 6:14-16 [1 Kings 8:23-53]
1 Samuel 2:1-3	2 Chron 6:18-21 [1 Kings 8:23-53]
2 Samuel 7:20-22 [1 Chron 17:18-20]	Nehemiah 1:5-7
2 Samuel 7:26 [1 Chron 17:24]	Nehemiah 9:5b-8
2 Samuel 7:28 [1 Chron 17:26]	Nehemiah 9:32-33
2 Samuel 22:2-3 (4-15) [Psalm 18]	Psalm 3:3-4
2 Samuel 22:26-32 [Psalm 18]	Psalm 3:8
2 Samuel 22:36 [Psalm 18]	Psalm 4:1
2 Samuel 22:47 [Psalm 18]	Psalm 5:7
1 Kings 8:23-25 [2 Chron 6:14-42]	Psalm 8:1,9a
1 Kings 8:27-30 [2 Chron 6:14-42]	Psalm 8:9a,1
1 Kings 8:59-60	Psalm 10:13-14
2 Kings 19:15 [Isaiah 37:16]	Psalm 10:16
2 Kings 19:17-19 [Isaiah 37:18-20]	Psalm 12:5-8
1 Chron 17:18-20 [2 Samuel 7:20-22]	Psalm 16:4-6
1 Chron 17:24 [2 Samuel 7:26]	Psalm 18:1-2 (3-14) [2 Sam 22]
1 Chron 17:26 [2 Samuel 7:28]	Psalm 18:25-31 [2 Samuel 22]

Psalm 18:35 [2 Samuel 22]

Psalm 18:46 [2 Samuel 22]

Psalm 21:13

Psalm 22:3-5

Psalm 22:26-31

Psalm 25:1-10

Psalm 26:8

Psalm 27:9-10

Psalm 28:6

Psalm 30:4-5

Psalm 31:2-3

Psalm 31:4-5 [Luke 23:46]

Psalm 31:9-14

Psalm 31:19-22

Psalm 32:7

Psalm 36:5-9

Psalm 38:21-22

Psalm 40:10

Psalm 40:16-17

Psalm 41:13

Psalm 43:2

Psalm 43:4

Psalm 44:4

Psalm 48:10

Psalm 51:14

Psalm 52:9

Psalm 54:6

Psalm 56:2

Psalm 59:9-17

Psalm 61:3-4

Psalm 65:5-7

Psalm 68:18-19

Psalm 68:24-27

Psalm 68:35

Psalm 69:16-17

Psalm 70:4-5

Psalm 71:3-7

Psalm 71:15-24

Psalm 73:26

Psalm 74:12

Psalm 77:12-20

Psalm 79:9

Psalm 80:1

Psalm 83:16-18

Psalm 86:8-10

Psalm 86:12-15

Psalm 89:52

Psalm 90:1-11

Psalm 94:1-2

Psalm 94:17-18

Psalm 101:1

Psalm 102:11-12

Psalm 102:21-24

Psalm 102:25-27 [Heb 1:10-12]

Psalm 102:28

Psalm 106:48 [1 Chron 16:36]

Psalm 109:21

Psalm 118:21

Prayers *of* Worship

Psalm 118:26 [Matt 21:9; 23:39b;   Psalm 119:167

Mark 11:9-10; Luke 13:35b;   Psalm 119:172

19:38; John 12:13]   Psalm 119:174

Psalm 118:28   Psalm 138:2

Psalm 119:12   Psalm 138:4-5

Psalm 119:24   Psalm 138:8

Psalm 119:39   Psalm 142:5

Psalm 119:48   Psalm 143:6

Psalm 119:57   Psalm 143:8

Psalm 119:68   Psalm 143:10

Psalm 119:70   Psalm 145:1-3

Psalm 119:72   Psalm 145:7-9

Psalm 119:75   Psalm 145:21

Psalm 119:77   Isaiah 37:16 [2 Kings 19:15]

Psalm 119:86   Isa 37:18-20 [2 Kings 19:17-19]

Psalm 119:89-93   Isaiah 63:16

Psalm 119:96-97   Jeremiah 12:1-2

Psalm 119:103   Jeremiah 14:8-9

Psalm 119:111   Jeremiah 17:13-14

Psalm 119:113-114   Jeremiah 17:17

Psalm 119:119   Jeremiah 20:11

Psalm 119:127-129   Lamentations 5:19

Psalm 119:137-144   Daniel 9:7

Psalm 119:151-152   Daniel 9:9

Psalm 119:156   Daniel 9:14

Psalm 119:159-163

Bibliography

Bounds, E. M. *The Complete Works of E. M. Bounds on Prayer.* Grand Rapids: Baker Book House Company, 1990.

Cho, Paul (David) Yonggi. "Yoido Full Gospel Church – South Korea," Worthy News, http://churches.gmttmedia.com/documents/302.html. (Accessed February 7, 2012).

Hayford, Jack. *Prayer is Invading the Impossible.* New York: Ballantine Books, 1977.

Henry, Matthew. *Commentary on the Whole Bible.* 1706.

Henry, Matthew. *A Method for Prayer.* Glasgow: D. MacKenzie, 1834.

Law, William. *A Serious Call to a Holy and Devout Life.* London: William Innys, 1732.

Lockyer, Herbert. *All the Prayers of the Bible.* Grand Rapids: Zondervan Publishing House, 1959.

Lord, Peter. *The 2959 Plan.* Agape Ministries, 1976.

Meyer, Joyce. *The Power of Simple Prayer.* New York: Faith Words, 2007.

Moody, D. L. *Prevailing Prayer: What Hinders It.* Chicago: Fleming H. Revell, 1884.

Murray, Andrew. *The Inner Chamber.* New York: Fleming H. Revell Company, 1905.

Nee, Watchman. *Let Us Pray.* New York: Christian Fellowship Publishers, Inc., 1977.

Prince, Derek. *Secrets of a Prayer Warrior.* Grand Rapids: Chosen Books, 2009.

Ravenhill, Leonard. *Revival God's Way.* Minneapolis: Bethany House Publishers, 1983.

Simpson, A. B. *Days of Heaven Upon Earth – A Year Book of Scripture Texts And Living Truths.* Brooklyn: Christian Alliance Publishing Co., 1897.

Stanley, Charles. *Handle with Prayer.* Colorado Springs: ChariotVictor Publishing, 1982.

ten Boom, Corrie. *Amazing Love.* Grand Rapids: Fleming H. Revell, 1953, 41.

ten Boom, Corrie. Quote only – no known publication.

Torrey, R. A. *How to Pray* (chapter 7).

Trueblood, D. Elton. BrainyQuote.com, Xplore Inc, 2012. *http://www.brainyquote.com/quotes/authors/d/d_elton_trueblood.html.* (Accessed April 24, 2012).

Author Biography

Being a believer for more than 30 years, Mark was ordained to the ministry, and licensed in 1984. He has never lost his fascination with all things God, especially His Holy Book. Via military service, retired U.S. Air Force, Mark and his wife ministered in several churches worldwide. Especially dear to him were his times with Awana and Bible Quiz and in Kwang Ju, South Korea. Also Okinawa, Michigan, Colorado, Saudi Arabia, San Antonio, and, well, everywhere! This is the third book he has compiled, along with two games, one being a Bible Book-by-Book card game. Also a former certified Texas public high school math teacher, Mark Rodriguez and his wife of more than three decades reside in a small south Texas town near San Antonio with several animals. Happy are they with their quiver full of children and grandchildren close at hand, but not too close. :-)